Bed & Breakfast

NORTH AMERICA

Bed & Breakfast

NORTH AMERICA

by Hal Gieseking

A Frommer Book
Published by Simon & Schuster, Inc.
NEW YORK

Copyright © 1985
by Hal Gieseking

All rights reserved
including the right of reproduction
in whole or in part in any form

Published by Frommer/Pasmantier Publishers
A Division of Simon & Schuster, Inc.
1230 Avenue of the Americas
New York, NY 10020

ISBN 0-671-53271-5

Manufactured in the United States of America

CONTENTS

PART I
Introducing Bed & Breakfast

1	Bed & Breakfast—the *Friendly* Revolution in Travel	13
2	How to Find Bed & Breakfasts	24
3	How to Use B&B Referral Agencies	42
4	National & International Help	46
5	How to be a B&B Guest	65
6	B&Bs Abroad	68
7	How to be a B&B Host	93

PART II
The Directory of B&B Reservation Service Organizations in North America

THE NORTHEASTERN STATES   109

    Connecticut / 111
    Maine / 115
    Massachusetts / 117
    New Hampshire / 130
    New York / 131
    Rhode Island / 144

THE MIDDLE ATLANTIC STATES 147

    Delaware / 149
    District of Columbia / 150
    Maryland / 152
    New Jersey / 153
    North Carolina / 154
    Pennsylvania / 156
    South Carolina / 163
    Virginia / 165

THE GREAT LAKES AREA 171

    Illinois / 173
    Michigan / 174
    Ohio / 176
    Wisconsin / 179

THE NORTHWEST & GREAT PLAINS 181

    Iowa / 183
    Minnesota / 184
    Montana / 185
    Nebraska / 186
    Oregon / 187
    South Dakota / 189
    Washington / 190

THE SOUTHEASTERN STATES 193

    Alabama / 195
    Florida / 197
    Georgia / 204
    Kentucky / 211
    Mississippi / 212
    Tennessee / 214

THE SOUTHWEST & SOUTH CENTRAL AREA 217

    Colorado / 219
    Kansas / 224

CONTENTS • 7

    Louisiana / 225
    Missouri / 228
    New Mexico / 233
    Texas / 234

CALIFORNIA & THE WEST   **241**

    Arizona / 243
    California / 245
    Utah / 260

ALASKA & HAWAII   **261**

    Alaska / 263
    Hawaii / 268

CANADA   **269**

    Alberta / 271
    British Columbia / 272
    Nova Scotia / 273
    Ontario / 276
    Quebec / 283

B&B PHONE BOOKING FORMS   **285-296**

INDEX   **297**

    Schools and Colleges / 300
    Major Businesses / 307
    Attractions / 312

Special Thanks To—

Gertrude Eber who spent many hours contacting and re-contacting B&B reservation services across the country and writing and compiling the results. This guidebook literally would not have been possible without her. Betty Oechsli who helped constantly and graciously with secretarial chores and organization . . . Vivian Holley who reported on B&B homes in the South for us . . . Eleanor Berman who sampled B&B homes in New England and Old England . . . Barbara Notarius for sharing her many insights about B&B travel . . . Bob Clive, Richard Mozzanica and Robert Tallon for their early help in bringing this book to life . . . and to Barbara Kouts, an agent and friend.

And most of all—to all the B&B reservation service organizations across North America who are helping to introduce the friendly revolution in travel.

PART 1

Introducing Bed & Breakfast

1
Bed & Breakfast—
The *Friendly* Revolution in Travel

- Travel across the U.S. and Canada, and stay in a B&B home for as little as $15 to $25 a night—breakfast included.
- Get "inside" tips from your hosts on the areas' best restaurants, shops, stores, sightseeing attractions.
- Make friends as you travel and become "part of the neighborhood" rather than paying guests at a hotel, welcomed only by an occasional bellman looking for a tip or a desk clerk who may not be able to find your reservation.
- Participate in activities with your host, which can range from shopping the local stores to sailing and lakeside picnics.
- Rather than staying in a cold, impersonal hotel with stain-resistant plastic furnishings, you may wake up in a colonial bedroom filled with antiques.

Many travelers in North America are waking up to the Bed & Breakfast way of travel.

There are an estimated 5,000 Bed & Breakfast homes now operating in the U.S., and the number is climbing almost daily. Many of the states we surveyed reported that the B&B movement was growing so fast they had trouble keeping any list of homes current.

Small wonder. Travelers have discovered what incredible

bargains B&B homes can be. The cost of a hotel room in the U.S. has climbed to an average of $56.69 a night (first quarter of 1984), with many rooms in major cities topping $100 to $150 per night. The B&B homes offer comfortable, homelike lodgings for as little as $15 to $25 per night per single, $20 to $50 per night double. It's true that you can also spend over $100 a night for some B&B rooms. But these are luxury exceptions in choice scenic locations, often with swimming pools, spas, and many other amenities.

But the real reason that the B&B way to travel has caught on is the sheer *friendliness* of many of the hosts. Vacationers and travelers are weary of the impersonality, coldness and rudeness of many travel personnel. They are tired of passing through some of the most hospitable areas of North America, and meeting no local person other than a bellman or hotel cashier. People who have become B&B hosts are often outgoing and friendly, and they take real joy in welcoming others into their homes and communities.

This welcome shows up in many ways.

In some California B&Bs, you may be greeted on arrival with good local wine and cheeses. In many homes the hosts serve far more than the typical Continental breakfast (juice, roll, coffee/tea). They introduce their guests to the local specialties. Not simply bacon and eggs but sourdough pancakes, English scones, fresh fruit platters, smoked meats, blueberry coffee cake, New England clam cakes, creamed cod on toast and many other luscious regional surprises you'd never find on a hotel breakfast menu!

Many of the hosts don't treat you like paying guests at all. Stay a few nights and you can practically become part of the family, gathering for cocktails around the fire in the evening with your hosts or even joining them for birthday parties and special local events. The stories I have gathered since I started researching this book indicate just how often hosts go out of their way to make their guests feel welcome.

Many hosts allow you laundry facilities. Others will act as your sightseeing guides. Some with small boats or even yachts take guests out on lakes, rivers, and oceans. Many will pick up guests at airports, bus and train stations. One host provides nightgowns and toothbrushes for guests whose luggage may have been lost by the airline. Many are happy to lend you bicycles for local touring, and give you maps, brochures, directions to interesting sightseeing. Still others give you membership cards to local country clubs, tennis clubs, swimming pools, etc. And when you want some company, they are often happy to oblige with breakfast or end-of-the-day conversations. As we said, this is a *friendly* revolution in travel.

Imagine the advantages of learning first-hand where the best restaurants are—from people who have lived in an area for years. You can learn what are the best times to visit DisneyWorld, which are the least crowded roads for New England leaf watching, which local stores are having sales. In these imperfect times, you also learn which local areas have high crime rates and should be avoided.

The hosts themselves are often fascinating people. Here is a random list of their occupations that I discovered in researching B&B organizations across North America: Journalists, investment bankers, linguists, painters, musicians (many), tennis pros and buffs, a world-renowned expert on Scotch whisky, doctors, lawyers, teachers (many), gardeners and gracious widows, widowers, divorced people who love to cook and entertain.

You know the hotel chain that proudly advertises "no surprises." Well, B&B homes are full of surprises, often very nice ones. When you check into some hotels, you know there is going to be a standard-size bed, a TV set, a scratch-proof, mar-proof dresser, and often the same graphics on the wall from hotel to hotel. But your room in a B&B home may have a cannonball bed from Colonial times, a working fireplace, family antiques that span the centuries, and often original artwork on all of the walls. The homes themselves are often unique. A number of B&B homes are listed on the National Historic Register. Others are not really houses at all but houseboats and yachts in which the hosts welcome you to a floating B&B. One B&B is a sailboat in the San Juan Islands of Washington State. Another is a spectacular solar-designed home with a 360-degree view of a canyon. There are also working ranches, Boston townhouses, New York luxury apartments, and remote Canadian farmhouses.

THE B&B EXPERIENCE

Here are some of the B&B homes and experiences other travelers have encountered recently.

Fireplaces and forest views in Wisconsin

In Door County, Wisconsin, you could swap stories with a retired host of a radio/TV show, in a lakeside redwood and native stone house. The view is spectacular, perched 300 feet above Green Bay. Beautiful grounds are all around you, with flower gardens and modern sculpture blending into evergreen forests. There are two guest rooms for B&B visitors. The first has a fireplace. The homemade continental breakfast is served in a glassed-in porch overlooking the water. The hosts' topics of conversation include music, literature and gardening. All of this Midwest luxury costs only $35 single; $45 to $55 double occupancy. You just couldn't match it in a hotel.

Ghostly B&B in Louisiana

The Myrtles is a beautiful old (1796) plantation on U.S. 61 near St. Francisville, LA. There are supposedly creaks and groans in the night, possibly the wanderings of Revolutionary War hero General David Bradford. But in the morning you waken to a good Southern-style breakfast, and can sit on the long veranda.

The Thomas Huckins House, 1705—in Cape Cod, MA.

A recent B&B guest reported, "This gray shingled colonial is located at 2701 Main Street in Barnstable, a charming old Cape Cod Village. It is the home of Burton and Eleanor Eddy, who have spent four years transforming their historic home from a wreck to a showplace. The house has the original wide floorboards, five fireplaces, and cubbies and crannies everywhere. The guest room downstairs has a walk-in fireplace, wood paneling painted Williamsburg blue, and is beautifully decorated with a blue paisley comforter on the bed, a big comfortable wing chair, an antique chest, a collection of German steins on the shelf over the fireplace and a cubby filled with Burt's handcarved birds (so appealing I bought one).

"The private bath, which is super-size, is in tan and green with handsome brass fittings, and on a brass openwork shelf, a collection of old advertising tins; a wooden container that once held chewing gum is now filled with fancy soaps.

"They are an intelligent and very interesting couple. He's a retired army career man. They've lived all over the country and in Germany. During their longest stint in one place, she got a Masters at the University of Kansas and taught history there. This was really like visiting lovely people in an extraordinary home. The accommodations were quite private, even to the separate entrance to hall to front door so you didn't have to go through the rest of the house to come and go. Even breakfast was exceptional—fresh fruit cup and homemade waffles."

Opera star's Georgia hideaway

Travel writer Vivian Holley visited Arden Hall, a B&B home built as a farmhouse in 1880 in Marietta, Georgia. She reports, "It's a two-story frame structure painted gray-green with dark green shutters and a red door. Marietta is an Atlanta suburb some 25 miles north of the city and home of the Kennesaw Mountain National Battlefield Park of Civil War fame. The house is on the National Register of Historic Places.

"It's furnished with antiques, oriental rugs and objets d'art collected in the owners' travels. Guests have the run of the house, including the warm, comfortable kitchen, which has been modernized but retains the original pine cabinets with white porcelain knobs. The three guest bedrooms, each with bath, are meticulously decorated down to the last needle-pointed pillow. One of the rooms is done in pink; its curtained double bed boasts an eyelet dust ruffle, plump pillows, and a comforter covered with tiny pink bows. Since the room's decor is feminine, the owner keeps some masculine trappings handy for a quick change for male guests. The owner's friend, opera star Roberta Peters, frequently occupies this room and her autographed photo hangs on the wall. Each room has heavily lined 'blackout' draperies for late sleepers."

As you can see, not your typical motel modern decor.

Philadelphia party

Recently, a young doctor from Milwaukee visited Philadelphia. He had sufficient travel funds to stay at a fashionable center city hotel for about $80 per night, or at a motel near the airport for about $45 a night. Instead, he chose a B&B private home for only $19 a night.

But the cost savings were only part of the story. He enjoyed a breakfast *in bed* of melon, fresh croissants with butter and jam, and hot coffee. (It was all delivered on a tray to his door.) That evening he joined his hostess and other guests at a going-away dinner party for a young foreigner (also a B&B guest) returning home.

"Breakfast at the Baker's—near Stone Ridge, NY"

When Fran Baker cooks breakfast in her 17th-century stone house, it's a feast. I started with fresh orange juice, followed by fresh picked rhubarb served with apples, raisins, bananas, and oranges. The main course was a cheddar cheese frittata, with hot homemade poppy seed bread served with a small round tub of butter and homemade strawberry jam or marmalade. With about four cups of hot coffee.

Everything tastes so fresh because much of it is grown right outside the kitchen, in a colonial garden (the same vegetables and fruits as were grown in colonial times) that Fran has created. After breakfast, Fran may give guests lessons in sketching. Other B&B guests that day included several stars of a national soap opera who had discovered a bucolic way to escape from a day of divorce, tragedy, and medical crises.

As you can see, B&B travel is not your typical run-of-the-mill travel. Of course, you could get a bad B&B—a poorly maintained house, surly people, a stale-roll for breakfast. But I've personally encountered all of these problems in modern, expensive hotels, and you probably have too.

B&B travel can be more fun and more personal and more relaxing than any kind of traveling you've ever done before. You can meet and make new friends all over the country and the world. You can also save a lot of money.

Talking about savings, think about this. Next time you and your spouse or friend have breakfast in a top hotel, add up the *total* cost, including the tip to the waiter and local sales tax. That cost alone may just about equal the cost of a typical Bed & Breakfast for two in many parts of the country.

This guidebook was written to help you make the most of your next trip. It does *not* list individual B&B homes which go in and out of business with some frequency. Also, we have no way of knowing the *quality* of these individual homes. (Some guidebooks, alas, list any B&B home that pays a *fee* to be included in the listings.)

Instead this guidebook contains the most comprehensive listings and descriptions of North American B&B reservation services ever published. Many of these services pre-inspect every single home on their list. We surveyed them *twice*—with a span of one year between each survey—to help ensure that we were including the most stable and long-lasting services of this fledgling cottage industry. Some asked if they had to pay to be included in this guidebook. We told them of course not. Our only criteria for their inclusion was how well they were serving the traveling public.

We found many of these reservation service organizations to be extremely conscientious, personally *pre-inspecting* the B&B homes included in their lists.

This guidebook also contains useful information for your next visit to a B&B overseas.

So come join the *friendly* revolution in travel—Bed & Breakfast. You're going to like it!

ANSWERS TO SOME COMMON QUESTIONS ABOUT B&B TRAVEL

Q. *"Is B&B travel a new idea?"*

A. Not at all. It's one of the oldest. In the 11th century, when monks and other pilgrims were walking to Rome or other holy sites, they frequently stopped overnight at private farms, monasteries and homes. After breakfast in the morning, they were on their way—the first B&B guests.

In recent years the B&B movement has spread throughout much of Europe. Europeans frequently stop at homes with "Bed & Breakfast" or "Zimmer Frei" (room free) signs posted on the front lawn.

In the American depression years of the 1930's, "tourist homes" sprang up all over the countryside. For as little as $2 you could have a modest room and sometimes an equally modest breakfast.

However, the current B&B movement is much different. While there are still many modest homes offering a room and breakfast, the quality of most accommodations (and breakfasts) is light years ahead of early tourist homes.

Q. *"I get confused. I see B&B signs on hotels."*

A. It is confusing. Many small inns have taken to calling themselves Bed & Breakfast places. These can be very pleasant but they are not the subject of this guidebook. When we say "B&B" we are talking about a room in a private home with at least a continental breakfast served to guests. It is the warmth and personality of the hosts and their interaction with guests that make the difference.

Q. *"Why should I make a reservation through a B&B reservation service organization? I see lists of individual B&B homes in books and brochures."*

A. You can, of course, make your own arrangements directly with a B&B home. Some of these we've seen can be very good. However, because of zoning and other problems with neighbors, often the best B&B homes *never* appear in any public list. The only way you can book them is through a reservation service organization.

The best of these organizations *pre-inspect* all prospective B&B homes before listing them.

Some of these organizations can occasionally be hard to reach. Many are small "mom and pop" or sometimes just "mom" operations. They have a list of B&Bs, a telephone and an answering machine. Sometimes you may not be able to reach them until after 6 p.m. at night because the owners of the service work during the day. However, with a little persistence, you can usually get through. Almost all of the organizations we have included in this guide have been in existence at least one year. We surveyed most of them *twice*, with a span of one year in between.

Q. *"Can I use a B&B home for business travel?"*

A. Of course, B&Bs are ideal for business travelers who want to reduce costs. The reservation service organizations included in this directory have listed many of the major corporations that are located near their B&B homes.

B&B homes are also ideal for parents visiting children at college, single women relocating to a new community, skiers, vacationers visiting specific scenic attractions, national parks and other recreation areas, and everyone who's tired of paying high hotel costs and sometimes getting second class, impersonal treatment.

Q. *"Can I travel with a pet?"*

A. Some B&B homes, especially in rural areas, do allow well-behaved dogs and cats to stay with their owners. Always ask about this, however, when you make your reservation. We know of one cat-owner who stayed in B&B homes all over the state of Colorado with Tabby joining him for breakfast every morning.

If you are allergic to dogs or cats, be sure to ask if any are in residence in the B&B home before you make your reservation.

Q. *"Are there any disadvantages to B&B travel?"*

A. Yes. There can be a lack of privacy. Sometimes you and your spouse or friend want to be alone together on vacation; the conversation of even a well-meaning hostess may be more than you want. You also may have to wait in line for a shared bathroom, just like home if you have a large family. You also may feel guilty staying too long in the shower when you know others are waiting.

You also may find a few B&B homes that are disappointing. Barbara Notarius, president of Bed & Breakfast USA Ltd., reported on her visit to one. "I recently went out on an appointment to visit one prospective B&B for my network. I arrived at the appointed time. The place was beautiful from the outside, handmade by a custom cabinet maker, very rustic and nestled in the woods by a running stream just outside a desirable country community. When I rang the bell, a woman came to the door and stared at me. I asked for the woman of the house from whom I had the first inquiry many weeks previously. The woman looked at me a bit bewildered and said, 'no,' and just stood there. So I asked for the husband who had given me detailed directions only a few days before. Again this woman said, 'no,' and continued to look at me. I finally said, 'Who are you? When will the family be back?' Her response was that she was a tenant, the family had a spat the day before. The wife had left and (the woman) thought the husband had gone off flying shortly before I arrived. Since they obviously had forgotten about the appointment, I asked to have a look at the house anyway. She didn't mind, so in I went. Furniture was practically non-existent, filth was everywhere, and even the room this woman was renting had only a sleeping bag over a piece of foam, no sheets."

Moral: It's a pretty good idea to have the B&B home inspected and approved by the reservation organization *before* you pull into the driveway.

2

How to Find Bed & Breakfasts

- Many of the most fascinating B&B homes never advertise or post a B&B sign.
- New sources of B&B information are springing up almost every week.

This book is the key to hundreds of the better B&B homes throughout the U.S. and Canada.

Why "better"?

Because most of the most luxurious or interesting or historic B&B homes won't risk angry confrontations with their neighbors by posting a Bed & Breakfast sign on their lawn, or advertising in a local publication. Even B&B homes that have received free publicity from a well-meaning reporter have encountered problems from zoning boards, health boards, and sometimes a whole block of people who have exaggerated fears about a "business" operating in the neighborhood.

Also, many B&B hosts feel much more secure if any prospective guests are pre-screened by a reliable reservations services organization. Otherwise they would be opening their homes to total strangers right off the street.

That's why so many of the really great B&B homes *never* are advertised or publicized. Some of these homes have swimming pools, country antiques and fireplaces in every room, and beautiful grounds. The way to find them is to call one of the reservation organizations listed in this book.

Use the unique *B&B Finder* cross index at the back of this guide. For example, if you are parents of a son at Atlanta University, you could simply turn to the "Schools and Colleges" section and find which reservation agencies offer B&B accommodations near this school. If you wanted to attend a Shakespeare play at the Stratford Festival in Ontario, Canada, turn to the "Attractions" section for your B&B reservation service. If you are a business person tired of the plastic sameness and $100-plus price tags of many hotels, check the "Major Business" section for listings of top corporations across North America and the B&B reservation organizations that have homes nearby. This service can be particularly valuable for women travelers who enjoy the security and comfort of a home environment when they're out of town.

If you ever do get stuck and can't contact a reservations organization operating in the area you want to visit, there are several alternatives.

First you can look in the local Yellow Pages phone directory. Reservation services and individual Bed & Breakfast homes will be listed under a new, separate "Bed & Breakfast" heading. For example, as of August 1984, these listings appeared in all 163 Yellow Pages editions published by New York State.

You can also write ahead to local chambers of commerce and state tourism offices. (You'll find a complete list of state tourism offices and their addresses on page___.) Many are now beginning to offer free lists of B&B homes or brochures about individual homes and farms.

Tourist information booths along state highways are also beginning to carry B&B brochures and information.

When you're visiting a resort area, stop in the local tourist office. Some can tell you about local availabilities and may even be able to book you into a B&B on the spot.

In some rural areas (where neighbors are more tolerant or friendly), you will see "Bed & Breakfast" signs in front of some homes.

You also can now get information about B&B accommodations from the American Automobile Association. In a newsletter to other AAA clubs, the National Travel Department of AAA wrote, "Due to the rapid growth of interest in Bed & Breakfast facilities, we decided to review our method for presenting B&B data to AAA Clubs. In the future, in order to insure that members receive current information pertaining to reputable B&B referral services, we will provide a listing of only those B&B referral services which screen their listings. In this way, the listing provided to clubs will reflect AAA's concern for property cleanliness, hospitable hosts and ethical operations." (NOTE: AAA really meant "reservation"—not "referral" agencies.)

As the B&B movement keeps growing (and in some areas it's starting to roar along, picking up new momentum with each day), you'll find more and more sources of information.

For information about finding Bed & Breakfast accommodations in foreign countries, turn to the chapter on "B&Bs abroad." This chapter contains a complete list of foreign tourist offices and their addresses, usually good sources of basic information before you go. You'll also learn how seasoned travelers overseas keep an eye peeled for "Zimmer Frei" and "chambre d'hote" signs to find some delightful B&Bs along their way.

When you're traveling in North America, take this guidebook along. It can introduce you to B&Bs all over the U.S. and Canada through a network of reservation service organizations. It's among the most friendly, inexpensive ways to travel today.

STATE TOURISM OFFICES

State tourism promotion offices often can supply useful help in locating B&B properties. These offices may go by different names such as Department of Industry & Trade, Bureau of Publicity, Department of Parks and Tourism, etc. You can find a complete list of tourism offices at the end of this chapter. A postcard may produce all of the information you need, plus background information and sometimes a free state highway map.

Here are a few examples of states that responded to our request for information on B&Bs.

ALABAMA
(Bureau of Publicity and Information)

Kim Richards of the Bureau wrote, "Bed and Breakfast is becoming more familiar in Alabama." And she sent some brochures to prove her point.

One example: you can have "Bed & Breakfast on Victorian Farm—The Rutherford-Johnson House" in Franklin, Alabama. There are four guest bedrooms furnished with original period pieces.

CALIFORNIA
(Department of Economic and Business Development)

The California Office of Tourism sends out a free brochure, "California Bed & Breakfast Inns." It primarily lists Bed & Breakfast inns (there are approximately 300 of these now operating). But it also includes a listing of reservation services that do refer you to private B&B homes.

DELAWARE
(Delaware Development Office)

At this time the state suggests travelers to Delaware contact Bed & Breakfast, Delaware at 1804 Breen Lane, Wilmington, DE 19810. Phone (302) 475-0340 from 3 to 5 p.m. daily.

GEORGIA
(Department of Industry & Trade)

Karin Pendley, Tourist/Communications Division, said, "The Bed and Breakfast movement is indeed spreading in Georgia. The practice dates back to the late 1960's in Savannah and is catching on in the rest of the state. Most travelers to Georgia would be advised to make B&B arrangements through the Chambers of Commerce or Convention and Visitors Bureaus in Atlanta, Athens, Clermont and Savannah."

The Department also distributes a "Georgia Inns and Bed and Breakfast Accommodations" report.

INDIANA
(Tourist Development Division)

The tourist office reports that a B&B list is available by mail. B&B homes that have brochures also distribute them at the 34 Tourist Information Centers located along the Indiana interstates.

IOWA
(Development Commission)

"Yes, we feel the Bed & Breakfast concept is growing here," said Paul Comer, Jr., Manager of Visitors and Tourism. We distribute a brochure ('Bed & Breakfast in Iowa Ltd.') for the private sector people who handle Iowa's program. This brochure moves in our mail 'free of charge' and at our seven welcome centers."

MAINE
(The Maine Publicity Bureau, Inc.)

Would you like to stay at The 1859 Guest House in Bridgeton? Or Boswell's Bight in Camden, Maine? Or the Cloverleaf Cottage ("No Cats") on Bailey Island? You'll find these and 40 other B&B homes with addresses and phone numbers in the "Maine Bed & Breakfast Places" folder. This free folder also identifies which homes are open year round and whether pets are allowed.

LOUISIANA
(Office of Tourism)

A number of plantation homes offer B&B accommodations. Some are very pleasant surprises. For example, you could stay at Old Lyons House at 1335 Horridge St. in Vinton, Louisiana. The brochure mailed by the tourist office offers this description:

"The owners invite you to be their guests in their delightful Queen Anne Home. The elaborate Eastlake ornamentation makes it one of the most unique and beautiful homes in Southwest Louisiana. Relax while sitting on the curved downstairs porch, or the ornate upstairs balcony. A cozy atmosphere is attained indoors by the spacious rooms with antique furniture and the warmth of the fireplaces. You'll surely want your photo taken on the graceful Eastlake staircase." You'll also share an unusual bit of history. "The house was noted to be one of the first places West of the Calkcasieu River to have electricity. When the electricity was installed, Mr. Lyons left his lights on and his doors open all night for the neighbors and surrounding community to come in and see what electric lighting was like."

Write the Office of Tourism for the free booklet, "River Trails, Bayous and Backroads." In addition to listing some of the plantations and historic homes that offer overnight accommodations and meals, the booklet is an excellent guide to off-the-beaten-track tourism in the state.

MASSACHUSETTS
(Department of Commerce and Development)

The B&B concept is slowly catching on in this state, with the number of B&B's and requests for information about them steadily increasing. The state issues a very useful listing, "Bed & Breakfast in Massachusetts" that is worth writing for. It includes not only B&B referral services but individual homes and B&B inns.

MISSOURI
(Division of Tourism)

Missouri reports that the B&B movement is definitely growing in that State, "although it probably isn't as advanced as in some others. There now is a Missouri Bed & Breakfast Association listed in our Missouri Guide." (Four independent Missouri referral agencies that operate now under one name—Missouri Bed & Breakfast Association, P.O. Box 31246, St. Louis, MO 63131—phone 314/868-2335 or 965-4328.) Homes listed include those in the Ozarks, including the Branson and Tri-Lakes area, St. Louis, and many other cities in Missouri and Southern Illinois.

MINNESOTA
(Minnesota Office of Tourism)

This state has just completed a new brochure of Bed & Breakfast homes and historic inns which is available free of charge. There is even a new association of historic B&Bs throughout Minnesota which is currently being formed.

NEBRASKA
(Travel & Tourism Division)

There are few B&Bs in the state so far, but the movement is slowly spreading. There is a Nebraska Bed and Breakfast Association which apparently has run into some opposition from state lodging interests who may not like the idea of paying guests being diverted to private homes. The tourism office will send out a brochure about this association, which tells you how to "travel the Old West Trails" and stay at farms, ranches and villages while visiting pioneer villages, historic parks and a Pony Express station.

If you're driving through Nebraska on I-80 during the summer months, you'll also find these brochures at state vacation information booths.

NEW MEXICO
(Tourism and Travel Division)

The state sends out a "Vacation Planner" with some useful information for vacationers. It does describe Bed & Breakfast places but these are primarily B&B inns. However, some of them are so small that they "qualify" as B&B homes. For example, "Rancho Arriba, run by Curtiss and Jessica Frank, attracts hiking enthusiasts due to its location at the gateway to the Pecos Wilderness. The inn is actually a small working farm and is known locally as the source of Truchas eggs, popular in health food stores."

NORTH CAROLINA
(Travel & Tourism Division, Department of Commerce)

The Tourism Department sends out a gaggle of brochures on B&Bs. Many feature B&B inns rather than individual homes, but some B&B hosts have prepared informal literature. For example, Jo Anne & Lee Green invite you to be their houseguests at Greenwood in Greensboro.

"Enjoy a fine European tradition; stay in an elegant private home and share a hearty continental breakfast with the family and other guests. We would enjoy meeting you and having you stay with us.

"You can spend a summer's afternoon at the swimming pool or a winter's evening in front of a roaring fire or take a leisurely walk along country roads."

The Greens of Greenwood are also in step with the times. Master Card and Visa are accepted.

OREGON
(Economic Development Department)

"The Oregon Report" sent free by this Department cheerfully reports, "The European style of in-home hospitality is sweeping Oregon, and now there are dozen of bed & breakfast facilities in operation throughout the state." They will also send you several brochures with information about B&B referral services.

RHODE ISLAND
(Tourism and Promotion Division)

Write for their free "Guide to Rhode Island." It contains a

complete list of accommodations throughout the state, including 45 B&B homes and inns.

TEXAS
(Texas Tourist Development Agency)

Texas is big in B&Bs, naturally. The tourist agency currently sends out a free list of Bed & Breakfast Associations and some individual inns and guest houses. Their major concern is that the number is growing so fast they're not sure the list is up to date.

Brenda Stone of the Tourist Development Agency suggests, "In addition to contacting our agency, travelers may visit one of 12 tourist bureaus upon entering Texas (they are located along the borders), where trained counselors answer questions and distribute brochures."

SOUTH CAROLINA
(Division of Tourism)

Do you want to visit relatives stationed at the Marines camp on Parris Island? You can stay with a retired marine just a short jog away, with a driving range and bass fishing on the 21-acre retreat.

Or would you like to stay deep in the heart of Historic Charleston, walking past period houses, walled gardens, with flowers everywhere?

These are some of the possibilities included in the free listings mailed out by the South Carolina Department of Parks, Recreation and Tourism.

There is a proliferation of B&Bs in Charleston as well as in many of the older towns.

VERMONT
(Vermont Travel Division)

Still another state heard from with an optimistic outlook. "The B&B movement is definitely on the rise here in Vermont," said Russel C. Smith, Information Officer for the Travel Division. "We receive requests on this type of lodging continuously." The state will send you a mailboxful of useful information for prospective B&B guests, all free, including a Vermont Travel Guidebook listing lodgings, attractions, and restaurants, a brochure on Vermont Country Inns (with bed & breakfast information), and the Official State Map. It's yours for a postcard.

VIRGINIA
(Division of Tourism)

The Bed & Breakfast movement began in Virginia during the Bicentennial (1976) when a former school teacher introduced a B&B reservation service called Guesthouses. B&Bs are now available all over the state, including the state capital of Richmond, Williamsburg, Alexandria, Lynchburg, the Blue Ridge Mountains, Norfolk-Virginia Beach, Chincoteague Island (home of the wild ponies), and the Eastern Shore.

Some of the more unusual trappings or features of B&B homes in Virginia include a "footed, monogrammed porcelain bathtub in a Charlottesville residence near Thomas Jefferson's home, Monticello," a four-poster bed in a home close to the church where Patrick Henry gave his famous "liberty or death" speech, and an antique cradle in a home in Williamsburg.

The state tourism office suggests contacting any of these reservation services for more information:

HOW TO FIND BED & BREAKFASTS • 35

Bed & Breakfast—Tidewater
P.O. Box 3343
Norfolk, VA 23514
(804) 627-1983 or 627-9409
Price range: $30 to $55 double

Bensonhouse of Richmond
P.O. Box 15131
Richmond, VA 23227
(804) 321-6277 or 649-4601
Price range: $30 to $60 double

Blue Ridge Bed & Breakfast
Rt. 1, Box 517
Bluemont, VA 22012
(703) 955-3955
Price range: $25 to $45 double

Guesthouses—Charlottesville
P.O. Box 5737

Charlottesville, VA 22905
(804) 979-7264
Price range: $32 to $72 double

Princely Bed & Breakfast
819 Prince Street
Alexandria, VA 22314
(703) 683-2159
Price range: $30 to $60 double

Sojourners Bed & Breakfast
3609 Tanglewood Lane
Lynchburg, VA 24503
(804) 384-1655
Price range: $36 double

The Travel Tree
P.O. Box 838
Williamsburg, VA 23185
(804) 229-4037 or 565-2236
Price range: $20 to $45 double

The tourist office will send more information about B&Bs and a handsome free booklet, "Virginia," which will whet your appetite for visiting this beautiful state.

WASHINGTON
(Department of Commerce & Economic Development)

"The Bed & Breakfasts are very popular and new ones are opening monthly in our state," says Bobbi Bennett, Tourism Program Specialist. "We distribute listing(s) to visit or information centers throughout the state of Washington, and we also use (them) to answer mail and telephone inquiries." The listings are more useful than most because they give precise directions to the B&B homes: "Take Highway 2 to Icicle Road. Up Icicle Road 1-½ miles to Wilson Road. Third house on the right. Two rooms. Open year round."

WEST VIRGINIA
(Governor's Office of Economic and Community Development)

In response to our request for information about B&Bs in West Virginia, the state sent us two brochures on individual homes. The most intriguing was a stay at the Kilmarnock Farm Retreat, a 300-acre Appalachian farm with brooks, meadows, deep forests, a 970-acre fishing lake and a resident population of deer, turkey, and grouse.

Says the brochure, "At Kilmarnock farm you will be personal guests (capacity is only two bedrooms) sharing delicious country fare—served family style—and lodging in a comfortable 19th-century farmhouse. The atmosphere is informal and relaxed: dress casually. Guests generally entertain themselves. Breakfast and dinner are served: a lunch is packed. International cuisine. Your own fish and game cooked and special diets are catered upon request. No pets please."

What do you do for recreation? Learn more about the Civil War. Or quilting. Or participate in the chores of a farm, everything from wood cutting to shearing a sheep. If you are a birdlover, you can see and hear songbirds such as the scarlet tanager, indigo bunting, bluebirds, and warblers. For more information, write the Kilmarnock Farm Retreat, Rt. 1, Box 91, Orlando, WV 26412. Phone 304/452-8319.

WISCONSIN
(Department of Development)

Gary Knowles, Director of the Bureau of Communications for the Division of Tourism, writes, "The Bed & Breakfast movement has definitely spread to Wisconsin; however, it's in its early stages of organization and as of this date there is no official directory of such establishments statewide. Bed & Breakfast establishments are becoming more popular in Wisconsin due to recently passed legislation that establishes guidelines and laws for operators."

WYOMING
(Wyoming Travel Commission)

The state is definitely gloomy about the B&B movement to date, saying that so far it "is nonexistent." Their current "Wyoming Vacation Guide" only lists one B&B and that is a Bed & Breakfast inn.

STATE TOURIST OFFICES

Alabama Bureau of Publicity &
  Information
532 S. Perry St.
Montgomery, AL 36130
  (800)ALA-BAMA

Alaska State Division of
  Tourism
Pouch E
Juneau, AK 99811
  (907) 465-2010

Arizona State Office of Tourism
3507 N. Central Ave., Suite 506
Phoenix, AZ 85012
  (602) 255-3618

Arkansas Division of Tourism
One Capitol Mall
Little Rock, AR 72201
  (501) 371-7777

California Office of Tourism
1030 13 St., Suite 200
Sacramento, CA 95814
  (916) 322-1396

Colorado Office of Tourism
1313 Sherman St., Rm. 500
Denver, CO 80203
  (303) 866-3045

Connecticut Dept. of Economic
  Development, Tourism
  Division
210 Washington St.
Hartford, CT 06106
  (203) 566-2496

Delaware State Travel Service
99 Kings Highway
Dover, DE 19901
  (302) 736-4271

Florida Division of Tourism
107 W. Gaines St., Rm. 505
Tallahassee, FL 32301
  (904) 488-5606

Georgia Tourist Division
P. O. Box 1776
Atlanta, GA 30301
  (404) 656-3594

Hawaii Visitors Bureau
441 Lexington Ave., Suite 1407
New York, NY 10017
  (212) 986-9203

Idaho Travel
State Capitol Building, Rm. 108
Boise, ID 83720
  (800) 635-7820

Illinois Office of Tourism
310 S. Michigan
Chicago, IL 60604
  (312) 793-4732

Indiana Tourism Development
  Division
440 N. Meridian St.
Indianapolis, IN 46204
  (317) 232-8870

Iowa Tourism & Travel Division
250 Jewett Building
Des Moines, Iowa 50309
  (515) 281-3100

Kansas Division of Travel
  Marketing
503 Kansas Ave., 6th Fl.
Topeka, KS 66603
  (913) 296-2009

Kentucky Department of
  Economic Dev.
Capitol Plaza Tower
Frankfort, KY 40601
  (502) 564-4930

Louisiana Office of Tourism
P. O. Box 44291, Capitol
  Station
Baton Rouge, LA 70804
  (504) 925-3853

Maine Publicity Bureau
97 Winthrop St.
Hollowell, ME 04347
  (207) 289-2423

Maryland Office of Tourism
  Development
1748 Forest Drive
Annapolis, MD 21401
  (301) 269-2686

Massachusetts Dept. of
  Commerce & Development
100 Cambridge St.
Boston, MA 02202
  (617) 727-3201

Michigan Travel Bureau
P. O. Box 30226
Lansing, MI 48909
  (800) 248-5700

Minnesota Tourism Bureau
419 N. Robert St.
St. Paul, MN 55101
  (612) 296-2755

Mississippi Dept. of Economic
  Development, Div. of
  Tourism
P. O. Box 849
Jackson, MS 39205
  (601) 359-3414

Missouri Division of Tourism
Truman State Office Building
P. O. Box 1055
Jefferson City, MO 65102
  (314) 751-4133

Montana Promotion Bureau
Department of Commerce
Helena, MT 59620-0144
  (406) 449-2654

Nebraska Travel & Tourism
  Division
P. O. Box 94666
Lincoln, NE 68509
  (402) 471-3111

Nevada Tourism Commission
State Capitol Complex
Carson City, NV 89710
  (702) 885-4322

New Hampshire Office of
  Vacation Travel
105 Loudon Rd.
Box 856
Concord, NH 03301
  (603) 271-2666

40 • INTRODUCING BED & BREAKFAST

New Jersey Division of Travel &
  Tourism
P. O. Box CN826
Trenton, NJ 08625
(609) 292-2470

New Mexico Tourism & Travel
  Div. Comm. & Indust. Dept.
Bataan Memorial Building
Santa Fe. NM 87503
(505) 827-5571

New York Division of Tourism
230 Park Ave., Suite 1155
New York, NY 10169
(212) 949-8429

North Carolina Travel &
  Tourism Division
430 N. Salisbury St.
Raleigh, NC 27611
(919) 733 4171

North Dakota Tourism
  Promotion Division
Capitol Grounds
Bismarck, ND 58505
(800) 437-2077

Ohio Office of Travel & Tourism
P. O. Box 1001
Columbus, OH 43216
(614) 466-8844

Oklahoma Tourism &
  Recreation Dept.
505 Will Rogers Building
Oklahoma City, OK 73105
(405) 521-3981

Oregon Tourism Division
595 Salem St.
Salem, OR 97310
(800) 547-7842

Pennsylvania Bureau of Travel
  Development
416 Forum Building
Harrisburg, PA 17120
(800) 237-4363

Rhode Island Dept. of
  Economic Development
7 Jackson Walkway
Providence, RI 02903
(800) 566-2484

South Carolina Dept. of Parks,
  Recreation & Tourism
1205 Pendleton St., Suite 113
Columbia, SC 29201
(803) 758-2536

South Dakota Division of
  Tourism
221 S. Central Ave.
Pierre, SD 57501
(800) 843-1930

Tennessee Department of
  Tourist Development
601 Broadway
P. O. Box 23170
Nashville, TN 37202
(615) 741-2159

Texas Tourist Development
  Agency
Box 12008, Capitol Station
Austin, TX 78711
(512) 475-4326

Utah Travel Council
Council Hall, Capitol Hill
Salt Lake City, UT 84114
(801) 533-5681

Vermont Travel Division
61 Elm St.
Montpelier, VT 05602
(802) 828-3236

Virginia Division of Tourism
202 N. Ninth St., Suite 500
Richmond, VA 23219
(804) 786-2051

Washington Tourism Division
101 Gen. Administration
  Building
Olympia, WA 98502
(206) 753-5600

Washington Convention and
  Visitors Association
1575 I St., N.W., Suite 250
Washington, DC 20005
(202) 789-7000

West Virginia Travel
  Development Division
1900 Washington St. East
Charleston, WV 25305
(304) 348-2286

Wisconsin Division of Tourism
123 W. Washington Ave.
P. O. Box 7970
Madison, WI 53707
(608) 266-7621

Wyoming Travel Commission
Frank Norris, Jr., Travel Center
Cheyenne, WY 82002
(307) 777-7777

TERRITORIES

Economic Dev. Plan & Tourism
  Office of American Samoa
P. O. Box 1147
Pago Pago, American Samoa
  96799

Guam Visitors Bureau
P. O. Box 3520
Agana, Guam 96910
(671) 646-5278

Mariana Visitors Bureau
P. O. Box 861
Saipan, Mariana Islands 96950
  6-7327

Puerto Rico Tourism Company
P. O. Box 44350, Old San Juan
  Station
San Juan, PR 00905
(809) 721-2400

Virgin Islands Division of
  Tourism
Box 1692
Charlotte Amalie, St. Thomas
U.S. Virgin Islands 00801
(809) 774-8784

3
How to Use B&B Referral Agencies

- B&B Referral agencies often publish directories to homes; you make your own reservations directly with these homes

The difference between B&B reservation organizations and B&B referral agencies/publishers is clear from their designations.

B&B reservation organizations maintain lists of B&B accommodations within certain geographic areas, publish borchures about these homes (without addresses), and require that the prospective guest make all reservations through the organization.

On the other hand, referral agencies simply refer you to B&B accommodations. You then have to contact the host of any home you want to visit and make all reservations and other arrangements yourself. The referral agencies make their profit from selling lists of B&Bs either in book or booklet form. Individual B&B hosts have to pay a fee to be included in some of these publications, a practice we don't happen to like from the standpoint of unbiased journalism. (No reservation organization referral agency listed in this book paid as much as a penny to be included.)

One disadvantage of these referral agency lists is that they may represent homes that have never been inspected by anyone. This means you may be strictly on your own when you select a B&B from a list. It could be a winner, or a run-down loser. As the carnival barker said, "You pays your money and you takes your chances."

However, some referral agencies are conscientious, and we'll indicate some we believe are doing a good job. We suggest you use a reservation organization, but if that is not always possible, a reliable list of B&B homes in the area you plan to visit could be a help.

Here are a few:

AMERICAN BED & BREAKFAST OF NEW ENGLAND
$4 postpaid
American Bed & Breakfast of New England
P.O. Box 983
St. Albans, VT 05478

This B&B directory lists homes in Vermont, New Hampshire, Massachusetts, The Adirondack/Olympic region of New York State, and Maine. Homes range in price from $18 to $24 single; $25 to $35 double. Note: Many of them are near excellent downhill and cross-country skiing areas, including Stowe, Killington, Smuggler's Notch, Mt. Snow and Jay Peak.

BED & BREAKFAST WEST COAST
$4.50 postpaid
Bed & Breakfast West Coast
Carpinteria, CA 93013

This small (32-page) directory describes B&B homes and small inns in California, Oregon, Washington, and Canada. Many of the listings are in the Santa Barbara area.

Listed homes include this attractive-sounding hideaway in Wedderburn, Oregon: "On the Oregon coast near the wild and scenic Rogue River, Ken & Lea invite you into their home. The bedroom has a double bed, private bath; the family parlor has a cozy fireplace. Homemade bran muffins and jams for your breakfast; good ocean or river fishing close by. Or you can jet back into the wilderness of the Rogue. Bird watching and beachcombing for driftwood are favorite activities around these parts."

E.P. TOBIN'S BED & BREAKFAST GUIDE.
$4.80 postpaid. Published in 1982.
A 1983 supplement is available for $2.
Available from: Tobin's B&B Guide
RD 2 Box 64
Rhinebeck, NY 12572

Mr. Tobin does not operate a referral agency as such. Strictly speaking he is a writer/publisher who updates and expands his guide regularly. We like his candid statement in his book, "I have visited each home to meet the hosts and ascertain the accuracy of the lodgings' descriptions. Time can change things and tastes do vary. I do offer a hope, but not a guarantee, that you enjoy your visit." B&B homes listed in the guide range from Maine to Florida.

The descriptions are folksy and informative. Here's how one B&B home in Millbrook, NY is described: "Our home was said to have been built by a bootlegger who kept his stock in the cellar. We prefer to focus on the upstairs and have added comfortable rooms there. Two miles east of Millbrook on U.S. 44, we are near the Town Park and swimming hole, where you can enjoy a refreshing dip or watch a ball game on most summer evenings. There is ice skating in winter (indoor or outdoor), with excellent hiking and biking on country roads. A mile from here is a field where deer love to browse and where we've seen as many as twenty-eight at one time. For bus travelers with reservations, we'll meet you at the depot in Millbrook."

EDUCATORS' BED & BREAKFAST AND HOME EXCHANGE DIRECTORY
$6.50 postpaid
Educators' Vacation Alternatives (EVA)
317 Piedmont Road
Santa Barbara, CA 93105

An informal network of teachers and education administrators open their homes to their peers in the educational world. Educators' Vacation Alternatives publishes a directory to these B&B homes (as well as possible home exchanges). You make all of your arrangements with the host family. Addresses and phone numbers are listed in the book. The definition of "teachers" is pretty broad. If you teach a course in adult education, for example, you could qualify. Said EVA, "Our main concern is really to find interesting guests who will have something in common with their educator hosts . . . Many hosts will meet guests. Some provide bikes, boats, etc. for recreation."

One of the more unusual homes in the current listing is a renovated 17-room home built in 1811 on 120 acres. It's near Penn State University, lakes, caves, Amish markets. Children are not only welcome but there are animals to pet. Another is an 1877 Chicago home filled with antiques, including a 100-year-old Steinway. There's even a marbled fireplace in the room.

TOWN & COUNTRY BED & BREAKFAST IN B.C.
(Directory of Home Accommodations in B.C.)
$5.95 (Canadian dollars) postpaid.
Publisher requests that only money orders are acceptable.
Available from: Box 46544 Stn. G
Vancouver, B.C. V6R4G6, Canada

This directory published in 1983 lists 124 host homes—"a wide variety of accommodations, from urban to rural, modest to luxurious . . . ." Rentals range from $18 to $25 single; $30 to $50 double (Canadian dollars).

4
National and International Help

- From many areas you can now book a B&B room across the country or across the world with a local phone call
- Want to stay in a beautiful B&B home for $10 a night? What's the catch? You have to be at least 50 years old.
- Want a B&B in the Virgin Islands? Or France? Or Mexico? Or Great Britain? A national reservation service could get it for you.

In recent months the trend among B&B reservation services has been toward consolidation. Some have merged. But more often, independent agencies have joined with other similar organizations to market their services under one name. For example, several B&B agencies in Missouri recently banded together under the name the Missouri Bed & Breakfast Association. This allows them to offer rooms across the whole state rather than in just one area. Other reservation organizations are joining together to offer complete tours that feature B&B homes. In addition several national organizations that offer specialized services to the traveling public and to the reservation organizations have come on the scene.

In the future many B&B organizations will be linked with each other in vast computer reservation networks that could allow you to book a trip all across North America or abroad with just one local call.

These are some of the major national organizations now operating:

AFFILIATED BED & BREAKFAST

This is a relatively new association of six independent reservation organizations that interview all prospective hosts and inspect the homes. One call to any of the agencies allows you to book anything from a log cabin to a B&B cattle ranch or even a yacht. Costs range from a low of $17 to a high of $75. Individual organizations also offer tour packages, including a six night (double occupancy) tour of the Rocky Mountains National Park. Tours to other national parks are also available.

You can obtain a complete list of host homes available by sending a large, self-addressed envelope (with 37¢ stamps) to any of these member organizations.

Bed & Breakfast Brookline/Boston
Box 732
Brookline, MA 02146
(617) 277-2292

Bed & Breakfast Texas Style
4224 W. Red Bird Lane
Dallas, TX 75237
(214) 298-5433

Bed & Breakfast—Rocky Mountains
P.O. Box 804
Colorado Springs, CO 80901
(303) 630-3433

Bed & Breakfast USA, Ltd.
49 Van Wyck St.
Croton, NY 10520
(914) 271-6228

Mi Casa Su Casa
Box 950
Tempe, AZ 85281
(602) 990-0682

Toronto Bed & Breakfast
P.O. Box 74
Station M
Toronto, Ontario M6S 4T2 Canada

(NOTE: You'll find more detailed information on most of these reservation services under their individual listings that appear in the appropriate geographic section of this guidebook.)

THE AMERICAN BED & BREAKFAST ASSOCIATION
P.O. Box 23294, Washington, DC 20026
Phone (202) 237-9777

This organization has been in business over two years, and calls itself a clearinghouse for B&B information, both for prospective guests and for reservation agencies and individual B&B homes.

As a traveler, you can subscribe to their services for $25 a year and receive two updated versions of a booklet called "Host List" and monthly newsletters about B&Bs in different sections of the country. The Host List includes names and addresses of reservation services, plus a listing of individual hosts.

If you are over 50 years old, you can join the Association's Evergreen Club. You agree to be a host yourself to other members of the club. In turn you can stay in other members' homes for only an honorarium of $10 single; $15 double. At present there are about 120 members across the U.S. and Canada, with about 30 new members joining monthly. The

NATIONAL & INTERNATIONAL HELP • 49

cost of joining is $20 annually. (*Note:* If you cannot host because of a lack of space, you can still join by paying annual dues of $35.)

The organization also holds seminars and publishes a newsletter called "Shoptalk" for reservation organizations and individual B&B homes.

This is not a reservation service as such. You would make all of your own reservations by using the information and phone numbers the organization supplies in its literature.

BED & BREAKFAST/ASSOCIATED RESERVATION SERVICES
125 Newton Road, Springfield, MA 01118
Phone: (413) 783-5111

This is an association of 22 reservation services. You can make one phone call to any of the members and book one of 3500 B&B homes from New England to Hawaii. When you call, you should describe the type of home you want. The reservation service will tell you what is available and the price range. You send in a deposit for the reservation directly to the service, and pay the balance due to the host when you arrive.

For a free list of all of the member reservation services, write to the address above.

THE BED & BREAKFAST LEAGUE LTD.
2855 29th St., N.W. Washington, DC 20008
Phone (202) 232-8718

The League is an unusual membership organization that is bringing stability and high standards to the Bed & Breakfast industry.

You can join the Bed & Breakfast League by completing an application with a personal reference and paying annual dues of $25. This gives you access to some 600 high quality B&B homes all over the U.S., as well as in Canada, Great Britain,

Bermuda, France, and New Zealand. The League is currently working on plans to offer B&Bs in Spain and Japan, as well as on yachts.

As a member, you can select the B&B home you want from descriptions in an annual "Host Directory" and in bi-monthly newsletters. Here is an example of one of the descriptions in the current directory in Studio City, California:

Rambling antique-filled home has been used as movie location. Handmade quilts on king-size bed in spacious guestroom. Two-bedroom suite occasionally available to sleep three or four. Swimming pool. Host is actor; hostess is TV producer. Very active. Informal family. Continental breakfast and complimentary wine. Walking distance to park, tennis, golf course, fine shops and restaurants. Universal Studios, 5 min; Hollywood, Beverly Hills, Westwood and downtown, 10 min.; LAX (Los Angeles Airport) 30 min.; Burbank Airport; 25 min. No smoking. Children over 14 welcome. Resident parrot, cats, dog. Guest pickups arranged."

The rate for each room was $90 to $100 per room, per night. However, this is a little misleading, since it was a special (inflated) rate for the Summer Olympics in Los Angeles. The rooms would undoubtedly be more reasonable now.

Mark Kauffman, Marketing Director of the League, said, "We encourage all of our hosts to serve, at a minimum, lavish continental breakfasts. Usually two croissants, fresh fruit juice, good quality jams and preserves, and coffee or tea.

Once you've made your selection, you can call a special toll free 800 number for members only to make your reservations. You pay for lodging in advance, by personal check or by Visa, MasterCard or American Express. All financial dealings are handled directly with the Bed & Breakfast League, Ltd.; never with the host. The League can make air and other travel arrangements for you, and plans tours abroad that include B&B homes.

NATIONAL & INTERNATIONAL HELP • 51

BED & BREAKFAST REGISTRY
P.O. Box 80174
St. Paul, MN 55108
Phone: (612) 646-4238

This organization now offers over 300 homes all over the U.S., with the heaviest concentration in California and Minnesota. Rates start as low as $12 per night for a single to $160 a night for two in a posh California hideaway. These homes are described and pictured in a nationwide directory which sells for $5.95 postpaid. You can order the directory; then call the Registry for reservations. You must send a deposit of one night's rental plus $10 for each additional night of your reservation. MasterCard and Visa are acceptable for this payment. The balance due is paid to the host when you arrive.

HOME SUITE HOMES
1470 Firebird Way
Sunnyvale, CA 94087
Phone: (408) 733-7215

This national reservation service offers some 300 homes across the U.S. with rates ranging from $30 to $100 per night. The upper range is primarily for the more expensive homes in California's wine country, Napa Valley. One of their more unusual B&B homes is a yacht with a hot tub, docked in Sausalito, California. Another is a luxury cabin totally surrounded by acres of giant redwoods. Alaska is one of the areas where many B&B's are becoming available.

Rhonda Robins, one of the owners of the service said, "A great deal of our reservations now comes from business travelers. We have a concentration of B&B homes in and around California's Silicon Valley. Because so much high tech is happening here, there are numerous conventions and meetings and the local hotels just can't handle all of the business. They call us to find B&B homes for the overflow. Business travelers are just beginning to realize how much money they can save using B&B homes."

This service formerly represented B&B homes abroad but has recently discontinued this because of foreign currency exchange problems.

For a list of available homes, send a stamped self-addressed envelope to Home Suite Homes.

NEW AGE TRAVEL (formerly International Spare Room)
P.O. Box 378
Encinitas, CA 92024
Phone: (619) 436-9977

This service currently represents about 130 B&B homes in the U.S. Average rates of these homes range from $25 single to $35 double. One of their real strengths seems to be Great Britain (over 600 B&B homes represented). They also offer a "smattering" of homes in Mexico, the Caribbean, and Europe.

Pam Davis is the owner of this service and she travels frequently throughout the U.S. and Europe to do her own personal inspections of homes on her list. For a free brochure that lists available homes and such basic information as types of room, whether children are allowed, rates, etc., send a stamped, self-addressed business envelope to New Age Travel.

Other reservation services that offer national and/or international listings include:

NATIONAL & INTERNATIONAL HELP • 53

American Historic Homes Bed & Breakfast
P.O. BOX 336, DANA POINT, CA 92629

Offers B&B Homes In:
500 locations throughout the United States

Reservations Phone: (714) 496-6953
Phone Hours: 9 a.m. to 5 p.m.   **Available:** Monday to Friday
Price Range of Homes:
Single: $25 to $65   Double: $35 to $85
Breakfast Included in Price:
Continental or full American . . . some specialties are cinnamon rolls, freshly ground coffee, smoked meats, fresh-baked breads, and "recipes from the Gold Rush days in Mother Lode country"
Brochure Available: For a fee, which is $1.00 (includes listings and descriptive sampler)
Reservations Should Be Made: 2 weeks in advance (last minute reservations accepted if possible)

B&B Bonuses.
  "You may choose to stay in an estate built in 1693 and occupied by the Marquis de Lafayette as his headquarters; a Federal-style home circa 1827 on the old Boston Post Road that includes a secret room under a trap door in the library for slaves escaping North; a lighthouse on the National Register of Historic Places; an opulent estate with a full view of San Francisco Bay three blocks from Fishermen's Wharf; a carriage house in Washington, DC, two miles from the White House. There are Queen Anne Victorians, Georgians, colonial plantations, and Cape style homes available throughout the country."

BABS (Bed & Breakfast Service)
P.O. BOX 5025, BELLINGHAM, WA 98227

Offers B&B Homes In:
Over 60 host homes nationwide, many in New England, Idaho, Washington, and Southern California

Reservations Phone: (206) 733-8642
Phone Hours: 7 a.m. to 9 p.m.   **Available:** 7 days a week
Price Range of Homes:
Single: $15 to $24   Double: $18 to $30 (children in own sleeping bag, $3)
Breakfast Included in Price:
Continental (juice, roll/toast, coffee), featuring blueberry coffee cake in some Pacific Northwest homes
Brochure Available: There is a book available for a fee, which is $3.75 postpaid, describing homes and listing local Referrers' phone numbers.
Reservations Should Be Made: 2 weeks in advance (last minute reservations accepted by phone to BABS or Referrers listed in BABS Travel Book)

B&B BONUSES

A Bavarian-style house on a lake in N.W. Washington, a solar home in Durango, Colorado, a 2,000 acre Montana ranch, and historic homes, are a sample of what is available.

Airport pickups can be made for a fee, and guests will be well supplied with maps, brochures, and other local information.

Bed & Breakfast Hospitality
823 LA MIRADA AVE., LEUCADIA, CA 92024

Offers B&B Homes In:
Across the U.S. (major cities and rural areas), Hawaii, New Zealand, Australia, Israel, Ireland, England, Scotland, France, Bermuda, Iceland, South Africa

Reservations Phone: (619) 436-6850
Phone Hours: 8 a.m. to 8 p.m.   **Available:** Monday to Saturday, no holidays

Price Range of Homes:
Single: $18 to $95   Double $36 to $110
Breakfast Included in Price:
Continental or full American . . . most hosts serve home-baked breads and muffins, fresh fruit in season, and farms serve their own eggs and produce.
Brochure Available: Free. International Directory is $7.95, including tax and handling (this also covers fee for those who wish to join this organization).
Reservations Should Be Made: 2 weeks in advance for the U.S.; 6 weeks for international (last minute reservations accepted if possible)

B&B BONUSES

The listings include sheep ranches in Australia, castles and manor houses in England, rural Irish village homes, kibbutz/monastery in Israel, beach areas in California, Florida, Hawaii, etc., ski areas, fresh and salt-water fishing areas, San Francisco Victorian homes, and many renovated and restored homes in the U.S., Europe, and other countries.

Occasional extras are airport and train pickups, gourmet picnic lunches and evening meals, sherry and high tea, sightseeing tours, horseback riding, restaurant and theater reservations.

Bed & Breakfast International
151 ARDMORE ROAD, KENSINGTON, CA 94707

Offers B&B Homes In:
San Francisco and all areas of tourist interest in California, including Los Angeles, Monterey Peninsula, San Diego, Wine Country, coastal and mountain regions; also, Seattle, Las Vegas, New York City, and Hawaii

Reservations Phone: (415) 525-4569 or 527-8836
Phone Hours: 8 a.m. to 5 p.m.   **Available:** Monday to Friday, till noon Saturday

Price Range of Homes:
Single: 20% discount on double rate   Double: $30 to $95
Breakfast Included in Price:
Full American . . . the famous sourdough bread is served in many of the San Francisco host homes.
Brochure Available: Free if inquirer sends stamped, self-addressed #10 envelope
Reservations Should Be Made: 2 weeks in advance preferred

B&B BONUSES:
Hosts live in modern apartments in city centers, in Victorian mansions, California Mediterranean-style homes on quiet, tree-lined streets, mountain chalets, beach houses, and a houseboat in Sausalito.

NATIONAL & INTERNATIONAL HELP • 57

Bed & Breakfast Society
330 WEST MAIN STREET, FREDERICKBURG, TX 78624

Offers B&B Homes In:
Network for reservations and worldwide B&B information includes the entire United States, Canada, Mexico, Europe, particularly Germany and Austria, and other foreign nations.

Reservations Phone: (512) 997-4712
Phone Hours: 10 a.m. to 5 p.m.   **Available:** Monday to Saturday
Price Range of Homes: Single: $25 to $100   Double: $35 to $125
Breakfast Included in Price:
Continental or full American . . . for guests who prefer to be left alone, there are private guesthouses with kitchen facilities and supplies, so they can fix their own breakfasts.
Brochure Available: Free if inquirer sends stamped, self-addressed #10 envelope (they also publish "Bed & Breakfast World Magazine" and "B&B World Directory," both of which are available for $5)
Reservations Should Be Made: As far as possible in advance (last minute reservations accepted if possible)

B&B BONUSES

"Our host homes and inns are spread all around the world. They are located in little towns, in the country on farms and ranches; one is an exotic game ranch; another is a 20-room guesthouse in Bavaria near the Alps, and another is a simple pioneer Texas cottage in a rustic setting."

Many of the hosts make arrangements for special diets and allergies, pickups to and from transportation centers, and assistance with sightseeing tours.

The Society also assists host homes to prepare to receive guests, and helps in the organization of Reservation Service Organizations (B&B agencies) anywhere in the world. The Society Tour office provides escorted B&B tours in cooperation with various types of organizations and special interest groups.

California Houseguests International, Inc.
18533 BURBANK BLVD.-P.O. BOX 190, TARZANA, L.A. CA 91356

Offers B&B Homes In:
California: Los Angeles area, Carmel, Santa Barbara, San Francisco, San Diego - and all over the world

Reservations Phone: (818) 344-7878
Phone Hours: 9 a.m. to 5 p.m.   **Available:** 7 days a week (collect calls to book reservations are accepted)

Price Range of Homes:
Single: $40 to $60   Double: $45 to $65
Breakfast Included in Price:
Special Continental breakfast: croissants, cheese, hot beverage, preserves, fresh fruit, with a flower
Brochure Available: Free if inquirer sends stamped, self-addressed #10 envelope
Reservations Should Be Made: 1 week in advance (last minute reservations accepted if possible)

B&B Bonuses

Many charming homes close to beaches, or in the cities with pools and other amenities, plus mansions and some large estates, are on this B&B's list in California.

Pickups from terminals, babysitting, extra meals, and kitchen privileges, are offered at a reasonable extra charge.

Christian Bed & Breakfast of America
P.O. BOX 388, SAN JUAN CAPISTRANO, CA 92693

Offers B&B Homes In:
All over the United States, in 350 cities

Reservations Phone: (714) 496-7050
Phone Hours: 8 a.m. to 5 p.m.   **Available:** Monday to Friday, and weekend evenings, 6 p.m. to 9 p.m.

Price Range of Homes:
Single: $15 to $40   Double: $20 to $55
Breakfast Included in Price:
Continental or full American . . . specialities offered in some areas, such as high English tea served on 100-year old china in prize winning table settings on Cape Cod
Brochure Available: For a fee, which is 50 cents
Reservations Should Be Made: 2 weeks in advance (last minute reservations accepted if possible)

B&B Bonuses

Their many host homes throughout the country include farms, ranches, oceanfront apartments, historic homes, and estates.

Regional sightseeing and cultural tours, wind-surfing and sailing excursions, picnic lunches, skiing, live music, and airport pickups, are some of the extras frequently offered.

CoHost, America's Bed & Breakfast
P.O. BOX 9302, WHITTIER, CA 90608

Offers B&B Homes In:
Throughout the U. S.—homes in Northern and Southern California, and many other states

Reservations Phone: (213) 699-8427
Phone Hours: 8 a.m. to 9 p.m.   **Available:** Any time on answering machine

Price Range of Homes:
Single: $20 to $60   Double: $25 to $65

Breakfast Included in Price:
Full breakfast . . . CoHosts specialize in regional foods, such as a typical Mexican breakfast with huevos rancheros and tortillas, or country biscuits and gravy with ham and eggs, or eggs Benedict and fruit compotes

Brochure Available: Free if inquirer sends stamped, self-addressed #10 envelope

Reservations Should Be Made: 2 weeks in advance (last minute reservations accepted if possible)

B&B Bonuses

Enjoy the hospitality of a Spanish-speaking, world-traveled bachelor who collects art and photographs, or feast on succulent crepes and delicate pastries with former owners of a popular restaurant, or, if you have children, stay at a home with large bedrooms, in a quiet neighborhood that is near Disneyland and Knott's Berry Farm, where the English hosts will welcome you back for tea afterwards.

For a moderate fee, arrangements are available to take guests to and from the airport by limousine. Many hosts are eager to provide sightseeing trips to the guest's choice of destination.

"Our rates do not fluctuate with seasons or special events . . . this is one of the areas in which we specialize and in which we are different from other B&B's."

Home Suite Homes
1470 FIREBIRD WAY, SUNNYVALE, CA 94087

Offers B&B Homes In:
All areas of the United States, mostly Northern California, particularly San Francisco, Monterey, Carmel, Santa Cruz, Silicon Valley, wine country

Reservations Phone: (408) 733-7215
Phone Hours: Any Hour   **Available:** 7 days a week
Price Range of Homes:
Single: $25 to $40   Double: $30 to $70
Breakfast Included in Price:
Continental or full American (varies according to individual home)
Brochure Available: Free
Reservations Should Be Made: 2 weeks (or less) in advance, last minute reservations accepted if possible

B&B Bonuses
"Many hosts will pick up at airports for a small fee ($5 to $10). Many will give extra meals and sightseeing. They will also make reservations for theaters or festivals."

Megan's Friends B'n B
1296 GALLEON WAY #2, SAN LUIS OBISPO, CA 93401

Offers B&B Homes In:
West Coast of U. S., and worldwide referrals (this is a private membership group with both exclusive listings of hosts limited to Megan's Friends members, and referral homes, which list themselves with other B&B's also)

Reservations Phone: (805) 544-4406
Phone Hours: Any time   **Available:** 7 days a week (regular office hours Monday to Friday, 10 a.m. to noon, 1 to 4 p.m.)

Price Range of Homes:
Single: $30 to $45   Double: $35 to $75
Breakfast Included in Price:
Full American . . . and many homes offer "Megan's Friends Special Recipes," which have been published as "Breakfast Recipe Guide From Megan's Friends" and may include such dishes as "Gordon's Gammon and Egg Toast"
Brochure Available: Free if inquirer sends stamped, self-addressed #10 envelope
Reservations Should Be Made: 3 weeks in advance (last minute reservations accepted if possible)

B&B Bonuses

To maintain strict standards of cleanliness and comfort, no smoking is permitted in Megan's homes. They range from a beachfront redwood with spectacular ocean view, to a solar-designed home with a 360-degree canyon view, to completely equipped honeymoon cottages along the Pacific coast.

Special acts of hospitality have included picnic lunches, invitations to join the host family at a concert, play, or tour, help in getting tickets, restaurant reservations, flowers . . . and gifts and cards to celebrate guests' birthdays and anniversaries.

Northwest Bed & Breakfast, Inc.
7707 S. W. LOCUST ST., PORTLAND, OR 97223

Offers B&B Homes In:
Oregon, British Columbia, Washington, California, Idaho, Montana, Nevada, and England

Reservations Phone: (503) 246-8366
Phone Hours: 9 a.m. to 6 p.m.   **Available:** Monday to Saturday
Price Range of Homes:
Single: $18 to $30   Double: $24 to $45
Breakfast Included in Price:
Full American (meats not necessarily included) . . . plus regional specialties such as clam fritters, sourdough pancakes, English scones, fresh fruit platter, depending on host
Brochure Available: Free if inquirer sends stamped, self-addressed #10 envelope
Reservations Should Be Made: In advance (last minute reservations accepted if possible)

B&B Bonuses

A few of their notable homes are an 80-acre working ranch serving food grown on the premises, an 1896 home in San Francisco with coffee and sherry available around the clock and French, Greek, and Spanish spoken; a sail boat in the San Juan Islands of Washington state, and a self-contained guest cottage adjoining the host's home, with a magnificent view of Cowichan Bay, BC, and salmon fishing as well as Indian longboat racing out front.

Many guests are picked up at the airport, and taken on sightseeing tours. Ask for their brochure of self-drive holidays on the West Coast.

P. T. International
1318 S. W. TROY ST., PORTLAND, OR 97219

Offers B&B Homes In:
48 states throughout the U. S.

Reservations Phone: (800) 547-1463 or (503) 245-0440 (Telex #277311)
Phone Hours: 8 a.m. to 5 p.m.   **Available:** Monday to Friday
Price Range of Homes:
Single: $20 to $129   Double: $30 to $200
Breakfast Included in Price:
Continental or full American, according to individual property
Brochure Available: Free
Reservations Should Be Made: Any time, last minute reservations accepted

B&B Bonuses

"We benefit the (B&B) traveler by offering information and reservations through any travel agency, or by calling our office toll-free from anywhere in the nation, excluding Oregon . . . brochures on request . . . assistance in trip planning . . . car rental information and reservations for most destinations."

(This organization represents, besides B&B homes, nearly 300 inns in our country.)

5

How to be a B&B Guest

- Use a reservation service organization that pre-inspects the homes on its lists.
- Some B&B homes offer free pick-up at airports and train and bus stations for travelers without cars.
- Use our B&B PHONE BOOKING FORM to help you get the B&B home that best matches your needs and pocketbook.

While enjoying the hospitality and warmth of a typical B&B home may be as easy as saying, "Pass the strawberry preserves," finding the right home for you and your family may require a little effort and advance planning.

First, we strongly recommend that you use a reservations service rather than taking pot luck as you drive along the road or call a home that you've seen listed in a book. Any reservation service worth its fee that it usually receives from each rental (from the B&B host, not you) will inspect the homes on its list. Or at a very minimum, the service will quickly drop any homes that guests have complained about frequently.

It's true that you may occasionally find a gem on your own simply by stopping at a "Bed & Breakfast" sign. But the odds are against you because many of the best B&B homes aren't listed.

We've repeated this warning in other parts of this guide because we truly believe that booking your B&B home through an established reservation service organization is the simplest, safest and ultimately the most satisfying way.

However, before you call any reservation service, you should write down your basic needs. In many cases the reservation service will send you a free or low-cost brochure that describes the homes and locations available. You then phone or write the reservation service after you've made the selection. You will usually be required to confirm the reservation by a minimum payment of the first night's rental. Some services may require full payment in advance.

But there may also be many times when you're making a spur of the moment vacation or business trip and the whole reservation process must be completed with one phone call. Because we wanted to make this guide a workbook that helps you truly enjoy the B&B experience to the fullest, we have included after the listings a "B&B Phone Booking Form." If you complete some of the information on the form *before* you call and then use the form to ask the right question of the reservation service, chances are you'll get the B&B that is just right for you.

After you have a confirmed reservation from the reservation service, always call the host. This is a very important call because it will be your first contact with this very important person. You can begin to establish a friendship with that first call. Have a map handy and you can ask specific questions about the most direct route to the B&B home.

Many B&B hosts offer pick up services to carless travelers, free or at a small fee. If you arrive by plane, bus, or train, you may be able to have the host meet you at the airport or station.

It is always a good practice (and often required) that you

pay the host any balance due for your entire B&B stay when you arrive. This also saves problems when you check out if the host is away.

Ask about the use of a house key, particularly if your host works and you want access to the house and your room during the day. You may be required to post a key fee.

Ask all about the use of the house and grounds. Some hosts give you kitchen privileges and allow you to fix your own breakfast whenever you're ready. One B&B guest surprised her host by making strawberry pancakes for her husband and the whole host family. "They were pleased," she said later. "But you could tell this wasn't their typical breakfast. They really thought I was serving them dessert."

There may be recreation facilities/equipment in the house and on the grounds—TV sets, stereos, barbeque pits, volley ball nets, swimming pool, sleds, etc. Find out if you're permitted to use them. Many hosts are happy to oblige.

In the house itself, is smoking permitted in your room? In certain areas? Or forbidden throughout the house. Do you have access to the family room, the living room, and the laundry facilities.

Never hesitate to ask if you need certain comfort items—an extra blanket for the bed, extra towels, etc. Some rooms have individual air conditioners or temperature controls. Ask for a demonstration of how to regulate them.

The host may give you a written set of "house rules." Follow them and treat the house as you would your own. Clear communication and common courtesy are the bases for a successful and happy B&B homestay.

Always sign the guestbook when you leave, with any personal comments about what you liked about the visit and your hosts. It's a great keepsake for the hosts. It also can lead to Christmas cards, social notes, and just possibly, a lifelong friendship.

6
B&Bs Abroad

- Sleep in a French country chateau in a room with one whole wall a fireplace, with a medieval timbered barn and green mountains right outside your three windows. Cost? About $16 a night for two, breakfast in an antique-filled kitchen included.
- Bed and Breakfast in a Cyprus Monastery high atop a craggy mountain - at no charge (a small donation is appropriate).
- Help herd a flock of the unique black sheep and sightsee glaciers. Then come home to a warm welcome on a B&B farm in New Zealand.

What can you and the Ambassador from Australia, the Secretary of Finance from Denmark, and the former Prime Minister of the Netherlands have in common?

You can all stay in a chambre d'hote in Normandy, France for about $12 to $16 a night. That is the cost for two people, who like the world statesmen, elect to stay in the 16th-Century farmhouse in the Village of Commes as the guests of the Leroys.

All of the statesmen named above did just that and signed the family's guestbook which is overflowing with notes of thanks, friendship, and photographs from all over the world.

The house is an ancient delight with huge sunny rooms filled with country antiques from different periods of French history. Madame Leroy may welcome her guests with some of the Calvados region's famous apple cider and apple cake. Not only apple orchards flourish in this rich Normandy soil. It is said to be so rich that a farmer thrusting a stick into the ground in the morning will find it filled with leaves in the afternoon. You may have trouble swallowing that local claim, but certainly not Madame Leroy's glorious breakfasts. On a typical country morning she may serve eggs, corn flakes, fresh pan bread, the freshest butter you've ever spread on bread, and homemade jams. You have your choice of cafe au lait (coffee with hot milk), tea or chocolate. The source of all these fresh dairy products will probably come in view during the day when a herd of cows leaves the 16th-century barn right across the courtyard.

Then the day is yours to explore Normandy. During the summer, you may want to head to the nearby beaches. The Leroy farm is also close to the D-Day landing areas and the Normandy American Cemetery. Near the farmhouse a signpost will direct you to Bayeux. You will want to take a full day to explore the 11th-century Cathedral and, of course, see the Bayeux Tapestry in the former Bishop's Palace. This magnificent 11th-century work of art is misnamed. It's not really tapestry but embroidery; colored wools on linen. Shown under glass, it depicts 58 historic scenes with astonishing perspective and freshness. Or you may decide to follow the plump red apple "route du Cidre" signs to ancient farmhouses where making the tart, bracing apple cider is a Normandy art. If you're lucky enough to be passenger rather than driver, you may also want to sample the potent Calvados apple brandy made and sold right on the farms.

The whole area offers many great restaurants. After all, this is France. But some B&B guests have learned that one of the very good "restaurants" in much closer to home—right in the Leroy's spacious dining room. For about $8 per person, the Leroys will serve a dinner that consists of soup, salad, meat with vegetables, cheese, and some more of that famous apple cake.

There are some 600 Bed & Breakfast style homes (chambre d'hotes) in Normandy. Some are in beautiful country chateaus surrounded by gardens and ponds. Others are in simple rustic farmhouses. All of them have wash basins in the room, include excellent breakfasts in the price, and—with the continuing strength of the dollar in Europe—all are incredible bargains. Prices range from a low of about $10 per night for one person to a little over $16 to $18 for two.

The local tourism office goes all out to encourage the development of these chambre d'hotes, paying owners 20,000 francs for each room they renovate and rent. No more than five rooms may be renovated, and the tourist office, through the use of its checkbook, helps to control standards and quality.

Said one tourist officer, "We call this 'green tourism'—living in the country and coming in contact with the French people. Personal contact is the key. Travelers, however, should remember that these people are not professional hotel keepers. Don't expect things a hotel staff might do, such as carry your bags or serve you breakfast in bed. But these French farm people can be so warm and friendly, and they love to meet people."

I personally experienced some of this warmth when I visited another Normandy B&B, Le Manoir du Champ Versant. This chateau is a 17th-century building that has already been featured in a coffee-table book of great French houses. The hostess is a lovely, animated French woman who speaks no English. But that doesn't matter. She takes you to some of the rooms that are available. One has a huge fireplace that dominates the room, and an equally huge country bed. The room and its antique furniture is a sun-filled joy. The light comes from three windows that look out over the surrounding countryside, a scene which includes an ancient timbered barn, herds of cattle, a large pond, and green hills. On learning that this room cost only about $16 a night for two, I was ready to abandon this guidebook and rent the place for the summer.

Unfortunately an American painter who lives on Central Park West in New York City had already seen the view, the bed, and the fireplace and booked it long-term.

While the settings may be rural, the reservations system for these chambre d'hotes is as modern as the computer in the local Caen office. For more information you could write to the French Tourist Office (see address at the back of this section) or directly to the Chambre d'Agriculture, Promenade de Sevigne, 140000 Caen, Normandy, France.

You also can simply look for the green "chambre d'hote" signs along the roadside. In certain summer months the rooms may already be booked. (Consider the case of the greedy long-term renter, the American painter.) But in spring and fall, you have an excellent chance of waking up to the smell of hot coffee and warm pan bread emanating from a rich country kitchen, such as that of Madame Leroy. Be sure to sign her illustrious guestbook.

Great Britain is almost the ancestral home of the whole B&B movement. For a number of years American travelers have stopped, slept and breakfasted in the honey-colored homes of the Cotswolds, in cottages rising right out of the mist of Scotland's Isle of Skye, and in every nook and quaint cranny of London.

Eleanor Berman, author of *Away for the Weekend: New England*, recently was touring Wales with her daughter and stopped at a B&B in Llangollen, Wales near the river Dee.

She reported, "Llangollen is a charming typical Welsh village of stone cottages, made particularly scenic by a river flowing through the center of town. Church Street parallels the river and runs right into the main shopping street—an ideal location—and Maew Mawr House and its proprietors are right out of central casting. A cozy home and rosy-cheeked, plump, white-haired couple who couldn't have been sweeter or more solicitous.

"Rooms are very big here and look out either at the river or the pleasant street. This isn't decorator decor, but has been done with obvious care. Each room has a color scheme carried through to curtains, linens and comforters atop each bed. Ours was pale violet. Another nice room was done in pale green. The bathroom was all in blue. Each room has an electric teapot and fixings for coffee or tea.

"Our hostess' first question after we checked in was 'What time will you want breakfast?' The meal was the usual hearty English morning fare of a fried egg, sausage *and* bacon, grilled tomato and toast. The very pleasant dining room looks out at the river. The mantel is covered with postcards from former guests all over the world.

"She then sat down with us and drew a careful map of the most scenic route to follow when we left. Then came out with us to the car park to watch for traffic for me so I could back out without any trouble, knowing I was still uneasy with my gear shift, left-drive car."

The cost? About $16 a night for two, with that breakfast of "sausage *and* bacon" included.

You will also find B&B's all over Germany and Austria. Most of these can be booked on the spot. You just look for the "Zimmer Frei" sign in front of the houses, and take your pick. You are always welcome to inspect the room before booking.

Surprisingly there are few, if any, B&B homes in Italy. However, you will find a number of moderately priced *pensions* which may be located in private homes but are essentially full-time commercial operations. The B&B concept has not yet spread to the Middle East to any great extent although the Egyptian tourism people are currently considering this idea. Some women in Greece (on the island of Lesbos) are trying to start the first B&Bs in that country.

B&B's are flourishing in many other parts of the world. In New Zealand you can stay in city and town B&Bs, or join a sheep-raising family on their farm. The country offers a free-wheeling B&B concept called "Go as You Please" (from Oct. 1

to March 31 each year). You buy a series of vouchers and a book listing all hosts. You call your host at least 24 hours in advance from anywhere along the road. You can travel by rental car, rail coach, air, or even bicycle.

Japan offers something similar to B&Bs. There are homestays in typical Japanese houses, often in rural areas. These are not for the super-comfort seekers. You may sleep on mats in a barely furnished room. Travel writer Jack Adler said, "It may not be for the first-time traveler to Japan. On my visit with my wife we made our own beds and had to bring our own soap and wash cloths. But we did prepare meals right in the room, and that was great fun."

If you plan to look for B&B accommodations abroad, you should first write to the country's tourist office in the U.S. Some of these, unfortunately, have a knee-jerk response to many letters and may send you a general brochure that doesn't even mention B&B's. But others are becoming much more sensitive to this "people's hotel" concept, and will send you very complete information.

You also can visit the regional tourist offices when you've arrived. These offices often have lists of area B&B homes, and some may even handle bookings for you.

In Europe a good source of B&B information is often the local bookstore (English-language section). On a recent visit to Paris I found a number of books and directories to B&Bs on the Continent, and for many areas of Great Britain. The Europeans long-ago discovered the economies and pleasures of the B&B.

FOREIGN TOURIST OFFICES

The tourism departments of various foreign countries and areas with offices in major U.S. cities can be very helpful when you're looking for B&B accommodations abroad. A complete list of these offices is at the back of this section.

Here are some of the particularly useful responses to our queries.

AUSTRALIA
(Australian Tourist Commission)

Australia is almost literally bursting with Bed & Breakfast opportunities.

An organization called Bed & Breakfast International plans and books a number of unusual home and ranch stays. A "homestay" includes your room in a private home. Breakfast is included and dinner may often by booked. You can also stay on a working sheep station or a cattle ranch. All of the homes included in the program have been personally inspected by Bed & Breakfast International.

Here are a few of the B&B programs you can choose:

"Meet the Aussies." You spend four days/three nights with a host family in Sydney, Melbourne, Adelaide, Brisbane, Perth, Canberra, Caires or a resort or country town. The price depends on the type of room and home you choose and ranges from about $60 to $75. Or you can spend a budget week in Sydney for about $13.50 a night. The organization will attempt to match you with a host who has similar interests.

It's even possible to combine a *flying* tour of the Australian outback with your B&B stay.

Bed & Breakfast International promises this idyllic-sounding vacation. "Imagine an elegant homestead, a large outback ranch, a personality-plus host, wildlife, and not a soul in sight for miles. But charter your host's light aircraft and he will take you to seldom visited, inaccessible areas plus fabulous Queensland boulder opal country. This is the Australia of wide open spaces, extensive livestock grazing, artesian water, kangaroos and emus, where man has a constant battle with nature." The cost for a four days/three nights ranchstay is about $225. Not cheap but could be quite an experience.

Did you ever hanker to milk a cow, shear and dip a sheep, or go for long hayrides into the countryside? You can do all this and more on a B&B stay in *Brooklyn*. Yes, Australia has one, too. The cost is only about $20 a day and includes *all* meals.

Like New Zealand, Australia also offers self-drive holidays which combine a rental car with stops along the way at B&B homes.

For further information on these and many other B&B accommodations and complete vacations in Australia, write for these free booklets: "Australia Farm Holidays" and "Australian Homestays and Ranchstays." These are available from the Australian Tourist Commission (address at the end of this section).

Bed & Breakfast International (Australia)
18-20 Oxford Street
P.O. Box 442, Woollahra
Sydney, N.S.W. Australia 2025
Telex: AA27229

For self-drive holidays—

PT International
1318 SW Troy
Portland, Oregon 97219

AUSTRIA
(Austrian National Tourist Office)

When traveling through Austria, keep your eye out for a sign "Zimmer Frei" or simply a sign with a white bed on a green background. These signs are usually hung at the front gate of private homes that offer Bed & Breakfast accommodations. When this sign is on display, it's the equivalent of an American motel sign flashing "vacancy."

Feel free to stop and ask to inspect the room (advance

reservations are extremely rare and usually impossible). If you like the room and the price, take it. The price is not hard to like—$8 to $15 a night for two people, including a Continental breakfast. A single traveler might pay as little as $5 per night.

You should pay your bill when you take the room, in Austrian Schillings. Don't expect a private bath. There is often only one bathroom in the whole house. But the rooms are usually very clean, and there is a wash basin in the room with hot and cold water.

BERMUDA

On a recent visit to Bermuda, I stopped in the Visitors Service Bureau in Hamilton, about a block from the Princess Hotel. The official greeter gave this advice to anyone looking for B&B in Bermuda. "We have a list of homes that visitors can book by stopping here."

The office also provides this information in letter form:

"More than one hundred families in all parts of the Island are registered with the Bermuda Chamber of Commerce. Some offer single or double rooms with or without breakfast. Others offer studio apartments, or one- and two-bedroom guest cottages. The rates are from $15 to $25 per person per day (double occupancy).

"Arrangements can be made by writing to the Visitors Service Bureau, Bermuda Chamber of Commerce, P.O. Box 655, Hamilton 5-31 Bermuda. We must know the exact dates of arrival and departure; number of people in your party; type of accommodation preferred and the maximum rate per person. "We will then book your accommodation and direct you to send a two-day deposit to your host to confirm the room.

"If you prefer to telephone and are prepared to accept a collect call when we have found a suitable home, much time will be saved. Our telephone number is 809-295-1430."

Editor's Note: There is one possible disadvantage to staying at a B&B in a remote location. Unless you ride a bicycle or a Moped, you may have real trouble getting around the island. There are no rental cars in Bermuda, and taxis are in short supply—usually available primarily at the airport and around major hotels. You can also call for a taxi but this can take some time. I was recently stranded for well over an hour in St. Georges, Bermuda, waiting in vain for a taxi I had called.

BULGARIA
(Bulgarian Tourist Office)

Mr. Ivan Dimov, Director of the Bulgarian Tourist Office in New York, says, "Private boarding houses with Bed & Breakfast or full board are available for tourists in every large town in Bulgaria." All reservations are made through Balkantourist. This organization also offers a wide range of services that include tours and trips for groups and individual tourists, motel or hotel accommodations, booking of minibuses and rent-a-cars.

The address of Balkantourist is 1 Vitosha Boulevard, Sofia 1000, Bulgaria. Att: Overseas Department. Telephone: 84-131 (Ext. 284), Telex: 865-22583(4).

CYPRUS
(Cyprus Tourism Organization)

Cyprus does not have any Bed & Breakfast homes as such but does have commercial guest houses. The tourism office also offers an intriguing alternative, Bed & Breakfast in a monastery. You can actually stay overnight for three nights without charge (although it is customary to leave a donation at the end of the stay).

For example, you could stay at the Kykko Monastery,

perhaps the most famous monastery in the world. The literature reports, "The Monastery was founded around 1100 AD . . . (and) possesses an icon of the Virgin Mary and Child, believed to have been painted by St. Luke."

You may also want to visit the Stavrovouri Monastery (founded in 327 AD) and situated high on a peak 25 miles from Nicosia. According to a belief held by many, there is still a fragment of the Holy Cross in the monastery. You can also see a huge wooden cross from 1476, carved with Biblical scenes. But couples would not make this a B&B stop. Because of the monastery's strict religious vows, women are permitted to visit only on Sundays. Men traveling alone can stay over on Mondays, Wednesdays, Fridays, and Sundays.

On a drive through Cyprus, you may want to plan your own breakfast picnic. Stop for homemade bread and a jar of the marvellous flavored honey that you can purchase from one of the monasteries.

CZECHOSLOVAKIA

According to Cedok Travel & Hotel Corporation (the company that arranges almost all travel to Czechoslovakia, "there is no possibility to accommodate travelers in homes on a bed & breakfast basis. Nevertheless for people traveling to Europe with a limited budget we have the following suggestions:

"1. Accommodations with (two meals daily—MAP) in three-star category hotels owned and operated by CEDOK cost between $37.50 and $52 per double room.

"2. During the summer months, a limited number of student dormitories is available, basically in Prague, Brno, Bratislava and Olomou as well as in some other cities. For each season a complete list including addresses is available from our national tourist office. Price is between $12 and $15 per person (double sharing). Breakfast is usually available in nearby restaurants on an individual basis."

DENMARK
(The Danish Tourist Board)

B&B homes are available in this delightful country. But the tourist office has no information or lists of them. Your best bet is to stop in one of the local tourist offices when you're traveling through Denmark. These offices can arrange private accommodations.

EGYPT
(Egyptian Tourist Authority)

Mr. Shawki Hussein, Director of the Egyptian Tourist Authority in New York, advises, "Staying with families is hardly practiced in Egypt. However, the Egyptian General Authorities for the Promotion of Tourism is currently exploring the possibilities to provide such means of accommodation."

FRENCH WEST INDIES—GUADELOUPE, MARTINIQUE
(French West Indies Tourist Board)

There are no Bed & Breakfast homes in the French West Indies. However, there are alternatives. These are some suggestions from the tourist office.

"On Guadeloupe the Relais Hotels de la Gaudeloupe are a group of small hotels and inns, some with as few as seven rooms, where guests receive the personal attention of the manager and where room with breakfast can be arranged. The association's address is: Chaine des Relais-Hotels de la Guadeloupe, Chateaubrun 97180, Sainte-Anne, Guadeloupe, FWI. Telex: 919913.

"For visitors wanting a home atmosphere, houses can be rented from Gites de France, but this is quite different from B&B. The houses range from modest weekend places to comfortable villas, either in villages or by the sea. Details are available through Mme Marcelle Lautric, c/o Guadeloupe Tourist Office, 5 Square de la Banque, Pointe-a-Pitre, Guadeloupe, 97110, FWI. Phone: 82-09-30.

"On Martinique La Chaine des Relais de la Martinique is comprised of small hotels, bungalows, and cottages. Some of these properties offer room and breakfast, others breakfast-making facilities. There is a central reservations service: Petite Hotellerie de la Martinique, Pavillon du Tourisme, rue Ernest-Deproge, 97200, Fort-de-France, Martinique, FWI. Phone: 71-56-11.

GERMANY
(German National Tourist Office)

"Hospitality is especially personalized in private Bed & Breakfast homes throughout Germany offering visitors clean and comfortable rooms from $8 to $16 (U.S.) nightly, per person, including a full breakfast!

"All Bed and Breakfast accommodations are inspected periodically by local tourist boards and must merit approval before being offered to the public. Homes must provide clean and comfortable rooms (some rooms have sinks with hot and cold running water). Bathroom facilities are often shared, although some homes provide a private bath.

"Breakfasts range from hearty to elegant. Guests can count on eggs, freshly baked rolls and bread; plenty of butter, jam, and marmalade; perhaps cold cuts and cheese; and, of course, coffee, tea, and hot chocolate."

After sending us all of this helpful information, the tourist office underlined with a heavy yellow pen this point—*"Infor-*

mation on available rooms is only obtainable from local tourist offices" which are usually within or near the rail terminals in cities. In smaller towns and villages tourist offices are located in or nearby the "Rathaus" (City Hall). A tourist office generally will give a visitor three listings, and also subsequent leads if the visitor isn't satisfied with the first round of inspection. Quite often homeowners will pick up rail travelers who telephone from the tourist offices.

"Bed & Breakfast rooms are available year-round in Germany. There are more choices in popular tourist areas from April through the summer, and many homes in the winter sports areas make rooms available during that season. In larger cities, a number of homes are suitable for business travelers. Accommodations are especially welcomed during periods when trade fairs and conventions are held, and during the peak season when major hotels are booked well in advance.

"Bed & Breakfast homes accept only cash. Rates are set by the home owners."

GREAT BRITAIN
(British Tourist Authority)

B&B homes are easy to spot. Just look for the sign "Bed & Breakfast" in the downstairs front windows of many homes. You may also see this sign on posts on the lawn or hanging on the garden gate. Breakfasts are a special treat because they almost always include a hot course such as bacon and eggs, plus toast and coffee or tea and marmalade. In rural areas these products may be just hours from the farm. You can 'book a bed ahead' at British Tourist Information Centers (stop before noon to arrange the evening's accommodations). For more information, write the Tourist Authority for their helpful booklet, "Bed & Breakfast in Britain."

INDIA
(Government of India Tourist Office)

If you're interested in booking a B&B in India, you should first write the Tourist Office in the U.S. for a list of brochures about the various areas. Mr. S. K. Kachroo then advises, travelers "can write to our offices in India. Their addresses are mentioned in each of the brochures. The local offices who maintain such lists can assist the traveler."

IRELAND
(Irish Tourist Board)

Catherine Cullen of the Public Relations Department of the Irish Tourist Board wanted to share this information with readers of this guidebook:

"All bed & breakfast homes listed in Irish Tourist Board guides have been inspected by our staff and are identified by an 'approved' sign (the word 'Approved' in red flanked, of course, by two green shamrocks).

"We have a comprehensive listing of all properties called 'Irish Homes.' Travelers may write to us for a copy.

"Reservations may be made by: a. writing to our reservations department—Central Reservations Service, Dublin Tourism, 14 Upper O'Connell Street, Dublin 1 (Ireland), phone: 01-747733. b. As holidaymakers drive through Ireland, they may make reservations at Irish Tourist Board offices which are located in almost every town. c. Simply asking at a home which displays the 'Approved' sign."

ISRAEL
(Israel Ministry of Tourism)

While there have been local programs that allow you to meet with the Israelis in their homes for conversation, B&B

programs have lagged behind. The Ministry of Tourism directed our inquiry to Excursions Limited, a U.S. tour company that recently recruited a number of families in Israel as Bed & Breakfast hosts. These homes are part of tours and can't be booked individually. Ms. Phillis P. Caro, President of the organization, said, "The traveler or their travel agent must contact Excursions Unlimited prior to departure for Israel to make the bookings. All Israel Government Tourist Offices, El Al offices, many travel agencies and most Jewish Community Centers will have brochures." For more information, write Excursions Unlimited, 2 Headley Way, Woodbury, NY 11797.

JAPAN
(National Tourist Office)

Minshuku are the Japanese equivalent of B&B. You can stay in a private home for around $20 per night, including breakfast and one other meal. "Creature comforts" are often modest. You may stay in a city apartment or a thatched roof cottage and sleep on Japanese mats on the floor. The Japanese National Tourist Organization will supply a list of these Minshuku accommodations.

NEW ZEALAND
(Tourist Office)

"Bed & Breakfast is booked a little differently in New Zealand than for instance, in England and Europe," says Diane Moir, Marketing Officer for the New Zealand Tourist Office in New York.

"One has to book through an agency such as the New Zealand Home Hospitality Ltd. (P.O. Box 309, Nelson. Telex: NZ3697 Attn HOMEHOSP Telephone: 54 85-727.; their services are fully described in the free brochure, New

Zealand Bed & Breakfast in Town and Country Homes). Or for a farm stay through the agencies listed on page 122 of the New Zealand Accommodation Guide. (Editor's Note: This free book is excellent; be sure to ask for it by name.) Both these guides are available to the general public from the tourist office."

"You can book such accommodations, either by writing directly to the agencies, or more easily and efficiently, through a travel agency contacting the New Zealand Tourist Office in San Francisco which handles all internal New Zealand reservations. (This reservation must be made through a travel agent and not by the traveler himself.) The address is: New Zealand Tourist Office, Alcoa Building, Suite 970, Maritime Plaza, San Francisco, CA 94111.

NORWAY
(Handled by Scandinavian National Tourist Offices)

Elin Bolann, Director of the Scandinavian Tourist Office, says, "Bed & breakfast is mostly only common in the cities. Most types of accommodations in the countryside offer breakfast and dinner. Unfortunately there is no list available of Bed & Breakfast homes in Norway. The best thing to do for travelers is to contact the local tourist offices in Norway, and ask there."

THE PHILIPPINES
(Office of the Tourism Director)

Marilen Paderon writes, "Our office maintains a list of accredited tourist establishments throughout the Philippines. However, our classification does not include bed & breakfast homes. We do have a number of inns, pensions, and lodges within Metro Manila and in the provincial areas which would probably be equivalent to your bed & breakfast homes in

North America. This list is available upon request through our office. Advance bookings may be made directly through our domestic field offices."

SRI LANKA
(Ceylon) (Ceylon Tourist Board)

As this book goes to press, this lovely land of "serendipity" is still a troubled place, riven by racial strife. However, when (or if) the civil breaches are healed, Sri Lanka will again be one of the more relaxing experiences of many travelers' around the world trip.

Sri Lanka has a "rooms in homes" program similar to the U.S. Bed & Breakfast concept. The Tourist Board in New York will send a free listing to all who write.

For example, you could stay with Mrs. Rohini Abeysekera in Colombo, in a room with air conditioning. Sea bathing is available. The accommodating Mrs. Abeysekera will also provide dry cleaning and laundry service, store your luggage while you visit other areas, and get you a taxi when needed.

SOUTH AFRICA
(South African Tourism Board)

Bed & Breakfast facilities can be booked by writing: Professional Holiday Services (Pty) Ltd, Suite 206, 6 Church Square, Cape Town, 8001, phone (021) 46-3829. Telex: 57-22747.

YUGOSLAVIA
(Yugoslav National Tourist Office)

B&B-type accommodations are available throughout this country, and are even organized and classified by the government. Prices range from $10 to $25, and that upper price limit is along the Adriatic Riviera. The major difference among the categories seems to be how much private time you get in the bathroom: Category 1A provides a room with private bath in a villa-type house; Category I applies to a room with bathroom shared with other guests on the floor; Category II ensures a room with bathroom facilities shared with guests and the host family; Category III enables you to stay in a house in one of the old citadels, with bathroom shared with the host families. You will pay a premium of about 30% for stays of less than three nights. The breakfast charge is extra.

To book one of these rooms in advance, you should first get free literature from the Yugoslav Tourist Office in New York which lists all of the local tourist offices in Yugoslavia. Then you write directly to the office in the area you want to stay. It is not possible to make reservations in the U.S. either through the tourist office or through any tour operators.

However, there is another possibility when you've arrived in Yugoslavia. You can stop at a local tourist bureau or travel agency in any major tourist area and ask to see a list of available private homes. Or when driving down the road, you can look for an appealing home with a "Soba-Simmer-Room" outside (meaning they have a room available).

GOVERNMENT TOURIST OFFICES

Andorran National Tourist Board
Andorra Information Center
1923 W. Irvingpark Rd.
Chicago, IL 60613

Antigua Tourist Board
610 Fifth Ave., Suite 311
New York, NY 10020
(212) 541-4117

Aruba Tourist Bureau
1270 Ave. of the Americas,
  Suite 2212
New York, NY 10020
(212) 246-3030

Australian Tourist Commission
636 Fifth Ave., Fl. 4
New York, NY 10111
(212) 489-7550

Austrian National Tourist Office
545 Fifth Ave.
New York, NY 10017-3642
 (212) 697-0651

Bahamas Tourist Offices
Ministry of Tourism
Box N-3701
Nassau, Bahamas
 (809) 322-7500

Barbados Board of Tourism
800 Second Ave.
New York, NY 10017
 (212) 986-6516

Belgian Tourist Office
745 Fifth Ave.
New York, NY 10151
 (212) 758-8130

Bermuda Department of
 Tourism
Front St.
P.O. Box 465
Hamilton, Bermuda
 (809) 292-0023

Bhutan Travel Service
120 E. 56 St.
New York, NY 10022
 (212) 838-6382

Bolivian Consulate General
10 Rockefeller Plaza
New York, NY 10020
 (212) 586-1607

Bonaire Information Office
1466 Broadway, Suite 903
New York, NY 10036
 (212) 869-2004

Brazilian Consulate General
630 Fifth Ave.
New York, NY 10020
 (212) 757-3080

British Tourist Authority
40 W. 57 St.
New York, NY 10019
 (212) 581-4708

British Virgin Islands Tourist
 Board
370 Lexington Ave.
New York, NY 10017
 (212) 696-0400

Bulgarian Tourist Office
161 E. 86 St.
New York, NY 10028
 (212) 722-1110

Canadian Govt. Office of
 Tourism
235 Queen St.
Ottawa, Canada K1A 0H6
 (613) 996-4610

Cayman Islands Department of
 Tourism
250 Catalonia Ave., Suite 604
Coral Gables, FL 33134
 (305) 444-6551

Ceylon Tourist Board
609 Fifth Ave., Suite 308
New York, NY 10017
 (212) 935-0369

Tourist Office of Chile
c/o Lan-Chile Airlines
Rockefeller Center
630 Fifth Ave., Suite 809
New York, NY 10111
(212) 582-3250

China, Republic of, Tourism
  Bureau
1 World Trade Center, Suite
  86155
New York, NY 10048
(212) 466-0691

Colombian Govt. Tourist Office
140 E. 57 St.
New York, NY 10022
(212) 688-0151

Costa Rica Embassy
2112 S. St., N.W.
Washington, DC 20008

Curacao Tourist Board
400 Madison Ave., Suite 311
New York, NY 10017
(212) 751-8266

Cyprus Tourist Office
13 E. 40 St.
New York, NY 10016
(212) 686-6016

Czechoslovak Travel Bureau
10 E. 40 St.
New York, NY 10016
(212) 689-9720

Danish Tourist Board
75 Rockefeller Plaza
New York, NY 10019
(212) 582-2802

Dominica Tourist Board
Caribbean Tourism Association
20 E. 46 St.
New York, NY 10017
(212) 682-0435

Dominican Tourist Information
  Center
485 Madison Ave.
New York, NY 10022
(212) 826-0750

Egyptian Tourist Authority
630 Fifth Ave.
New York, NY 10111
(212) 246-6960

Finnish Tourist Board
75 Rockefeller Plaza
New York, NY 10019
(212) 582-2802

French Govt. Tourist Office
610 Fifth Ave.
New York, NY 10020
(212) 757-1125

French West Indies Tourist
  Board
610 Fifth Ave.
New York, NY 10020
(212) 757-1125

German National Tourist Office
747 Third Ave.
New York, NY 10017
(212) 308-3300

Consulate General of Ghana
Trade and Investment Office
19 E. 47 St.
New York, NY 10017
(212) 832-1300

Greek National Tourist
  Organization
Olympic Tower
645 Fifth Ave., 5th Fl.
New York, NY 10022
(212) 421-5777

Consulate General of Guatemala
57 Park Ave.
New York, NY 10016
(212) 686-8513

Haiti Govt. Tourist Bureau
1270 Ave. of the Americas
New York, NY 10020
(212) 757-3517

Hong Kong Tourist Association
548 Fifth Ave.
New York, NY 10036
(212) 869-5008

Hungarian Travel Bureau
630 Fifth Ave.
New York, NY 10111
(212) 582-7412

India Govt. Tourist Office
30 Rockefeller Plaza, 15-n.
  Mezzanine
New York, NY 10112
(212) 586-4901

Indonesia Consulate General
5 E. 68 St.
New York, NY 10021
(212) 879-0600

Irish Tourist Board
590 Fifth Ave.
New York, NY 10036
(212) 869-5500

Israel Ministry of Tourism
350 Fifth Ave.
New York, NY 10118
(212) 560-0650

Italian Govt. Travel Office
630 Fifth Ave.
New York, NY 10111
(212) 245-4822

Jamaica Tourist Board
866 Second Ave.
New York, NY 10017
(212) 688-7650

Japan National Tourist
  Organization
630 Fifth Ave.
New York, NY 10111
(212) 757-5640

Jordan Tourist Information
  Center
535 Fifth Ave.
New York, NY 10017
(212) 949-0060

Kenya Tourist Office
424 Madison Ave., 6th Fl.
New York, NY 10017
(212) 486-1300

Korea National Tourism
  Corporation
460 Park Ave., Suite 400
New York, NY 10022
  (212) 688-7543

Embassy of Laos
2222 S St. N.W.
Washington, DC 20008
  (202) 232-6416

Liberian Consulate General
820 Second Ave.
New York, NY 10017
  (212) 687-1025

Luxembourg National Tourist
  Office
801 Second Ave.
New York, NY 10017
  (212) 370-9850

Malaysian Tourist Information
  Centre
Transamerica Pyramid, 5th Fl.
600 Montgomery St.
San Francisco, CA 94111

Mauritius Tourist Information
  Service
2 W. 45 St., Suite 803
New York, NY 10036
  (212) 921-2944

Mexican Ministry of Tourism
405 Park Ave., Suite 1002
New York, NY 10022
  (212) 755-7261

Monaco Govt. Tourist and
  Convention Bureau
20 E. 49 St.
New York, NY 10017
  (212) 759-5227

Moroccan National Tourist
  Office
521 Fifth Ave., Suite 2800
New York, NY 10017
  (212) 421-5771

Netherlands National Tourist
  Office
576 Fifth Ave.
New York, NY 10036
  (212) 245-5321

New Zealand Tourist Office
Tishman Westwood Building
10960 Wilshire Boulevard
Los Angeles, CA 90024
  (213) 477-8241

Consulate General of Nigeria
575 Lexington Ave.
New York, NY 10022
  (212) 715-7200

Northern Ireland Tourist Board
40 W. 57 St., 3rd Fl.
New York, NY 10019
  (212) 765-5144

Norwegian National Tourist
  Office
75 Rockefeller Plaza
New York, NY 10019
  (212) 582-2802

Pakistan Consulate General
12 E. 65 St.
New York, NY 10021
   (212) 879-5800

Panama Govt. Tourist Bureau
19 W. 44 St., Suite 709
New York, NY 10036
   (212) 869-2530

Peruvian Consulate
10 Rockefeller Plaza, Suite 729
New York, NY 10020
   (212) 265-2480

Philippine Ministry of Tourism
556 Fifth Ave.
New York, NY 10036
   (212) 575-7915

Polish National Tourist Office
500 Fifth Ave.
New York, NY 10110
   (212) 391-0844

Portuguese National Tourist
   Office
548 Fifth Ave.
New York, NY 10036
   (212) 354-4403

Romanian National Tourist
   Office
573 Third Ave.
New York, NY 10016
   (212) 697-6971

Scandinavian National Tourist
   Offices
75 Rockefeller Plaza
New York, NY 10019
   (212) 582-2802

Senegal Govt. Tourist Bureau
Pan Am Building
200 Park Ave.
New York, NY 10166
   (212) 682-4695

Singapore Tourist Promotion
   Board
342 Madison Ave.
New York, NY 10173
   (212) 687-0385

South African Tourist
   Corporation
747 Third Ave., 20th Fl.
New York, NY 10017
   (212) 838-8841

Spanish National Tourist Office
665 Fifth Ave.
New York, NY 10022
   (212) 759-8822

St. Lucia Tourist Board
41 E. 42 St., Suite 315
New York, NY 10017
   (212) 867-2950

St. Maarten-Saba-St. Eustatius
   Tourist Office
445 Park Ave., Suite 902
New York, NY 10022
   (212) 688-8350

St. Vincent and the Grenadines
   Tourist Board
Eastern Caribbean Tourist
   Association
220 E. 42nd St.
New York, NY 10017
   (212) 986-9370

Consulate General of the
  Republic of Suriname
Empire State Building, Suite
  718
350 Fifth Ave.
New York, NY 10118
  (212) 947-2940

Swedish Tourist Board
75 Rockefeller Plaza
New York, NY 10019
  (212) 582-2802

Swiss National Tourist Office
608 Fifth Ave.
New York, NY 10020
  (212) 757-5944

Tanzania Tourist Corporation
201 East 42 St.
New York, NY 10017
  (212) 986-7124

Togo Information Service
1625 K Street, N.W.
Washington, DC 20006
  (202) 659-4330

Tourism Authority of Thailand
5 World Trade Center, Suite
  2449
New York, NY 10048
  (212) 432-0433

Trinidad and Tobago Tourist
  Board
400 Madison Ave., Suites
  712-14
New York, NY 10017
  (212) 838-7750

Turkish Tourism and
  Information Office
821 UN Plaza
New York, NY 10017
  (212) 687-2194

Turks and Caicos Islands Tourist
  Board
Caribbean Tourism Association
20 E. 46 St.
New York, NY 10017
  (212) 682-0435

Uruguay Consulate
301 E. 47 St., Suite 19A
New York, NY 10017
  (212) 753-8193

U.S.S.R. (Intourist)
Travel Information
  Office/U.S.A.
630 Fifth Ave.
New York, NY 10111
  (212) 757-3885

Venezuelan Govt. Tourist
  Bureau
450 Park Ave.
New York, NY 10022
  (212) 355-1101

Yugoslav National Tourist Office
630 Fifth Ave., Suite 210
New York, NY 10020
  (212) 757-2801

Zambia National Tourist Board
235-237 E. 52 St.
New York, NY 10022
  (212) 758-9450

7

How to Be a B&B Host

- Some hosts make up to $10,000 a year. But the majority earn far less. However, they do make a lot of new friends from around the world.
- Take advantage of possible tax deductions when you use part of your home as a business.
- Expect the unexpected. B&B people have hosted everyone from motion picture and soap opera stars to casual visitors who ask to be married in their home!

A surprising number of people want to become B&B hosts and turn one or two spare rooms in their house into guestrooms. Some are widows, widowers, divorcees, and single people who are burdened by the rising costs and taxes of home ownership. The idea of earning anywhere from $15 to $80 per night for a room (depending on the quality and location of the home) can be very appealing.

Others are simply "empty nesters" whose children have gone off to college or careers and left them with extra rooms and an abnormally quiet house. They like the idea of meeting new people from around the U.S. and the world. Many of these hosts are college professors, doctors, lawyers, world travelers, company presidents, as well as automobile mechanics, shop foremen, secretaries, and bus drivers—a generous cross section of America.

Other people who become B&B hosts are frustrated inn keepers or restaurant owners. Many dream of one day owning their own inn on a mountain or designing their own restaurant serving "new American cuisine." Becoming a B&B host allows a person to at least partially satisfy some of these dreams.

However, before you go into this business (and it *must* be a business, not a hobby, if you hope to qualify for possible tax deductions on your house), you should look at the pro's and con's with your eyes wide open. You may want to follow Ben Franklin's wise advice. Write down all of the positives you can think of on one sheet, all of the negative factors on another. Then look at both of them together. You may then quickly see what your decision should be.

Here are some things you should consider:

1. Don't expect to make much money. In fact, one B&B association estimated that only about 10% of the B&B homes make a profit at present. However, as every business person knows, "profit" is relative. You might make attractive and useful improvements in your home, such as new carpeting, drapes, furnishings. You might qualify for depreciation of your house (and furnishings) for tax purposes. However, be sure that you really do operate as a business. If the IRS rules that you are pursuing B&B as a hobby, wave goodbye to any tax deductions. That means you have to make *serious* efforts to rent the room regularly.

2. Look at your home objectively. Does your spare room(s) have a good double or twin beds? Are the furnishings in good condition? Is there adequate closet space? Will your guests have access to a private bath, or will the bathroom be shared with the family and other guests? One knowledgeable hostess said, "Always sleep at least once in the room you plan to use for your B&B service. You may be surprised by street noises,

or a too bright light in the early morning streaming in the windows—things you would be aware of only if you stayed in your own room." Often one of the key factors in how often the room is rented is the location of your home. If it is in or near a major interstate highway, a major city, scenic attraction, college, hospital, or major corporations, your chances of renting it regularly increase dramatically. Some reservation agencies have told us that a few B&B homes in really remote areas may only be rented about once a year!

3. Poll your whole family. How do they feel about having guests? Remind them that they may lose some privacy in their own home and that they may have to wait in line to use the bathroom. Everyone may have to cooperate to keep the whole house clean (particularly the bathroom) for the arrival of guests. This may be the time for a good family discussion before you make any decision. Do you have a pet. A dog that protects the home by nipping strangers could cost you a law suit.

4. Talk with a good lawyer or someone in local government who is familiar with regulations that may govern B&B operations. The real problem is that zoning laws across the country are often very vague about B&B homes. Some zoning laws seem to permit occasional boarders in a home. At other times, riled neighbors who fear that their property value or privacy may be threatened by strangers coming into the neighborhood, may contact the local zoning board for a ruling. Recently one woman in La Jolla, California began to operate a B&B business in her home. She posted notices locally. Some incensed neighbors brought suit against her. Although she fought the legal action vigorously, her lawyers eventually advised her to close the business. These zoning laws are in flux all over the nation. However, some B&B homeowners are also winning their cases and getting favorable rulings from zoning

boards. This is particularly true in states that are actively encouraging the growth of the B&B movement as a way of stimulating more tourism.

Also ask your attorney to check local public health/safety laws/regulations that may apply to any commercial application of your home. For example, some areas may require smoke detectors throughout your home.

5. If you do decide to become a B&B host, you now must decide whether you want to operate independently or want to be connected with a local or national reservation service. *We strongly recommend that you register your home with a reservation service.* If you operate as an independent, you must advertise and promote your home in some way to attract guests. That could mean putting small ads or generating publicity in local newspapers and magazines. You might even put a small sign in front of your home. Unfortunately all of these activities could raise red flags for your neighbrs or local officials. There is another problem. With your phone number on public display in an ad or in one of those books that describes independent B&B homes, you could be subject to unwelcome calls at any time of the day or night. You also would have little opportunity to screen the people who come into your home to spend the night. Instead you would be much better off using a reservation service that does not list your address or phone number in any of their literature. Let the reservation service pre-screen prospective guests. (Before you sign up for any reservation service, ask about their screening activities.) You may want a service that handles all of the financial details, even accepting credit card payments, and forwards a check to you. A service typically charges you a small annual fee to cover administration/advertising costs plus a percent of each rental (often 20% to 30%). When a service regularly brings you business and conscientiously screens prospective guests, they are more than worth their keep. If the service seems to be

choosy about selecting homes for their network and wants to come out for a personal inspection of your home, be thankful! It means the service really cares about offering attractive accommodations to the public, and you are in very good hands. Some of the larger services even hold seminars and annual meetings for B&B hosts. This whole business is still in its infancy, and hosts are learning from each other. This guide contains one of the most complete listings of reservation services now operating. Turn to one operating in your area. If none, consider one that offers B&B listings across the U.S. (See chapter 4, "National and International Help").

6. Check your home insurance coverage with your insurance agent. Tell him frankly what you plan to do. Ask what kind of coverage you have and how you would be protected if a paying guest were injured in your home. As the B&B movement grows, the insurance industry is becoming aware of the problems and drafting special new policies. We have deliberately listed the most negative factors, not to discourage you but to be sure that you understand that becoming a B&B host is not as simple as deciding you want to do it. That decision involves a commitment, and some careful attention to detail to avoid the pitfalls. However, there can be enormous personal rewards. Many of the stories we have heard from B&B hosts have been heartwarming. One hostess described the young lady who came to their Bed & Breakfast and liked their home so much that she asked to be married there. Other home owners have met people from around the world who became fast friends. Barbara Notarius, president of Bed & Breakfast USA, Ltd. frequently offers her home as a B&B. She told of her first guest, a retired mining engineer from Australia. He had spent much of his life in remote areas of the world such as New Guinea and had hundreds of stories to tell. Soon Barbara's husband was skipping work so he could drive the guest

around town. On another occasion, several of her house guests were musicians. Before they went to bed at night, they gave a chamber concert for Barbara and her family. "What a privilege!" she said.

But hosts also have to learn to be resilient and expect the unexpected. One hostess received a booking from a young woman for two people. When the two women arrived (one an actress who had recently appeared in a successful avant garde film), they announced that they were gay and wanted to share a double bed. The hostess accommodated them, and had food for conversation at the next eight bridge parties with her friends. (If you operate a B&B home, you have to decide in advance if you will accept unmarried couples, singles, etc. This is another advantage of using a reservation service that knows your preferences.) Joan Brownhill, President of Pineapple Hospitality reservation service in New Bedford, Massachusetts, tells how she selects B&B homes and hosts. "We send out a 'Host Home' preliminary packet which tells of our philosophy as an agency. There is a form to be completed that gives a profile of the prospective host, and answers such basic questions as to whether the host will accept children and pets. Two interviewers then visit the home by appointment to check everything out. If it meets the standards we've set, we sign an agreement with the new B&B home. An annual fee to the agency is collected."

Even when you are listed with an agency and want additional guests, there are a number of ways you could discreetly attract a number of guests:

■ If you are close to a local college, call or write the personnel office or office of student housing. Describe your home, its location, and room availability. Often visiting parents need an economical place to stay, especially with today's college costs being what they are. There also may be visiting professors or alumni who would welcome a home atmosphere. You might have some very stimulating guests.

- Contact the personnel office or corporate travel department of major corporations. Transferrees and other visiting employees might make excellent pre-screened guests. Women business travelers are particularly receptive to the relaxed B&B concept.
- Talk with local real estate agents. They may have out-of-town prospects who need a place to stay while looking for a new home. You'll not only earn extra income by providing hospitality, but you may also be making friends with new neighbors.
- Ask previous guests back. When you find particularly appealing and thoughtful guests, invite them back in the summer or winter. Always keep a guest book and ask them to write their comments. You may be pleasantly surprised how many Christmas/Holiday cards you receive from guests who enjoyed your hospitality. *Note:* If your guest originally came from a reservation service organization, you should ask them to re-book through this organization rather than directly with you. The few dollars you would lose in commission is more than made up by keeping the goodwill of the reservation service that is advertising and generating business for you.

Some tips for hosts—
"THE GIFT OF HOSPITALITY"
1. Show room and house and give guests an opportunity to unload their belongings.
2. Offer a drink/beverage and see if anything else is needed.
3. Take care of business, such as collecting money, signing the guest book and contracts, giving a receipt (preferably within 20 minutes of guests' arrival).
4. Answer questions and mention nearby attractions.
5. Supply guest with an information sheet containing questions and answers about your local area.

6. Collect brochures on sightseeing for your local area, as well as your state, and have them available for guests.
7. Offer a "Sue's Special:" picnic basket breakfast in bed.
8. Collect menus from popular restaurants to leave in guests' room.
9. Make coffee early. Find out when guests arrive what they prefer to drink in the morning. A thermos of coffee outside the door, so the first cup of coffee can be drunk in bed, is a real treat for the real coffee drinker.
10. Put an umbrella stand with loan umbrellas near the door and tell guests about it.
11. Set up a game corner (garage sales are a wonderful source of these and other handy items).
12. Place extra toilet articles (small sample sizes) in drawers.
13. Use liquid soap in the bathroom so that no guest has to use anyone else's soap.
14. Special guest tray including a fruit bowl, drinking glass, tissues, etc.
15. Have on hand books and magazines for your guests to read.
16. A hair dryer, make-up mirror, and curling iron from a garage sale may be lifesavers for your female guests.
17. Have newspapers on hand.
18. Have a good map on hand.
19. Copy the section of your local map showing your home and circle your house, restaurants, attractions, movies, etc., and run off enough copies so that each guest can take one with him/her.
20. Collect articles from your newspaper's attractions section and keep in a folder easily available to guests. Copies hold up better than newsprint originals.
21. Collect discount coupons from nearby attractions and restaurants for guests.
22. Save fast-food discount coupons, too.
23. Leave a note on guests' desk or bureau telling where they

can order take out pizza. Let them know if it's all right to eat on your deck or patio.
24. Deliver ice water to guests' room in the evening.
25. Have iced tea available in the refrigerator or let them know that they can always boil themselves hot water for tea or instant coffee.
26. Help your guests to feel comfortable in your home. Assure them that they should ask if there is something they need—extra towels, more pillows, etc.
27. Copy your special B&B recipes so guests can take them home.
28. Invite guests to watch you do your hobbies/special interest activities (such as stained glass, pottery, etc.).
29. If you have an historic home, guests may be interested in its history and architecture. Take a course about tracing the history of your home and keep the results of your work accessible.
30. See if the historical society or other town group has a walking tour of the community published that your guests can take.
31. Be sensitive to your guests' need for privacy and space. Don't ever make a guest feel that he's there to amuse you. Be available for those who want to talk but in touch enough to recognize when a guest just wants to be left alone.
32. B&B attracts a lot of folks looking for romance. If your setting is conducive to this, encourage it. Offer guests some privacy in front of the fireplace, put out a decanter with a little after dinner liqueur, etc. Flannel sheets are wonderful in cold climates.
33. Let your guests get to know you as an individual—your way of life, your part of the country.

(Suggestions from *Rocky Mountains-Bed & Breakfast* hosts, reprinted with the permission of Kate Peterson and Barbara Notarius).

COMMONLY ASKED QUESTIONS ABOUT HOSTING

Q. *"How much should I charge for the room?"*

A. The rate depends on several factors. The most important is location. Even a modestly furnished room in a modest house that is close to a popular ski slope can often command a premium rate. The condition of the room, its furnishings, and the general appearance of your home also should be considered. If the room has a private bath instead of a shared bath, you can also charge more. However, you want to be sure that the rate you charge is competitive and doesn't drive business away. Check the rates of other B&B homes in your area. Also, find out the rates of local hotels and motels. You rate should generally be lower than hotel rates. Travelers expect B&B rates to be bargains.

Q. *"What about income tax deductions?"*

A. If your home is only used for B&B hosting 14 or less nights per year, you may not have to pay any income tax on what you make. However, if a room in your home is rented more than 14 nights a year, then you would have to declare all income. You would also be entitled to deductions that could range from depreciation on your furnishings, fees paid to reservation service organizations, stamps, phone calls, etc. You also may be able to claim depreciation on your house and a percent of certain house cleaning/home maintenance costs. You should make (and report) a profit at least two out of every five years, or the government may claim your B&B operation is a hobby—not a business—and disallow any business deductions. To avoid problems, work with a good accountant who can help you interpret the current IRS rules.

Q. *"Should I tell my neighbors I operate a B&B home?"*

A. No. Not unless you are a would-be Perry Mason anxious to plead your case before a local zoning board.

Q. *"Should I charge sales tax?"*

A. Check with local authorities about this. It may be necessary for you to get a tax number and collect sales tax on all B&B rentals. Don't follow the human tendency to just keep mum about any rentals or income. You could become liable for back taxes and penalties.

Q. *"I have to leave for work early in the morning. How can I fix breakfast for guests or give them access to the house should they return while I'm away?"*

A. You could leave breakfast ingredients in the refrigerator and give your guests kitchen privileges for a do-it-yourself meal. Some hosts also give their guests a key, charging a "key fee" of $5 or $10 (which is refunded when the guest returns the key). For your own security, you may give the guest a key only to the regular lock, not a deadbolt lock, if you have one. You then have the security of locking the deadbolt without worrying about any unreturned keys that might be floating around.

Q. *"What about the possibility of theft? I am letting strangers into my home."*

A. Theft could happen. However, at least so far, B&B guests seem to be an unusually honest group of people. In talking with B&B hosts, we have yet to hear of an incident where a guest has taken as much as a teaspoon. (In contrast, talk with any major city hotel, which regularly loses a large quantity of towels and room service silverware and linen in the luggage of departing guests). You would want to use some common sense in protecting your personal belongings. If your guests have active children, you might want to store away any obvious breakables. You also can get an extra measure of security by having all prospective guests screened by the reservation service organization. Many of these organizations ask guests for personal references.

Q. *"Should I print a 'brochure' on my B&B home?"*

A. It really isn't necessary. You might want to do a simple letter on your stationery which describes your home and the breakfast you serve, tells of any 'house rule' restrictions (such as no smoking, no pets, etc.), and gives directions to your home. Offset print a quantity and send some to your reservation service organization. Or mail one to the guest who calls and asks for directions or more information.

Q. *"Will I make much money as a B&B host?"*

A. As we've said before, you probably *won't* make a high income as a host. However, we have been told of hosts who make up to $10,000 a year. Others who are close to scenic attractions, major cities, resort areas, etc. reliably make several hundred extra dollars each month. One hostess recently used her B&B earnings to pay for an all-expense safari in Africa. But there are also some B&B homes in remote locations that are only rented as little as once a year. Like the real estate people love to say about selling a house, the three most important factors are location, location, location.

Much of your reward of being a B&B host will come from meeting other people. Kate Peterson, Coordinator of Bed & Breakfast Rocky Mountains, shared this letter she had received from one of her new hosts:

"Dear Kate,

"Clyde and I just wanted to let you know how delighted we are with our first experience hosting bed and breakfast travelers. The couple from Houston left just this morning. I know we have made new friends. They were so comfortable with us that they have already decided to return in June to stay. It's amazing to me that they have even referred some of their friends to us—all this in just the last few days. Yesterday was really special. It was my birthday. When I got home in the afternoon, they had a birthday card and a delicate dried flower arrangement waiting for me. I was truly touched. Kate, we want to thank you for making this opportunity possible for us and for others. We are looking forward to the next bed and breakfast travelers we can serve.

Sincerely,
Fairley

These are the *real* rewards of becoming a B&B host.

PART II

Directory of B&B Reservation Service Organizations in North America

Special note to readers. Be sure to check the "B&B Bonuses" section of each listing. This is designed to give you an edge over other people calling the same reservation service. It describes some of the B&B homes that the services themselves consider their most appealing. Ask about them. Also you will learn about special services available from many B&B hosts for the asking.

NORTHEASTERN STATES

Connecticut
Maine
Massachusetts
New Hampshire
New York
Rhode Island

Connecticut

Seacoast Landings Bed & Breakfast Registry
133 NEPTUNE DRIVE, GROTON CT 06340

Offers B&B Homes In:
Southern Connecticut towns, villages, and cities

Reservations Phone: (203) 442-1940
Phone Hours: 8 a.m. to 8 p.m.   **Available:** 7 days a week
Price Range of Homes:
Single: $30   Double: $40 to $70
Breakfast Included in Price:
Continental (juice, roll/toast, coffee), except for one inn which serves full breakfast and juice or coffee served in bed
Brochure Available: Free
Reservations Should Be Made: 2 weeks in advance (last minute reservations accepted if possible)

Scenic Attractions Near the B&B Homes:
Mystic Seaport and Aquarium, Ocean Beach Amusement Park, schooner and deep-sea fishing tours, miles of shoreline homes, submarine base

Major Businesses Near the B&B Homes:
Pfizer, Electric Boat, Underwater Sound Lab, Millstone Nuclear Plant base

Major Schools, Universities Near the B&B Homes:
Connecticut College, Coast Guard Academy

B&B Bonuses

For an unusual experience, you can stay on a houseboat that sleeps four to eight people. It is moored in a quaint village, but the captain is flexible and will move the boat if desired, to nearby Fisher's Island or Block Island.

Groton offers a unique opportunity to tour a submarine—don't miss it!

Nutmeg Bed & Breakfast
222 GIRARD AVE., HARTFORD, CT 06105

Offers B&B Homes In:
Throughout Connecticut, 125 homes

Reservations Phone: (203) 236-6698
Phone Hours: 9 a.m. to 6 p.m.   **Available:** 7 days a week
Price Range of Homes:
Single: same as double   Double: $25 to $70
Breakfast Included in Price:
Continental or full American—many homes serve full breakfast, often featuring nut breads and croissants
Brochure Available: $2.00 for a complete Directory
Reservations Should Be Made: 2 weeks in advance (last minute reservations accepted if possible)

Scenic Attractions Near the B&B Homes:
Mystic Seaport, Sturbridge Village, etc. (guests are sent description of attractions in area they are visiting, before arrival)

Major Businesses Near the B&B Homes:
Hartford, Aetna, Travelers, and many other insurance companies, IBM, GE

Major Schools, Universities Near the B&B Homes:
Yale, Wesleyan, Trinity, Coast Guard Academy, and Hotchkiss, Kent, Pomfret, Lakeville, Choate, Rosemary Hall, Wallingford and Miss Porter's Farmington prep schools.

B&B Bonuses
A home in Old Wethersfield dates back to 1873. The young couple who has proudly preserved it will be glad to lend their bicycles to guests who wish to explore the old town. A country home at the entrance to Penwood Forest offers jogging, skiing, swimming, hiking, and "11 goats who cut the grass and answer to their names!" French, Yiddish, German, and Hungarian are a few of the languages spoken. One hostess "felt like a mother again" as she packed picnic lunches and cooked dinners for a lovely Hong Kong family with small children.

"Long-term accommodations available for corporate re-location (price adjustment)."

Bed & Breakfast, Ltd.
P.O. BOX 216, NEW HAVEN, CT 06513

Offers B&B Homes In:
Throughout Connecticut

Reservations Phone: (203) 469-3260
Phone Hours: 5 p.m. to 7 p.m.   **Available:** Monday to Friday, and weekend mornings

Price Range of Homes:
Single: $20 to $25   Double: $35 to $40
Breakfast Included in Price:
Continental or full American; varies with individual home
Brochure Available: Free if inquirer sends stamped, self-addressed #10 envelope
Reservations Should Be Made: 1 week in advance (last minute reservations accepted if possible)

Scenic Attractions Near the B&B Homes:
New Haven Coliseum, Long Wharf Theater, Powder Ridge ski area, Shubert Theater, Connecticut shore, Mystic Seaport, Peabody & British Art Museums, antique shops, historic country villages

Major Businesses Near the B&B Homes:
Bic Pen, Aetna Insurance

Major Schools, Universities Near the B&B Homes:
Yale, Wesleyan, Southern Connecticut State, Albertus Magnus, Hopkins, Choate, Milford Academy, Hampden Hall, Coast Guard Academy

B&B Bonuses

One of the homes is a Victorian in-town residence that has been on the local house tour for two years. It is filled with antiques as well as contemporary touches, is near beaches and convenient to Routes I-95 and I-91.

Some hosts offer a welcome cocktail or tea, fresh fruit and chocolates, and menus from local restaurants.

Covered Bridge Bed & Breakfast
BOX 380, WEST CORNWALL, CT 06796

Offers B&B Homes In:
Goshen, Kent, Sharon, Lakeville and other towns in the northwest corner of Connecticut; the Berkshires—Sheffield, Stockbridge, Williamstown—in Massachusetts; Shaftsbury in Vermont; Clinton and Essex in Southern Connecticut

Reservations Phone: (203) 672-6052
Phone Hours: 9 a.m. to 8 p.m.   **Available:** 7 days a week
Price Range of Homes:
Single: $30 to $50   Double: $35 to $75
Breakfast Included in Price:
Continental (juice, roll/toast, coffee)
Brochure Available: Free
Reservations Should Be Made: 3 weeks in advance (last minute reservations accepted if possible)

Scenic Attractions Near the B&B Homes:
Tanglewood Music Festival, Williamstown Theater, Jacob's Pillow, Sharon Playhouse, Appalachian Trail, white water canoeing, skiing, antiques, Lime Rock car racing, state parks.

Major Schools, Universities Near the B&B Homes:
Colleges: Williams, Bennington, Simon's Rock at Bard
Prep Schools: Hotchkiss, Kent, Salisbury, Berkshire, Indian Mountain Gunnery

B&B Bonuses
There are three antique-filled National Register homes, a working farm with large pond, mountain views, and horse trails with "homemade everything for breakfast," and a beautifully restored historic Colonial with four-poster bed, in Stockbridge (where you can see Norman Rockwell's home and paintings).

"Our hosts know how to balance friendliness with respect for the privacy of their guests."

CONNECTICUT / MAINE • 115

Maine

Bed & Breakfast Down East, Ltd.
BOX 547—MACOMBER MILL RD., EASTBROOK, ME 04634

Offers B&B Homes In:
Maine, statewide; including Acadia National Park, Mt. Desert Island area, coastal, inland, rural, lakeside, island, small towns and villages

Reservations Phone: (207) 565-3517
Phone Hours: 8 a.m. to 8 p.m.   **Available:** Any day at any reasonable hour

Price Range of Homes:
Single: $25 to $35   Double: $35 to $55
Breakfast Included in Price:
Most hosts give guests a choice between Continental and full American . . . some specialties served are blueberry scones, popovers, and "toad-in-a-hole"
Brochure Available: $1.00 for brochure and 3-page host list
Reservations Should Be Made: 2 weeks in advance (last minute reservations accepted if possible)

Scenic Attractions Near the B&B Homes:
Acadia National Park, Jackson Laboratory, Bar Harbor, scenic coastal areas, historic sites, museums, hiking trails

Major Businesses Near the B&B Homes:
St. Regis Paper Co., Bucksport Bath Iron Works (shipbuilders)

Major Schools, Universities Near the B&B Homes:
U. of Southern Maine, Portland, Gorham, Colby College, Waterville, Bates College, Lewiston, Bowdoin

B&B Bonuses
A 1785 country home with attached barns is on the National and State Register of Historic Places. Original murals by Jonathan Poor grace the stairway and hall, and there are 50 acres of woods for hiking, horseback riding, and swimming in a spring-fed pond. The hosts of another home with passive solar/wood heating are enthusiastic organic gardeners. And if you'd like to catch your own lobsters, a lobsterman-host will take you out on his boat (after a hearty country breakfast in the family's 150-year-old farmhouse) for a small fee.
One hostess spent three days driving a partially-disabled man and his wife all around her area.

Bed & Breakfast of Maine
32 COLONIAL VILLAGE, FALMOUTH, ME 04105

Offers B&B Homes In:
The state of Maine

Reservations Phone: (207) 781-4528
Phone Hours: Answering machine to 5 p.m.—5 p.m. to 11 p.m. "live"
Available: All times
Price Range of Homes:
Single: $25 to $45   Double: $31 to $70
Breakfast Included in Price:
Full American . . . "We encourage hearty breakfasts, if not hearty, at least fresh breads and real butter . . . blueberry pancakes are popular and fresh fruit cups or jams."
Brochure Available: Free
Reservations Should Be Made: 2 weeks in advance (last minute reservations accepted if possible)

Scenic Attractions Near the B&B Homes:
Daily cruise to Nova Scotia, clambakes, lobster festivals, craft shows, foliage tours, art festivals, island cruises, coastal resort activities

Major Schools, Universities Near the B&B Homes:
U. of Maine, Bates College, Maine Maritime, N.E. College, Westbrook College

B&B Bonuses

A mid-1800's historic home is nestled by a lovely harbor. It features a sauna, and there is a canal and a sailboat for guests. Hearty gourmet breakfast daily.

One host takes guests for a free sail on his 28-foot boat, weather permitting. He will also cook lobsters for a patio party, if desired.

Massachusetts

Mayflower Bed & Breakfast, Ltd.
P.O. BOX 172, BELMONT, MA 02178

Offers B&B Homes In:
Greater Boston area which includes the suburbs of Cambridge, Belmont, and Needham, also City of Boston

Reservations Phone: (617) 484-0068
Phone Hours: 11 a.m. to 6 p.m.   **Available:** Monday to Friday
Price Range of Homes:
Single: $30 to $45   Double: $50 to $75
Breakfast Included in Price:
Mostly Continental ... in certain cases, a full breakfast may be served for an extra charge, including bacon, eggs, etc.
Brochure Available: No
Reservations Should Be Made: 2 weeks in advance (last minute reservations accepted if possible)

Scenic Attractions Near the B&B Homes:
Habitat (environmental education center in Belmont), Audubon Highland Sanctuary, all Boston historic homes and attractions

Major Businesses Near the B&B Homes:
Genrad, Digital Equipment, Wang, Raytheon, and many hi-tech industries on Routes 128 and 2.

Major Schools, Universities Near the B&B Homes:
Belmont Hill School, Buckingham Nichols, Harvard, Babson, MIT, Lesley

B&B Bonuses
  Homes are generally owned by professional people who have accumulated interesting artifacts from travels around the world. However, the stress in this B&B is on ambience, atmosphere, and warm and intelligent hosts, rather than "things."
  Some instances of warmth and hospitality have included drinks served on arrival, invitations to family outings, complimentary brochures, and sight-seeing tours.

Bed & Breakfast Associates Bay Colony, Ltd.
P.O. BOX 166, BABSON PARK BRANCH, BOSTON, MA 02157

Offers B&B Homes In:
Boston, Cambridge, surrounding suburbs, Plymouth, Cape Cod

Reservations Phone: (617) 449-5302
Phone Hours: 10 a.m. to 5 p.m.   **Available:** Monday to Friday (out to lunch between 12 and 1:30)

Price Range of Homes:
Single: $25 to $50   Double: $30 to $65
Breakfast Included in Price:
Continental (juice, roll/toast, coffee)
Brochure Available: Free—for complete host directory, send $2 plus SASE
Reservations Should Be Made: 2 weeks in advance (last minute reservations accepted if possible)

Scenic Attractions Near the B&B Homes:
Boston's Freedom Trail, Faneuil Hall Marketplace, Beacon Hill, Lexington, Concord, Plimouth Plantation

Major Businesses Near the B&B Homes:
Prime Computer, Digital, Raytheon, industrial complexes on Rte. 495 and Rte. 28, Massachusetts General Hospital, Massachusetts Eye and Ear Hospital

Major Schools, Universities Near the B&B Homes:
Harvard, MIT, Boston U., Tufts, Wellesley College, Boston College, Simmons College, Northeastern U.

B&B Bonuses
   Some of the outstanding homes are a penthouse condominium in Boston's exclusive Back Bay (restored by a husband/wife architect team), a 200-year-old cottage just outside Harvard Square where the hostess serves breakfast on a tray in the cozy guestroom, and a gracious 14-room Colonial on 30 country acres overlooking gardens, bridle paths, and horse paddocks.
   Hosts have been known to arrange a picnic on the Charles River, pick up guests from Logan Airport, and a special few will spend the day showing historic Boston to visitors.

Bed & Breakfast, Brookline/Boston
21 MONMOUTH COURT, BROOKLINE, MA 02146

Offers B&B Homes In:
Boston proper, including Beacon Hill, Back Bay, Brookline, Cambridge; also in nearby Chestnut Hill, Newton, and Belmont; and Cape Cod.

Reservations Phone: (617) 277-2292
Phone Hours: 8 a.m. to 6 p.m.   **Available:** 7 days a week
Price Range of Homes:
Single: $25 to $40   Double: $40 to $55
Breakfast Included in Price:
Continental breakfast can include homemade jams such as "Beach Plum" on Cape Cod, cranberry muffins, croissants, cereal, "Anadama bread"—several hosts serve full breakfasts
Brochure Available: Free (for Accommodations Lists, send $1.00 and stamped, self-addressed envelope)
Reservations Should Be Made: Any time, "first come, first served"

Scenic Attractions Near the B&B Homes:
All of Boston's attractions are minutes away by subway; Museum of Fine Arts, Gardner Museum, and Fenway Park are especially convenient to several host homes

Major Businesses Near the B&B Homes:
Many businesses are nearby in Boston financial district

Major Schools, Universities Near the B&B Homes
Harvard, Boston U., Tufts, Simmons, Wheelock, plus centers for international visitors and studies

B&B Bonuses

From the gracious homes of exclusive Beacon Hill, Back Bay, Brookline, and Cambridge to a turn-of-the-century brick row house in Boston, there are accommodations for every need.

Several hosts speak foreign languages, and many have extended extra care and hospitality to patients of nearby hospitals. "Children can usually be accommodated."

Greater Boston Hospitality

P.O. BOX 1142, BROOKLINE, MA 02146

Offers B&B Homes In:
Boston, Cambridge, Brookline, Newton, Needham, Wellesley, Winchester, Marblehead, Salem, Swampscott, Charlestown, Belmont, Brighton, Massachusetts

Reservations Phone: (617) 734-0807
Phone Hours: 24 hours a day   **Available:** 7 days a week
Price Range of Homes:
Single: $25 to $40   Double: $30 to $60
Breakfast Included in Price:
Full American, which may include homemade peach preserves and scones, hot chocolate, buttermilk pancakes, bagels with smoked salmon and cream cheese, croissants . . . and a vegetarian/macrobiotic home serves fresh carrot juice, rice muffins with tofu cream cheese, hot oatmeal, apple-pear crunch, brown rice, tea or coffee
Brochure Available: Free
Reservations Should Be Made: 2 weeks in advance (last minute reservations accepted if possible)

Scenic Attractions Near the B&B Homes:
Boston Symphony, Boston Pops, Boston Ballet, Christian Science Church, Kennedy Library, Museum of Fine Arts, Isabella Stuart Gardner Museum, Faneuil Hall, Quincy Market, Freedom Trail, Chinatown, Beacon Hill, N.E. Aquarium

Major Businesses Near the B&B Homes:
Polaroid, Digital, IBM, Gillette, Stone & Webster, Monsanto, Teradyne, Raytheon, GTE, Arthur D. Little, Honeywell, Genrad, Itek, General Electric

Major Schools, Universities Near the B&B Homes:
Harvard, MIT, Boston U., Boston College, Emmanuel, Lesley, Pine Manor, Northeastern, Simmons, Wellesley, Massachusetts College of Art, New England Conservatory, Tufts, Babson, Brandeis

B&B Bonuses

A red brick Georgian carriage-house is located on a cul de sac in a fine old Boston residential area. Each guest room is on a separate floor with private bath and glass doors opening onto a large patio, where you can breakfast in summer.

Among the interesting hosts are a former concert pianist who frequently plays for guests, and a world-renowned expert on Scotch whiskey. Some little extra touches given here and there are maps of the area, candy, fruit, and mints, late afternoon wine and cheese, and an available washer and dryer.

Bed & Breakfast Areawide (Cambridge & Greater Boston)
73 KIRKLAND STREET, CAMBRIDGE, MA 02138

Offers B&B Homes In:
Cambridge and Greater Boston, including all towns and cities in eastern Mass., as well as Cape Cod, Nantucket, and Martha's Vineyard

Reservations Phone: (617) 576-1492 or 868-4447
Phone Hours: 9 a.m. to 6 p.m.   **Available:** Monday to Friday, and between 2 and 5 on weekend afternoons

Price Range of Homes:
Single: $21 to $55   Double: $28 to $65 (Apts., $30 to $100)
Breakfast Included in Price:
Full American (juice, eggs, bacon, toast, coffee, and many other choices)
Brochure Available: Free if inquirer sends stamped, self-addressed #10 envelope
Reservations Should Be Made: Same day reservations gladly accepted

Scenic Attractions Near the B&B Homes:
All Boston attractions, and beaches, lakes, islands, skyscrapers

Major Businesses Near the B&B Homes:
Digital, Wang, IBM, RCA, Raytheon, Prime Computer, Arthur D. Little, Polaroid, John Hancock, Gillette, Blue Cross/Blue Shield, major hospitals

Major Schools, Universities Near the B&B Homes:
22 major universities in the Boston area, including Harvard, MIT, Boston U., Lesley College

B&B Bonuses

To make sure guests are placed to their best advantage, this B&B agency likes them to phone ahead to discuss their particular needs and preferences. Many hosts provide a wide range of services, such as use of their memberships in social and athletic clubs, museums, and libraries; and baby-sitting, gourmet meals (including special diets), use of musical instruments, in-home laundry, and secretarial services.

Prospective guests are required to join this organization for a fee of $5.00 for a one-year membership.

House Guests, Cape Cod
BOX 8, DENNIS, MA 02638

Offers B&B Homes In:
Entire area of Cape Cod, plus the islands of Nantucket and Martha's Vineyard

Reservations Phone: (617) 398-0787
Phone Hours: 10 a.m. to 7 p.m.   **Available:** 7 days a week
Price Range of Homes:
Single: $22 to $36   Double: $32 to $48
Breakfast Included in Price:
Varies from continental to full American, with most hosts allowing "guests' choice." Almost all serve home-baked breads using native berries, and local fresh fruit is frequently served.
Brochure Available: Send $1.00 for complete directory in book form
Reservations Should Be Made: 2 weeks in advance (more notice needed for July and August holiday weekends)—last minute reservations accepted if possible

Scenic Attractions Near the B&B Homes:
National Seashore, National Register homes, Sandwich, whale-watching cruises, museums, old railroad train trips, deep-sea fishing

Major Schools, Universities Near the B&B Homes:
Cape Cod Community College

B&B Bonuses

You can sleep in the oldest home in Harwich, built in 1730. The hostess operates an antique shop in a converted carriage house. Or for a real old-fashioned family atmosphere, you can have the run of a house on the beach with big porches and old iron bedsteads, in Falmouth.

All sports and ferries to the islands are nearby, and you may get a surprise "fancy breakfast" on weekends. Many hosts will save you parking fees, etc., by driving you to and from the ferries from other locations. Other hospitable extras may include use of membership cards for museum tours, loans of bicycles, and afternoon tea or wine.

MASSACHUSETTS • 123

Bed & Breakfast in Minuteman Country
8 LINMOOR TERRACE, LEXINGTON, MA 02173

Offers B&B Homes In:
Lexington, Concord, Cambridge, Newton, and Brookline, in Massachusetts

Reservations Phone: (617) 861-7063
Phone Hours: 9 a.m. to 5 p.m.   **Available:** Monday to Friday
Price Range of Homes:
Single: $35 and up   Double: $40 and up
Breakfast Included in Price:
Continental or full American—it varies according to each individual home
Brochure Available: Free
Reservations Should Be Made: 2 weeks in advance (last minute reservations accepted if possible)

Scenic Attractions Near the B&B Homes:
Historic Lexington-Concord area, homes of Emerson and Hawthorne, Walden Pond, Thoreau Lyceum, museums, beaches, canoeing on Concord River

Major Businesses Near the B&B Homes:
Companies on American Technology Highway, Hewlett-Packard, Digital Equipment, Polaroid

Major Schools, Universities Near the B&B Homes:
Cambridge, Harvard, MIT, Boston U.

B&B Bonuses

Many homes are within easy drive of Harvard, MIT, Boston U., etc. Enjoy breakfast in the greenhouse of an 1884 Victorian home, or browse among the antiques and hand-crafted articles in a Colonial home enhanced by a woodland setting.

"Our host families are truly exceptional. Gracious, warm, and friendly, each has something special to offer, such as speaking a foreign language, and one host arranged a one-year-old birthday party for a guest's baby."

Pineapple Hospitality, Inc.
384 RODNEY FRENCH BLVD., NEW BEDFORD, MA 02744

Offers B&B Homes In:
Throughout New England—Massachusetts, New Hampshire, Connecticut, Rhode Island, Maine, Vermont (some are small inns)

Reservations Phone: (617) 990-1696
Phone Hours: 9 a.m. to 5 p.m.   **Available:** Monday to Friday
Price Range of Homes:
Single: $27 to $45   Double: $33 to $59 ($60 to $85 in high-demand areas)
Breakfast Included in Price:
Continental or full American. Hosts may serve cranberry maple syrup over hot cereal in Vermont, or grilled Portuguese sweetbread or Irish soda bread, in some areas.
Brochure Available: Free (special New England Host Home Directory-$3.32 ppd.)
Reservations Should Be Made: 2 weeks in advance (last minute reservations accepted if possible)

Scenic Attractions Near the B&B Homes:
White Mountains, Martha's Vineyard, Nantucket, Newport mansions, Sturbridge Village, Mystic Seaport, fall foliage, Boston attractions, Plymouth, Cape Cod

Major Schools, Universities Near the B&B Homes:
Harvard, Yale, Dartmouth, Brown, Rhode Island School of Design, Boston College, Phillips Academy in Andover

B&B Bonuses

Many of the homes reflect the history of New England, such as a New Bedford whaling captain's home built in 1815, and an 1875 textile magnate's mansion in Fall River, Mass. A home in New Hampshire is in the area where the movie "On Golden Pond" was filmed. And in Kennebunk, Maine, you can stay at a sea captain's home that was built in the 1700's!

You can also spend a nautical overnight on a 41-foot yacht on Cape Cod! And ask about their "New England Experience"—a unique way to see all the best of New England and experience their hospitality in a fascinating variety of home settings.

Host Homes of Boston
P.O. BOX 117, NEWTON, MA 02168

Offers B&B Homes In:
Greater Boston area, primarily Newton, with host homes also in Cambridge, Brookline, and Needham

Reservations Phone: (617) 244-1308
Phone Hours: 8 a.m. to 7 p.m.   **Available:** 7 days a week (or answering machine with same-day call back)

Price Range of Homes:
Single: $32   Double: $45
Breakfast Included in Price:
"Hearty" Continental (may include home-baked muffins, scones, or croissants) or full American, depending on individual home
Brochure Available: Free
Reservations Should Be Made: 2 weeks in advance (last minute reservations accepted if possible)

Scenic Attractions Near the B&B Homes:
"All the cultural, recreational, and educational offerings of Boston," including the Fine Arts Museum, Museum of Science, Boston Symphony, Boston Pops, Quincy Market, Old Sturbridge Village, harbor cruises

Major Businesses Near the B&B Homes:
GTE, Sylvania, Honeywell Information Systems, Gillette, John Hancock, Polaroid, high-tech businesses on Route 128

Major Schools, Universities Near the B&B Homes:
Boston College, Boston U., Harvard, Simmons, Suffolk, Brandeis, Bentley College

B&B Bonuses
"A small but complete (and completely charming) guest apartment in Boston's Back Bay offers top locations on a fine residential avenue, privacy (guests prepare own breakfast with stock provided), and surroundings and decor that are reminiscent of a past era."

Other homes offer spacious family quarters and play area with view of the Boston skyline, or a home near a lake with its own swimming pool, "among the many happy choices."

New England Bed & Breakfast, Inc.
1045 CENTRE ST., NEWTON CENTRE, MA 02159

Offers B&B Homes In:
Boston and other special places in New England

Reservations Phone: (617) 498-9819 or 244-2112
Phone Hours: 10 a.m. to 10 p.m.   **Available:** 7 days a week (498-9819 is a 24-hour service)

Price Range of Homes:
Single: $21 to $37   Double: $33 to $53
Breakfast Included in Price:
Continental (juice, roll/toast, coffee)
Brochure Available: Free
Reservations Should Be Made: 2 weeks in advance (last minute reservations accepted if possible)

Scenic Attractions Near the B&B Homes:
All Boston attractions, sand and dunes of Cape Cod, mountains and streams of New Hampshire and Maine, rolling hills of Vermont, Freedom Trail, historic Concord and Lexington, theaters, museums

Major Businesses Near the B&B Homes:
Major teaching hospitals, Lahey Clinic, Wang Laboratory, Interface, Massachusetts General Hospital

Major Schools, Universities Near the B&B Homes:
Harvard, Boston College, Boston U., Berkeley School of Music, Lesley, Northeastern U., La Salle, Bentley, Brandeis U.

B&B Bonuses
  All host homes are located in safe, convenient neighborhoods, near public transportation to the city. Friendly hosts serve lots of "TLC" such as inviting a couple and their seven-year-old son to Christmas brunch with 20 other private house guests, last Christmas.
  Frequently hosts drive guests to airport, bus stops, and hospitals.

Be Our Guest, Bed & Breakfast
P.O. BOX 1333, PLYMOUTH, MA 02360

Offers B&B Homes In:
Plymouth and neighboring towns of Hingham, Scituate, Kingston, Duxbury, Middleboro, and Marshfield

Reservations Phone: (617) 746-1208
Phone Hours: 8:30 a.m. to 10:30 p.m.   **Available:** 7 days a week
Price Range of Homes:
Single: $24 to $40   Double: $32 to $50
Breakfast Included In Price:
"Continental breakfast is served, but most hosts serve a good, healthy breakfast . . . pancakes and blueberries, zucchini bread (homemade, vegetables from garden), and croissants are the favorites"
Brochure Available: Free
Reservations Should Be Made: 2 weeks in advance preferred, but will make reservations same day as arrival in town

Scenic Attractions Near the B&B Homes:
Plimouth Plantation, "The Mayflower" ship, Plymouth Rock, Cranberry World, Commonwealth Winery, Edaville Railroad, Plymouth Wax Museum, historic homes, beaches, state parks, whale watching, deep-sea fishing, sailing

Major Businesses Near the B&B Homes:
Ocean Spray, Halliday Corp., Pilgrim Nuclear Plant, Commonwealth Electric

Major Schools, Universities Near the B&B Homes:
Bridgewater State College, all major Boston universities within 30 to 60 miles

B&B Bonuses

In a setting reminiscent of "On Golden Pond," a house panelled in knotty cedar throughout, with center chimney fireplace and cathedral ceiling, affords splendid views of the pond. If you prefer ocean views, you can stay at an elegantly decorated Dutch Colonial, with decks off every room.

From an invitation to dinner with the family, to baby-sitting the children and letting them watch "Star Wars" on the home video, to fixing a guest's car that had broken down, hosts have gone beyond the call of duty many times.

Bed & Breakfast Cape Cod
P.O BOX 341, W. HYANNISPORT, MA 02672

Offers B&B Homes In:
Throughout Cape Cod

Reservations Phone: (617) 775-2772
Phone Hours: 9:30 a.m. to 5 p.m.   **Available:** 7 days a week
Price Range of Homes:
Single: $24 to $40   Double: $32 to $70
Breakfast Included in Price:
Continental or full American . . . home-grown specialties such as native berry preserves and homemade bread and muffins are often served
Brochure Available: Free
Reservations Should Be Made: 2 or 3 weeks in advance (last minute reservations accepted if possible)

Scenic Attractions Near the B&B Homes:
Cruises to Martha's Vineyard and Nantucket, Heritage Plantation, Sandwich Glass Museum, Cape Cod National Seashore, Audubon Sanctuary, Cape Playhouse, Melody Tent, Falmouth Playhouse, golf courses, deep-sea fishing, lake trout fishing, sandy beaches

Major Schools, Universities Near the B&B Homes:
Woods Hole Oceanographic Institute, Cape Cod Community College, Cape Cod Conservatory of Music and Art, Boston universities and colleges (1½ hour drive)

B&B Bonuses

In Hyannisport, a 20-room turn-of-the-century estate overlooking Nantucket Sound is near the Kennedy compound. Each guest room has a water view, and guests are free to use the TV den, glassed-in summer room, and laundry facilities. A breakfast of gourmet treats like eggs Benedict, or apple pancakes, or steak and eggs—even strawberries with champagne—is served in the elegant dining room.

A "bird-watcher's delight" is a home near a salt marsh and a picturesque wooden bridge leading to an ocean beach called "Cockle Cove." Antiques, wide floor boards, and rag rugs complete the picture.

One hostess took a sick husband's place and spent the afternoon with her guest, touring the art galleries.

Hampshire Hills Bed & Breakfast Association
P.O. BOX 307, WILLIAMSBURG, MA 01096

Offers B&B Homes In:
The hills of western Massachusetts

Reservations Phone: (413) 634-5529
Phone Hours: After 6 p.m.   **Available:** Each home must be phoned directly; obtain numbers from brochure or call above
Price Range of Homes:
Single: $19 to $30   Double: $24 to $40
Breakfast Included in Price:
Continental or full American, varies with individual homes (regional specialties often served are local maple syrup, farm fresh eggs, and homemade blueberry muffins)
Brochure Available: Free if inquirer sends stamped, self-addressed #10 envelope
Reservations Should Be Made: 2 weeks in advance (last minute reservations accepted if possible)

Scenic Attractions Near the B&B Homes:
William Cullen Bryant Homestead, Historic Deerfield, DAR State Park, Chesterfield Gorge, Jacob's Pillow Dance Festival, Tanglewood Music Center, Williamstown Theater, Sterling Clark Museum, cross-country and downhill skiing, hiking trails, cycling, canoeing, tennis, golf

Major Schools, Universities Near the B&B Homes:
Smith College, Amherst, Hampshire, Mt. Holyoke, U. of Massachusetts, Deerfield Academy, Eaglebrook Prep

B&B Bonuses

   Enjoy home-grown foods in a 200-year old farmhouse, stroll to a general store, or eat a real American breakfast served in a country kitchen, heated by a wood stove. "Guests may awaken to the ba-a-a-ing of sheep, or the chimes of an antique Seth Thomas clock."

   Hosts are more than willing to assist with directions to points of interest, hiking trails, bicycling areas, dinner recommendations, swimming holes, and tennis courts.

New Hampshire

New Hampshire Bed & Breakfast
RFD 3, BOX 53, LACONIA, NH 03246

Offers B&B Homes In:
29 communities throughout New Hampshire

Reservations Phone: (603) 279-8348
Phone Hours: 1 p.m. to 8 p.m.   **Available:** Monday to Friday
Price Range of Homes:
Single: $15 to $32   Double: $20 to $50
Breakfast Included in Price:
Most homes serve full American breakfasts, including organically grown foods, real maple sugar, homemade cheese, pies, ice cream . . . others serve Continental
Brochure Available: For a fee, which is $1.00
Reservations Should Be Made: 2 weeks in advance (last minute reservations accepted if possible)

Scenic Attractions Near the B&B Homes:
Lake Winnipesaukee, Lake Sunapee, White Mountains, Merrimack Valley, ski areas, arts and crafts shows, historic sites and museums

Major Schools, Universities Near the B&B Homes:
Dartmouth College, Tilton Academy, Plymouth State College, Colby-Sawyer College, Keene State College, New Hampton School, Holderness, Brewster Head, St. Paul's, Concord schools

B&B Bonuses

Each of the homes offers something special, such as a copper bathtub, farm animals, maple sugaring, lakefront and mountain views, tennis courts, swimming pools, private beaches, museum tours, cross-country skiing, and antiques.

Some past surprises have included tour of the lake by boat, picnics, cookouts, special dinners, complimentary cocktail, and would you believe, breakfast in bed!

New York

Bed & Breakfast U.S.A. Ltd.
P.O. BOX 606, CROTON-ON-HUDSON, NY 10520

Offers B&B Homes In:
All over New York State

Reservations Phone: (914) 271-6228
Phone Hours: 7:30 to 9 p.m.   **Available:** Monday to Friday
Price Range of Homes:
Single: $20 to $30   Double: $30 to $60 (weekly rates, approx. $140 single, $210 double)
Breakfast Included in Price:
Full American (juice, eggs, bacon, toast, coffee)
Brochure Available: Fee is $1.00 if inquirer sends self-addressed #10 envelope with 37¢ stamp
Reservations Should Be Made: 3 weeks in advance (last minute reservations accepted if possible)

Scenic Attractions Near the B&B Homes:
Sleepy Hollow Restorations, Lyndhurst Castle, Rye Playland, Caramoor Music Festival, Murcoot Park, Boscobel and Hyde Park mansions, Croton Clearwater Revival, Cold Spring antiquing, Baseball Hall of Fame, Howe Caverns, Corning Glass, Saratoga, Vanderbilt Mansion, ice caves

Major Businesses Near the B&B Homes:
IBM, Texaco, General Foods, Nestles, Stauffers, GE, Pepsi

Major Schools, Universities Near the B&B Homes:
Sarah Lawrence College, Iona College, Manhattanville, Pace, Vassar, Westchester Community College, SUNY New Paltz, Ithaca College, Cornell U., Hamilton, Colgate, Skidmore, Russel Sage, Rensselaer Polytechnic Institute, Elmira colleges

B&B Bonuses

You wouldn't expect to find a 15-room Norman castle within walking distance of shopping and trains, but they have one in New Rochelle. A 200-year-old farm house on eight acres boasts a swimming pool, and there is even a 52 foot sailing yacht.

Many hosts enjoy driving into New York City with guests, for a Broadway show or other big-city activities. Interpreters and baby-sitters are often provided. (This agency charges a $15 booking fee for non-members; members pay $25 yearly, and no fee to book)

Alternate Lodging
P.O. BOX 1782, EAST HAMPTON, NY 11937

Offers B&B Homes In:
Eastern Long Island, New York State

Reservations Phone: (516) 324-9449
Phone Hours: 7:30 a.m. to 6 p.m.   **Available:** 7 days a week
Price Range of Homes:
Single: $26 to $60   Double: $39 to $85
Breakfast Included in Price:
Continental (juice, roll/toast, coffee)
Brochure Available: Free
Reservations Should Be Made: 3 weeks in advance (last minute reservations accepted if possible)

Scenic Attractions Near the B&B Homes:
Montauk Lighthouse, Amagansett Marine Museum, Sag Harbor Whaling Museum, Guild Hall summer theater, landmark homes, Watermill Museum

Major Schools, Universities Near the B&B Homes:
Southampton College

B&B Bonuses
The Hamptons have long been the "playground of the famous." Enjoy a "spectacular" home in the dunes with swimming pool and tennis courts, or relax in the ambience of a 100-year-old house with an up-to-date swimming pool.

"Our hosts are friendly, remarkable people. There have been instances when they have loaned their family car to a guest that was without transportation. Most homes have bikes to loan."

NEW YORK • 133

Hampton Bed & Breakfast Registry
P.O. BOX 695, EAST MORICHES, NY 11940

Offers B&B Homes In:
Long Island, especially the Hamptons, Huntington, and the Moriches

Reservations Phone: (516) 878-4439 or 367-4707 (answering service—288-3390)
Phone Hours: 9 a.m. to 9 p.m.   **Available:** 7 days a week
Price Range of Homes:
Single: $20 to $40   Double: $36 to $120
Breakfast Included in Price:
Continental (juice, roll/toast, coffee) . . . certain homes will provide country breakfasts
Brochure Available: For a fee, which is $1.00
Reservations Should Be Made: 2 weeks in advance (last minute reservations accepted if possible)

Scenic Attractions Near the B&B Homes:
Museums, historic homes, game farms, nature trails, health spas, beaches, theaters, tennis and golf courses

Major Businesses Near the B&B Homes:
Grumman, Hazeltines, Brookhaven Laboratories, Huntington-Melville Industrial Park

Major Schools, Universities Near the B&B Homes:
Hofstra, Adelphi, Southampton, St. Josephs Colleges

B&B Bonuses

You can arrange for an excursion on a cabin cruiser owned by one host, or enjoy the pool in an attractive modern home.

Several hosts help in planning tours and chauffeuring. They have been known to invite their guests to share a meal or an evening.

Bed & Breakfast Rochester
BOX 444, FAIRPORT, NY 14450

Offers B&B Homes In:
Around the Rochester area, and down into the Finger Lakes of New York State

Reservations Phone: (716) 223-8510 or 223-8887
Phone Hours: 9 a.m. to 9 p.m.   **Available:** "Any time within reason"
Price Range of Homes:
Single: $20 to $35   Double: $30 to $45
Breakfast Included in Price:
Continental, which may include apple muffins, apple oatmeal, German coffee cake, and other specialties
Brochure Available: Free if inquirer sends stamped, self-addressed #10 envelope
Reservations Should Be Made: 2 or 3 weeks in advance (last minute reservations accepted if possible)

Scenic Attractions Near the B&B Homes:
Eastman House of Photography, Strong Toy Museum, Genesee Country Museum, Letchworth Park, Sonnenberg Gardens, Lake Ontario, wineries, fishing derbies

Major Businesses Near the B&B Homes:
Eastman Kodak, Xerox, Corning Glass

Major Schools, Universities Near the B&B Homes:
U. of Rochester, Brockport, Geneseo, St. John Fisher, Rochester Institute of Technology, Nazareth

B&B Bonuses

Guests have exclusive use of the lower level (2 bedrooms and private bath) in a raised-ranch home on the beach at Lake Ontario. Breakfast with a view of the lake framed by graceful willows. The hosts are English. In a summer cottage on the beach at Keuka Lake, a college professor and his artist wife completed the remodeling of an old grape barn from the early 1800's. Some of the levels feature built-in double decker beds and a treehouse with screened tent. This is available in July and August only.

Nightgown and toothbrushes were once provided for guest whose luggage had gone astray. Hosts will often pick up at the airport, and drive guests around town.

Cherry Valley Ventures, A Bed & Breakfast System, Inc.
6119 CHERRY VALLEY TURNPIKE, LAFAYETTE, NY 13084

Offers B&B Homes In:
The entire state of New York, with the exception of New York City and Long Island

Reservations Phone: (315) 677-9723
Phone Hours: Any time   **Available:** 7 days a week
Price Range of Homes:
Single: $20 to $30   Double: $28 to $38 (ask about special weekly, monthly and salesman's rates)
Breakfast Included in Price:
At present more than 90% of their homes serve full breakfast, the others serve Continental
Brochure Available: No
Reservations Should Be Made: At least 2 weeks in advance (last minute reservations accepted if possible)

Scenic Attractions Near the B&B Homes:
Niagara Falls, Corning Glass, Saratoga Raceway and Center for Performing Arts, Baseball Hall of Fame, Howe Caverns, Shaker Museum, Finger Lakes, Thousand Islands, Syracuse Dome, Song Mountain Ski & Alpine Slide, Woods Valley, Cockaigne, Kissing Bridge, cross-country and downhill ski resorts

Major Businesses Near the B&B Homes:
GE, Sylvania, Chrysler, Carrier, Kodak, Crucible Steel, Xerox, Crouse-Hinds, dairy industry

Major Schools, Universities Near the B&B Homes:
Syracuse U., Lemoyne, Alfred State College, U. of Buffalo, Cornell U., Rochester Institute of Technology, Colgate, Hamilton, Ithaca College, SUNY at Oneonta, Hobart and William Smith College, Cazenovia College

B&B Bonuses

The hostess of an elegant contemporary home with 45-foot high ceilings loves to treat people like royalty. She will serve you a gourmet meal with choice of three entrees in the formal dining-room, at no extra charge!

An English tearoom and gift shop are part of a Federal-style 1807 home with three bedrooms, each with a walk-in fireplace. Stage-coach tours and horse-back riding are very nearby.

North Country Bed & Breakfast Reservation Service
P.O. BOX 286F, LAKE PLACID, NY 12946

Offers B&B Homes In:
Adirondack Mountains, Northern New York State, a few in other parts of New York and New England

Reservations Phone: (518) 523-3739
Phone Hours: 11 a.m. to 8 p.m.   **Available:** "Call any time—evenings always good"
Price Range of Homes:
Single: $12 to $50   Double: $24 to $100 and up
Breakfast Included in Price:
Continental or full American, depending on individual home . . . some specialties served are Adirondack flapjacks, berries in season, homemade breads and pastries, jams, jellies, New York maple syrup
Brochure Available: Free
Reservations Should Be Made: 2 to 3 weeks in advance (last minute reservations accepted if possible)

Scenic Attractions Near the B&B Homes:
Winter and summer sports, mountains and lakes, in Adirondack State Park, 1980 Winter Olympics sports facilities, The North Pole (Santa's home), Whiteface Highway, Adirondack Museum, Camp Topridge

Major Schools, Universities Near the B&B Homes:
U.S. Olympic Training Center, New York State Alpine Training Center, Trudeau Institute, W. Alton Jones Cell Science Center, Lake Placid Center for the Arts, St. Lawrence U., Clarkson, SUNY at Potsdam and Pittsburgh, Paul Smith's College, North Country Community College, Northwood School, North Country School

B&B Bonuses

Live like a millionaire with a marble bath and balcony off your room, in a house in the Adirondacks. Breakfast served on the patio overlooking the lake, as well. For something a little more rustic, after being greeted by their Old English sheepdog, you and your knowledgeable hosts will enjoy an evening around the wood stove planning your next day's activities. Great French toast from the Jenn-Aire griddle at this one!

Beverages and other special treats are frequent; so are guided skiing, fishing, and shopping trips, and help with emergency travel problems; and "lots of friendly conversation."

The B&B Group (New Yorkers at Home, Inc.)
301 EAST 60TH STREET, NEW YORK, NY 10022

Offers B&B Homes In:
Manhattan, and a few from May to December in the Hamptons (Long Island)

Reservations Phone: (212) 838-7015
Phone Hours: 9 a.m. to 4 p.m.   **Available:** Monday to Friday (no Saturdays, Sundays, or holidays)

Price Range of Homes:
Single: $35 to $55   Double: $50 to $75 (Apts. $65 to $135)
Breakfast Included in Price:
Continental (juice, roll/toast, coffee) in host homes only, not apts.
Brochure Available: Free if inquirer sends stamped, self-addressed #10 envelope
Reservations Should Be Made: 1 to 2 weeks in advance (no last minute reservations)

Scenic Attractions Near the B&B Homes:
Lincoln Center, United Nations, Theater District, SOHO, Greenwich Village, Central Park, Museum Row, New York Academy of Sciences, Cooper-Hewitt Mansion, World Trade Center, Wall Street, South Ferry, South St. Seaport

Major Businesses Near the B&B Homes:
Bloomingdale's, Macy's, Gimbels, GE, Lever House, stock market, commodities exchanges, brokerage houses, banking institutions, investment firms

Major Schools, Universities Near the B&B Homes:
NYU, Columbia U., Hunter College, Fordham U., Baruch College, John Jay U.

B&B Bonuses

This B&B is very popular with London visitors, having been written up in many of the London papers. It offers convenience to all the excitement of the "Big Apple" to people from all over the U.S. and Canada as well. Apartments are on the prestigious East Side of Manhattan, Greenwich Village, the up-and-coming West Side, and for those who prefer the summer waterfront, there are some host homes in the Hamptons.

Some hosts take time to show their guests around, and most provide maps and directions to special stores and restaurants in N.Y.C., and points of interest in their own areas.

Bed & Breakfast in the Big Apple (Urban Ventures, Inc.)

P.O. BOX 426, NEW YORK, NY 10024

Offers B&B Homes In:
Over 500 accommodations in New York City

Reservations Phone: (212) 594-5650
Phone Hours: 9 a.m. to 5 p.m.   **Available:** Monday to Friday; Saturday 9 a.m. to 3 p.m.

Price Range of Homes:
Single: $25 to $60   Double: $32 to $85
Breakfast Included in Price:
Continental (juice, roll/toast, coffee)
Brochure Available: Free
Reservations Should Be Made: 2 weeks in advance (last minute reservations accepted if possible)

Scenic Attractions Near the B&B Homes:
Broadway theater, Central Park, skyscrapers, famous restaurants, and all the many other Big Apple attractions

Major Schools, Universities Near the B&B Homes:
Columbia U., NYU, Pace College

B&B Bonuses

From a penthouse apartment in Greenwich Village to a duplex on exclusive Park Avenue, you can live like a real New Yorker. Friendly hosts have provided such personal services as lending guests umbrellas and clothing appropriate for the season.

New World Bed & Breakfast Ltd.
150 5TH AVENUE, SUITE 711, NEW YORK, NY 10011

Offers B&B Homes In:
Manhattan—New York City

Reservations Phone: (212) 675-5600
Phone Hours: 8:30 a.m. to 5 p.m. **Available:** 7 days a week; 24 hour answering service

Price Range of Homes:
Single: $35 to $65   Double: $45 to $75
Breakfast Included in Price:
Continental (juice, roll/toast, coffee)
Brochure Available: Free
Reservations Should Be Made: 2 weeks in advance (last minute reservations accepted if possible)

Scenic Attractions Near the B&B Homes:
All of New York City's attractions—theater, museums, business districts, Statue of Liberty, etc.

Major Schools, Universities Near the B&B Homes:
New York U., Columbia U., City College, The New School

B&B Bonuses

You can choose from East Side luxury apartments, Greenwich Village "pads", a brownstone duplex, accommodations on an island in the East River, a Soho loft, and apartments overlooking the Hudson and East Rivers. The host roster includes writers, artists, architects, actors, linguists, business people, journalists, etc.

A Washington attorney involved in a court case in downtown Manhattan was delighted to have his wish come true—a B&B apartment two blocks away from the courthouse!

Rainbow Hospitality
9348 HENNEPIN AVE., NIAGARA FALLS, NY 14304

Offers B&B Homes In:
Niagara Falls, Lewiston, Youngstown, Wilson east to Rochester, Buffalo suburbs south to Pennsylvania

Reservations Phone: (716) 283-0228 or 283-4794
Phone Hours: 9 a.m. to 6 p.m.   **Available:** All days except Saturday & Sunday (Saturday, 9 a.m. to 12:30 p.m.)

Price Range of Homes:
Single: $18 to $25   Double: $27 to $50
Breakfast Included in Price:
Continental or full American, according to individual home
Brochure Available: Free if inquirer sends stamped, self-addressed #10 envelope
Reservations Should Be Made: 2 weeks in advance (last minute reservations accepted if possible)

Scenic Attractions Near the B&B Homes:
Niagara Falls, Lewiston Art Park, Fatima Shrine, Fort Niagara, Kleinhans Music Hall (Buffalo), four large amusement complexes, lakes, rivers, convention centers, antique and outlet shopping, museums and art galleries, winter sports

Major Businesses Near the B&B Homes:
Carborundum, Hooker, DuPont, Union Carbide, Bell Aero Systems

Major Schools, Universities Near the B&B Homes:
Niagara U., SUNY at U. of Buffalo, Buffalo State, Canisius College

B&B Bonuses

Experience the atmosphere of an elegant old Victorian-style home with gables and wrap-around verandas, overlooking the Niagara River toward Canada. The host family can direct guests to nearby cultural or recreational activities of all kinds. "Our hosts are people who have a genuine desire to share their hospitality, rather than simply renting a room."

Some "extras" are transportation, sightseeing, babysitting, laundry, sailboat charter, and hosts and hostesses who speak several languages.

Bed & Breakfast of Long Island
P.O. BOX 312, OLD WESTBURY, NY 11568

Offers B&B Homes In:
Eastern Long Island Hamptons Beach area, Amagansett, Montauk, Sag Harbor, E. Quoque, Garden City, Glen Cove, Seaford, Valley Stream, Mystic CT

Reservations Phone: (516) 334-6231 or 334-8499
Phone Hours: 9:30 a.m. to 4 p.m.   **Available:** Monday to Saturday, some holidays

Price Range of Homes:
Single: $25 to $65   Double: $40 to $125
Breakfast Included in Price:
Continental or full American, plus regional specialties like homemade beach plum jam and blueberry muffins, waffles, buttery croissants
Brochure Available: Free if inquirer sends stamped, self-addressed #10 envelope
Reservations Should Be Made: 2 weeks in advance (last minute reservations accepted if possible)

Scenic Attractions Near the B&B Homes:
Sag Harbor Customs House, Whaling Museum, John Drew Theater, Guild Hall Art Exhibits, Home Sweet Home Museum, Parrish Museum, Shinnecock Indian Reservation, Halsey Homestead, Montauk Hither Hills State Park, sport fishing, Watermill Old Mill Museum & Windmill

Major Businesses Near the B&B Homes:
Brookhaven National Laboratories, Doubleday Inc., IBM, Avis Car Rental, Newsday Publishers

Major Schools, Universities Near the B&B Homes:
Hofstra, Adelphi, SUNY at Stony Brook, Southampton College, Bowling College, C. W. Post College, Kings Point Marine Academy

B&B Bonuses

   A historic 1882 landmark house designed by famous architect Stanford White, is filled with old-world craftsmanship like leaded glass windows and wood panelling. A floor-to-ceiling fireplace sets another home apart. A cottage on the bay with its own beach, pool, and Jacuzzi, offers breakfast in the dining room overlooking the water.
   Guests have enjoyed treats like hot cider, wine, homemade clam chowder, and coloring books with crayons, for the children.

A Reasonable Alternative, Inc.
117 SPRING STREET, ROOM 6, PORT JEFFERSON, NY 11777

Offers B&B Homes In:
Nassau and Suffolk counties, along the North and South, from Great Neck to Greenport, from Hempstead to the Hamptons

Reservations Phone: (516) 928-4034
Price Range of Homes:
Single: $20 and up, no fixed rate, depending on season, area, and amenities
Breakfast Included in Price:
Continental (juice, roll/toast, coffee); occasional extras and regional specialties are provided in some homes
Brochure Available: Free if inquirer sends stamped, self-addressed #10 envelope
Reservations Should Be Made: 2 weeks in advance (last minute reservations accepted if possible)

Scenic Attractions Near the B&B Homes:
Bethpage Recreation Village, Hargreaves Vineyards, Sag Harbor Whaling Museum, Sag Harbor Museum and Custom House, Game Farm and Zoo, Fire Island National Seashore, Montauk Lighthouse, Jones Beach, Westbury Music Fair, Stony Brook Museum Complex, Sagamore Hill, Vanderbilt Planetarium, Sunken Meadow State Park

Major Businesses Near the B&B Homes:
Brookhaven National Laboratories, Rte. 110 Industrial Complex, Hauppage Industrial Complex

Major Schools, Universities Near the B&B Homes:
Hofstra, Adelphi, C. W. Post, SUNY at Stony Brook

B&B Bonuses

A Historic home in the three-village area features a brass bed, enclosed brick patio, and barn. And how about a 36-foot cabin cruiser that sleeps six, or a restored Victorian farmhouse?

One host was unusually helpful when the husband of a South American guest family was in a severe auto accident, getting him to the hospital, taking care of their baby, and in general staying on call until relatives could arrive to take over.

Bed & Breakfast of Central New York
1846 BELLEVUE AVENUE, SYRACUSE, NY 13204

Offers B&B Homes In:
Syracuse and Central New York State

Reservations Phone: (315) 472-5050
Phone Hours: 8 a.m. to 9 p.m.   **Available:** 7 days a week
Price Range of Homes:
Single: $25 to $32
Breakfast Included in Price:
Continental or Full American may be served (breakfast varies with individual home)
Brochure Available: Free
Reservations Should Be Made: 2 weeks in advance (last minute reservations accepted if possible)

Scenic Attractions Near the B&B Homes:
Finger Lakes, Thousand Islands, Green Lake and Letchworth State Parks, Civic Center, Everson Museum, downhill and cross-country skiing

Major Businesses Near the B&B Homes:
GE, Carrier Corp., Allied Chemical, Crouse & Hinds, Upstate Medical Center

Major Schools, Universities Near the B&B Homes:
Syracuse U., Lemoyne College, Onondaga Community College, Maria Regina College, Cazenovia College

B&B Bonuses

"Syracuse now offers the European concept of hospitality, with charming accommodations in private homes." An "old stagecoach house" has fireplaces not only in some bedrooms but in the kitchen, too!

Pickups, sightseeing, antique tours, etc., can be arranged, sometimes for a fee.

Rhode Island

Castle Keep Bed & Breakfast Registry
44 EVERETT ST. NEWPORT, RI 02840

Offers B&B Homes In:
Aquidneck Island—Newport, Middletown, and Portsmouth in Rhode Island

Reservations Phone: (401) 846-0362
Phone Hours: 8 a.m. to 8 p.m.   **Available:** 7 days a week
Price Range of Homes:
Single: $25 to $40   Double: $35 to $75
Breakfast Included in Price:
Full American (juice, eggs, bacon, toast, coffee) and various special dishes, at host's discretion
Brochure Available: Free
Reservations Should Be Made: 2 weeks in advance, 3 weeks in summer (last minute reservations accepted if possible)

Scenic Attractions Near the B&B Homes:
America's Cup Races, Naval War College, Topiary Gardens, at least five major boat shows a year, and "the largest collection of restored and lived-in historic Colonial homes in America"

Major Businesses Near the B&B Homes:
Ancillary Software, companies with naval contracts

Major Schools, Universities Near the B&B Homes:
St. George's, Portsmouth Abbey prep schools, Salve Regina, Roger Williams College

B&B Bonuses
    Besides the largest collection of restored Colonial homes in America, Newport is famous for its fine beaches and harbors. One host home is a spectacular French chateau on the water, overlooking the entire yachting center, and another more modern home in right on the starting line for the 12-meter races. See what it's like to live like a millionaire yachtsman!

Guest House Association of Newport
BOX 981, NEWPORT, RI 02840

Offers B&B Homes In:
Newport only

Reservations Phone: Each home on their list must be called directly, for reservations; call (401) 846-5444 for other information
Price Range of Homes:
Single: $35 to $120   Double: $35 to $120
Breakfast Included in Price:
Continental (juice, roll/toast, coffee)
Brochure Available: Free
Reservations Should Be Made: 2 weeks in advance in winter, a month or more in summer or fall (last minute reservations accepted if possible)

Scenic Attractions Near the B&B Homes:
Nine National Historic Landmarks, Victorian "gilded age" mansions, Touro Synagogue (first in America), Cliff Walk, beaches, wharf dining and shopping areas

Major Businesses Near the B&B Homes:
Raytheon, Transcom, Naval Underwater Systems Center

Major Schools, Universities Near the B&B Homes:
Naval War College, Salve Regina College, St. George's Prep, St. Michaels, Portsmouth Abbey

B&B Bonuses
   All of the guest houses in the association have historical significance, most have been built in the mid-19th century and been furnished with antiques and period pieces. "The Wayside," a Georgian mansion on famed Bellevue Avenue, has a private pool, the "Brinley Victorian" has two parlors and a library, and "The Cliffside" near Cliff Walk and the beach, boasts an elaborately carved Victorian center staircase.

At Home in New England
BOX 25, SAUNDERSTOWN, RI 02874

Offers B&B Homes In:
Coastal areas near New Haven, CT: Providence, RI; Boston, MA; Portsmouth, NH; Southern Vermont

Reservations Phone: (401) 294-3808
Phone Hours: 8 a.m. to 5:30 p.m. **Available:** Monday to Friday, Saturday will return taped calls

Price Range of Homes:
Single: $28 to $45   Double: $38 to $60
Breakfast Included in Price:
Full American, which may include cranberry and blueberry muffins, johnnycakes, clam cakes, pancakes and Vermont maple syrup, blueberry buckle, and occasional New England specialties like creamed cod on toast and lobster quiche
Brochure Available: Free
Reservations Should Be Made: 3 weeks in advance (no last minute reservations accepted)

Scenic Attractions Near the B&B Homes:
Plymouth Rock, Mayflower Site, Minuteman National Historic Park, Roger Williams Park and Zoo, Newport mansions, Manchester, VT ski area, Mystic Seaport and Submarine Base, New Haven—British Art Center, Peabody Museum

Major Schools, Universities Near the B&B Homes:
Harvard, MIT, Brown U., Boston U., U. of New Hampshire, Yale U., U. of Rhode Island, U.S. Coast Guard Academy

B&B Bonuses

An 1825 Federal-style townhouse on the National Register, is located in a small, historic fishing village, furnished by an expert with antiques; the host owns an antique shop in town. In Vermont, a charming restored 18th-century cape is surrounded by pine-covered hills and overlooks a pond and vegetable and flower gardens. Guests have use of the entire second floor. Sports, shopping, art galleries and summer theaters abound in the area.

Hosts' interests and accomplishments range from investment counselling, journalism, sailing, painting, equestrian sports to "gardening on a grand scale," music, and tennis.

MIDDLE ATLANTIC STATES

Delaware
District of Columbia
Maryland
New Jersey
North Carolina
Pennsylvania
South Carolina
Virginia

Delaware

Bed & Breakfast of Delaware
1804 BREEN LANE, WILMINGTON, DE 19810

Offers B&B Homes In:
City and suburbs of Wilmington, Newark, Odessa, Lewes, in Delaware; Chadds Ford and other towns in nearby Pennsylvania and Maryland

Reservations Phone: (302) 475-0340
Phone Hours: 3 p.m. to 6 p.m.   **Available:** 7 days a week (any hour on answering service)
Price Range of Homes:
Single: $18 to $30   Double: $35 to $45 (beach homes to $65 in summer)
Breakfast Included in Price:
Full American (juice, eggs, bacon, toast, coffee)
Brochure Available: Free
Reservations Should Be Made: 2 weeks in advance (last minute reservations accepted if possible)

Scenic Attractions Near the B&B Homes:
Winterthur, Longwood Gardens, Brandywine River Museum, Hagley Museum, Nemours, Old New Castle, beach resorts, Philadelphia attractions

Major Businesses Near the B&B Homes:
E. I. duPont, Hercules, Inc., ICI, Avon, Cigna Insurance, W. L. Gore Associates, Hewlett-Packard, Chase Manhattan Bank, Beneficial Finance Corp., Franklin Mint, Philadelphia Navy Yard, Dover Air Force Base

Major Schools, Universities Near the B&B Homes:
U. of Delaware, Delaware Law School, West Chester U.

B&B Bonuses
   "Beautiful restored 18th- and 19th-century homes furnished with authentic antiques" are the specialty of this B&B. Some hosts have served as docents at major museums.
   Occasional extras are sightseeing tours, tennis and golf club privileges, and gourmet dinners.

District of Columbia

Bed 'n' Breakfast Ltd. of Washington, DC
P.O. BOX 12011, WASHINGTON, DC 20005

Offers B&B Homes In:
In Washington, DC: Georgetown, DuPont, Logan, and Thomas Circles, Capitol Hill, Upper Northwest; in nearby Virginia and Maryland: Chevy Chase and Bethesda

Reservations Phone: (202) 328-3510
Phone Hours: 9 a.m. to 1 p.m.   **Available:** Monday to Friday, occasional Saturdays
Price Range of Homes:
Single: $30 to $65   Double: $40 to $75
Breakfast Included in Price:
Most serve Continental, but a few homes serve full breakfasts, and several hostesses serve beaten biscuits, ham and eggs, and other specialties
Brochure Available: Free
Reservations Should Be Made: As soon as possible (last minute reservations accepted if possible)

Scenic Attractions Near the B&B Homes:
White House, Capitol Building, Smithsonian, Library of Congress, and all other Government buildings

Major Schools, Universities Near the B&B Homes:
Georgetown U., George Washington U., School of Advanced International Studies of Johns Hopkins, Catholic U., Trinity College, Howard U.

B&B Bonuses
From lovely homes on broad lawns away from the hustle and bustle of town, to prestigious Georgetown and Logan and DuPont Circle homes in the city, there are accommodations to please everyone.

Some extra services often provided are skirt hangers in closets, use of blow-dryers, hot rollers, and curling irons, telephone answering, receipt of packages for guests, and short-term luggage storage. All hosts give free DC tourist brochures.

Sweet Dreams & Toast, Inc.
P.O. BOX 4835-0035, WASHINGTON, DC 20008

Offers B&B Homes In:
Annapolis, Chevy Chase, and Bethesda in Maryland; McLean, Arlington, Alexandria in Virginia; and District of Columbia

Reservations Phone: (202) 483-9191
Phone Hours: 11 a.m. to 6 p.m.   **Available:** Monday to Friday, except holidays

Price Range of Homes:
Single: $25 to $40   Double: $35 to $60
Breakfast Included in Price:
Continental (juice, roll/toast, coffee)
Brochure Available: Free
Reservations Should Be Made: 2 or 3 weeks in advance (last minute reservations accepted if possible)

Scenic Attractions Near the B&B Homes:
National Zoo, The Smithsonian, John F. Kennedy Center for the Performing Arts, U.S. Capitol and all national buildings open to the public (National Archives, Bureau of Printing and Engraving, etc.), Arlington Cemetery, Mount Vernon, Children's Museum

Major Businesses Near the B&B Homes:
U.S. Government agencies, National Institutes of Health, and in Annapolis, U.S. Naval Academy and Westinghouse Oceanic

Major Schools, Universities Near the B&B Homes:
Howard U., George Washington U., Georgetown U., U. of District of Columbia, Catholic U. (Washington); U.S. Naval Academy, St. John's College (Annapolis)

B&B Bonuses

A quiet antique-filled suburban Maryland home can accommodate a family of four. The host speaks Spanish and French. If you prefer to be in the heart of Washington, a restored Victorian home is within a mile of the Capitol-Smithsonian area.

Numerous restaurants and excellent transportation characterize the area.

Maryland

Sharp-Adams, Inc., "The Maryland Registry"
33 WEST STREET, ANNAPOLIS, MD 21401

Offers B&B Homes In:
Annapolis, Baltimore, and 45 other cities and towns throughout Maryland

Reservations Phone: (301) 269-6232 or 261-2233
Phone Hours: 9 a.m. to 5 p.m.   **Available:** Monday to Friday
Price Range of Homes:
Single: $28 to $48   Double: $33 to $58 (yachts, $58 to $75)
Breakfast Included in Price:
Continental or full American, depending on individual host home
Brochure Available: Free
Reservations Should Be Made: 3 weeks in advance suggested (no reservation requests accepted with less than 24 hours notice)

Scenic Attractions Near the B&B Homes:
Baltimore Inner Harbor, Chesapeake Bay, Annapolis Naval Station, hiking and biking along the C&O Canal, big league sports, horse racing, historic homes

Major Businesses Near the B&B Homes:
U.S. Fidelity & Guaranty, Crown Petroleum, Martin Marietta, World Airways, Rouse & Co., Black & Decker, Perdue, Inc.

Major Schools, Universities Near the B&B Homes:
Johns Hopkins, Goucher College, U.S. Naval Academy, St. John's College, Washington College, U. of Maryland

B&B Bonuses

An exclusive feature of this agency is "B&B by Boat." You can enjoy accommodations on a safely moored yacht, or cruise along Chesapeake Bay and visit with different hosts along a charted route. Other excursions offered are chartered sails on Chesapeake Bay, biking and hiking itineraries including a ferry ride and lunch at a country inn; and guided goose and duck hunting expeditions. (This year, 1984, Maryland celebrates its 350th anniversary).

Ask about Sharp-Adams' two travel packages: "The Maryland Sampler" and "The Mid-Week Weekend," with special rates.

New Jersey

Bed & Breakfast of New Jersey

SUITE 132, 103 GODWIN AVENUE, MIDLAND PARK, NJ 07432

Offers B&B Homes In:
Entire state of New Jersey, mostly northern and central, as well as Atlantic coastline

Reservations Phone: (201) 444-7409
Phone Hours: 9 a.m. to 8 p.m.   **Available:** 7 days a week
Price Range of Homes:
Single: $20 to $75   Double: $30 to $90
Breakfast Included in Price:
Continental or full American (juice, eggs, bacon, toast, coffee); breakfasts vary from simple continental to elaborate festivities with lots of home-baked specialties
Brochure Available: Free if inquirer sends stamped, self-addressed #10 envelope
Reservations Should Be Made: 2 weeks in advance (last minute reservations accepted if possible)

Scenic Attractions Near the B&B Homes:
All sports, entertainment, cultural, and recreational activities to be found in New Jersey

Major Businesses Near the B&B Homes:
New Jersey is headquarters for many hundreds of the world's leading corporations

Major Schools, Universities Near the B&B Homes:
Fairleigh-Dickinson U., Rutgers U., Princeton U.

B&B Bonuses
"A beautiful old mansion on a hill, overlooking the ocean, was the home of a famous New Jersey painter (his paintings are in the National Art Gallery in Washington, D.C.). Beautifully redone, it is now run by his two granddaughters, and is famous for its warmth, hospitality, and wonderful location."

One of the gracious hosts ran a relocation service for three years, and is a gold mine of information about the New Jersey metropolitan areas. She loves to drive guests around, pointing out sights they might otherwise miss.

North Carolina

Charlotte Bed & Breakfast Association
1700-2 DELANE AVENUE, CHARLOTTE, NC 28211

Offers B&B Homes In:
Charlotte, NC

Reservations Phone: (704) 366-0979
Phone Hours: 9 a.m. to 5 p.m.   **Available:** Monday to Saturday
Price Range of Homes:
Single: $20 to $40   Double: $30 to $55 (top seasonal rate) (Suite—$44)
Breakfast Included in Price:
Continental (juice, rolls/toast, coffee)
Brochure Available: No
Reservations Should Be Made: 2 weeks in advance, deposit required; last minute reservations accepted if possible

Scenic Attractions Near the B&B Homes:
Discovery Place, Mint Museum, Nature Museum, Asheville/Biltmore Home

Major Businesses Near the B&B Homes:
IBM, Digital, Celanese

Major Schools, Universities Near the B&B Homes:
U. of North Carolina, Queens College, Central Piedmont Community College

B&B Bonuses
  This B&B agency is in the process of expanding into nearby areas such as Southern Pines, Beaufort, Tryon, Chapel Hill, Raleigh/Durham, and Lake Wylie, SC. One of their Charlotte homes is "simply but elegantly appointed, with contemporary paintings and furniture."
  Hosts will usually make airport pickups and returns, and may offer tours, if given sufficient notice.

B&B in Greensboro
201 W. BESSEMER AVE., GREENSBORO, NC 27401

Offers B&B Homes In:
Greensboro, NC

Reservations Phone: (919) 272-6248
Phone Hours: 8 a.m. to 8 p.m.   **Available:** 7 days a week
Price Range of Homes:
Single: $35 to $50   Double: $40 to $70
Breakfast Included in Price:
Breakfasts may include fresh seasonal fruits, melted natural cheese on whole wheat muffins, eggs, homemade bran muffins, juice, tea, coffee
Brochure Available: Free
Reservations Should Be Made: Prefer 2 days' notice, last minute reservations accepted if possible)

Scenic Attractions Near the B&B Homes:
North Carolina Zoological Park (natural environment zoo), Blandwood Estate, Greensboro Historical Museum, Green Hill Center for N.C. Art

Major Schools, Universities Near the B&B Homes:
U. of North Carolina at Greensboro

B&B Bonuses
"Enjoy comfort, character, and style at the home of a host eager to recommend antiques, fine crafts, and cultural activities, as well as the best in restaurants." This is in a restored elegant home in historic Fisher Park district, one mile from the heart of downtown Greensboro. The host is a runner, too, so scenic running routes and/or companion runner are available.

Offered on a fee basis are: transportation to and from airport, dinner featuring nouvelle cuisine, arts and crafts tour, and transportation to Old Salem in Winston-Salem.

156 • THE MIDDLE ATLANTIC STATES

Pennsylvania

Bed & Breakfast of Southeast Pennsylvania
P.O. BOX 278, RD #1, BARTO, PA 19504

Offers B&B Homes In:
Easton, Pa. west thru Bethlehem, Allentown, Kutztown, Reading, to Hershey, south to French Creek State Park, Boyertown, Bally, E. Greenville, Quakertown and Souderton

Reservations Phone: (215) 845-3526
Phone Hours: All day **Available:** 7 days a week
Price Range of Homes:
Single: $15 to $35   Double: $30 to $55
Breakfast Included in Price:
Continental or full American (one hostess serve a vegetarian, or macrobiotic breakfast)
Brochure Available: For a fee, which is $1.00
Reservations Should Be Made: 2 weeks in advance (last minute reservations accepted if possible)

Scenic Attractions Near the B&B Homes:
Canal Museum, historic Bethlehem, Dorney Park Velodrome and Art Museum, French Creek State Park, Hopewell Village, Hershey Chocolate Factory, Antique Car Museum, Kutztown Folk Festival, Reading shopping outlets

Major Businesses Near the B&B Homes:
Bethlehem Steel, Mack Truck, Air Products, Western Electric, Bally Block, Boyertown Casket, Drug Plastics, Gilbert Commonwealth, Carpenter Technology, Rockwell International (textile machine works), Brown Printing East, Knoll International, Pillsbury Co., Bally Case & Cooler

Major Schools, Universities Near the B&B Homes:
Lehigh, Lafayette, Moravian, Allentown, Cedar Crest, Muhlenberg, Albright, and Alvernia colleges; Kutztown U., Perkiomen School

B&B Bonuses

Meet a hostess who teaches in a one-room Amish school; she will welcome you in a new log cabin home with all modern conveniences, and a large porch where children can stay overnight in their own sleeping bags. Or would you prefer an 18th-century farmhouse with sheep, overlooking a stream filled with watercress? Or a chalet furnished with antiques that started life as a railroad station?

"Guests should complete section of brochure relating to their interests, for information of host home."

Bed & Breakfast of Philadelphia
BOX 680, DEVON, PA 19333-680

Offers B&B Homes In:
Center City Phila., all four surrounding counties of Bucks, Chester, Montgomery, and Delaware, including Main Line, New Hope, Doylestown, Valley Forge, West Chester, Chadds Ford, & Chestnut Hill, Wilmington (Delaware), Moorestown & Riverton (New Jersey)

Reservations Phone: (215) 688-1633
Phone Hours: 9 a.m. to 9 p.m.   **Available:** Monday through Friday, some weekend hours

Price Range of Homes:
Single: $25 to $35   Double: $35 to $55 (family rates in specific homes)
Breakfast Included in Price:
"Gourmet" Continental or full breakfasts, which may include quiches, Philadelphia sticky buns, scrapple, other host specialties and regional fare
Brochure Available: Free (detailed listings directory is $5.00)
Reservations Should Be Made: 1 week in advance or sooner; last minute reservations accepted, according to availability

Scenic Attractions Near the B&B Homes:
Valley Forge National Park, Independence Hall and National Park, Philadelphia Museum of Art, Franklin Institute, Rodin Museum, Longwood Gardens, Winterthur Museum & Gardens, Hagley Museum, Brandywine River Museum (Wyeth paintings), Skippack Village, Mennonite and Amish country

Major Businesses Near the B&B Homes:
Valley Forge and Ft. Washington industrial parks, NCR, Prudential, GE Space Labs, all major Philadelphia corporation headquarters and industrial complexes

Major Schools, Universities Near the B&B Homes:
U. of Pennsylvania, Drexel U., Temple U., Haverford, Bryn Mawr, Villanova, Swarthmore, Eastern, Beaver, Cabrini, St. Josephs, La Salle and Rosemont colleges; Philadelphia Textile College, Jefferson Medical School, Wills Eye Hospital, American College of Physicians, Presbyterian Hospital, Dufreye Medical Center

B&B Bonuses
    Accommodations for every taste include a turreted Victorian row home, a 300-acre working dairy farm, a 200-year-old farm house, a renovated grist mill, and a Mennonite farm. Some homes have been shown on ABC-TV, Hal Linden's show, "For Your Information," and others featured in national magazines and local papers.

Bed & Breakfast in Lancaster, Harrisburg, and Hershey Areas
463 NORTH MARKET STREET, ELIZABETHTOWN, PA 17022

Offers B&B Homes In:
Lancaster County, including Lancaster, Strasburg, nearby towns, Elizabethtown, Mount Joy, and others; Dauphin County homes in Hershey, Middletown, Harrisburg, and Hummelstown; Lebanon County homes in Annville and Palmyra; Southeastern PA

Reservations Phone: (717) 367-9408
Phone Hours: 7 a.m. to 10 p.m.   **Available:** 7 days a week
Price Range of Homes:
Single: $30 to $50   Double: $35 to $60
Breakfast Included in Price:
Continental or full American, many Lancaster area farm homes provide Penn. Dutch country breakfasts, with their own cured hams and sausages and breads and rolls baked early the same morning, special gourmet breakfasts served at a historic home in Annville
Brochure Available: Free if inquirer sends stamped, self-addressed #10 envelope
Reservations Should Be Made: 2 weeks in advance preferred, or one week (no last minute reservations accepted)

Scenic Attractions Near the B&B Homes:
Pennsylvania Farm Museum, Amish Homestead, Strasburg Railroad, Dutch Wonderland, Hershey Park, Hershey Museum of American Life, Hershey Rose Gardens, William Penn Museum, Antique Automobile Club of America, Zoo America, Chocolate World, many shopping outlets

Major Businesses Near the B&B Homes:
Armstrong, Kelloggs, Howmet, Hershey Foods Corp., Bethlehem Steel

Major Schools, Universities Near the B&B Homes:
Franklin & Marshall College, Millersville U., Elizabethtown College, Lebanon Valley College, Capitol Campus of Penn State, M.S. Hershey Medical Center of Penn State, Harrisburg Area Community College

B&B Bonuses

A historic home in Hershey offers the luxury of a bedroom with private powder room and porch decorated in "Laura Ashley" style. Or tour the dairy and herb and craft shop in a farm home in Mount Joy. Besides country breakfast, a herbal luncheon is available here, with advance reservation.

Many Lancaster farm hosts will custom-tailor sightseeing tours to meet the guest's particular interests. Another hostess provides round-trip transportation to and from her farm home and Harrisburg International Airport, for only $10.

Bed & Breakfast of Chester County
P.O. BOX 825, KENNETT SQUARE, PA 19347

Offers B&B Homes In:
Brandywine Valley, from the Philadelphia suburbs to Penn Dutch country

Reservations Phone: (215) 444-1367
Phone Hours: Any time   **Available:** 7 days a week
Price Range of Homes:
Single: $18 to $35   Double: $25 to $50
Breakfast Included in Price:
Continental or full American, depending on individual home; a specialty is Penn Dutch scrapple mushroom quiche; "Kennett Square is the mushroom capital of the world"
Brochure Available: For a fee, which is $1.00
Reservations Should Be Made: At least one week in advance preferred—"we try to accommodate immediately, or as soon as possible"

Scenic Attractions Near the B&B Homes:
Longwood Gardens, Winterthur, Wyeth Brandywine River Museum, Delaware Natural History Museum, Valley Forge, Brandywine Battlefield, Phillips Mushroom Museum, Penn Dutch country

Major Businesses Near the B&B Homes:
Hewlett-Packard, Burroughs

Major Schools, Universities Near the B&B Homes:
West Chester U., Lincoln U., Widener College, U. of Delaware, Penn State at Lima

B&B Bonuses
   An antique-laden 1836 farmhouse situated in the middle of 275 acres of pastoral beauty also offers such modern amenities as a swimming pool, hot tub in a greenhouse, and TV's in the rooms. "The delightful hostess loves to meet and entertain new people, offering a full country breakfast with homemade goodies." If you appreciate a view of horses grazing in pastures, you can feast your eyes from a Victorian mansion, circa 1840, and then take a dip in the pool.
   Hosts are glad to direct guests to local restaurants and sights—one even took a French lady to the hairdresser!

Center City/Bed & Breakfast
1908 SPRUCE STREET, PHILADELPHIA, PA 19103

Offers B&B Homes In:
Center City of Philadelphia, some outside city

Reservations Phone: (215) 735-0881 or 923-5459 or 735-1137
Phone Hours: 9 a.m. to 6 p.m.   **Available:** 7 days a week, except holidays

Price Range of Homes:
Single: $20 to $45   Double: $35 to $65
Breakfast Included in Price:
Continental or Full American (juice, eggs, bacon, toast, coffee). Full breakfast is served at certain host homes.
Brochure Available: Free
Reservations Should Be Made: 2 weeks in advance (last minute reservations accepted if possible)

Scenic Attractions Near the B&B Homes:
Independence Hall, Betsy Ross House, Liberty Bell, Fairmount Park, Carpenter's Hall, Rodin Museum, Franklin Museum, Amish Country, Philadelphia Art Museum, Philadelphia Zoo

Major Businesses Near the B&B Homes:
Cigna, Bell Telephone, Rohm & Haas, GE, Smith Kline, Beckman, Sperry Univac

Major Schools, Universities Near the B&B Homes:
U. of Penn., Temple U., Drexel Institute, Moore College of Art, largest number of medical schools in mid-Atlantic area

B&B Bonuses

   A restored town house furnished with antiques and canopied beds was mentioned in a recent issue of *National Geographic*. An elegantly furnished high-rise apartment affords a spectacular view, and a house "right out of Charles Dickens" is situated in a cobblestone courtyard with gaslight-type lanterns.
   Hosts will help locate parking space, make club membership privileges available, and some will serve "famous Rachelle's brownies" with milk at bedtime.

Rest & Repast Bed & Breakfast Service
P.O. BOX 126, PINE GROVE MILLS, PA 16868

Offers B&B Homes In:
Central Pennsylvania

Reservations Phone: (814) 238-1484
Phone Hours: 8 a.m. to 10 p.m. (best to call evenings—daytime answering machine)
Available: Monday to Friday, most weekends and holidays
Price Range of Homes:
Single: $20 to $27   Double: $28 to $37 Football Weekends—$35 to $47 (2 night minimum for Homecomings)
Breakfast Included in Price:
Continental or full American . . . almost half of the hosts serve full breakfasts, including Penn Dutch specialties, home-grown eggs, and home-made sausage
Brochure Available: Free
Reservations Should Be Made: 2 weeks in advance (last minute reservations accepted if possible . . . 3 to 6 months in advance for football weekends, especially Homecomings)

Scenic Attractions Near the B&B Homes:
Penns Cave, Indian Caverns, Woodward Cave, 28th Division Military Shrine & Museum, Governor Curtin Mansion Village, Four Wineries, Belleville Amish Market, Boalsburg (home of Memorial Day)

Major Businesses Near the B&B Homes:
Corning Glass works, HRB Singer, C-Cor Electronics, Martin Marietta

Major Schools, Universities Near the B&B Homes:
Penn State, Bucknell

B&B Bonuses
   One host has a herb farm, shop, and trading post in his home. Three other homes (with two pending) are on the National Historic Register, "beautifully furnished and lovingly restored." The hosts are glad to share their extensive knowledge with their guests.
   "Each host home has been inspected for comfort, cleanliness, and individual charm."

Country Cousins Bed & Breakfast Registry
228 WEST MAIN ST., WAYNESBORO, PENNSYLVANIA 17268

Offers B&B Homes In:
South Central Pa., from Susquehanna to Bedford—and a few homes in West Virginia

Reservations Phone: (717) 762-2722
Phone Hours: 1 p.m. to 6 p.m.   **Available:** Monday to Saturday, some weekends

Price Range of Homes:
Single: $20 to $40   Double: $30 to $56

Breakfast Included in Price:
Some Continental or "self-serve"—others full American (juice, eggs, bacon, toast, coffee); some homes serve breakfast quiche with local apples and sausage, or Pennsylvania scrapple; and some hosts serve local hot cider in winter

Brochure Available: Free if inquirer sends stamped, self-addressed #10 envelope

Reservations Should Be Made: 10 days in advance (last minute reservations accepted if possible)

Scenic Attractions Near the B&B Homes:
Appalachian Trail, Ski Liberty, Gettysburg, Caledonia State Park, Blue Ridge Mountains, Blue Knob Ski Resort, James Buchanan's birthplace (in Mercersburg); Totem Pole Playhouse, Cowan's Gap State Park, Belgian Orchestral Organ, hang gliding, factory outlets, York Fairgrounds, Allenberry Playhouse

Major Businesses Near the B&B Homes:
Grove Manufacturing, Frick Company, Landis Tool Co., Landis-Teledyne Machine Co., Fort Ritchie, Leterkenny Army Depot, T. B. Woods, Pet Foods, Knouse Corp., Hanover Foods, Mack Truck, Fairchild, Tab Books, Musselman Foods, Regency Printers

Major Schools, Universities Near the B&B Homes:
Mercersburg Academy, Gettysburg College, Shippensburg U., Penn State (Mont Alto Campus), York and Wilson Colleges, Dickinson College and School of Law, U.S. Army War College at Carlisle

B&B Bonuses
   Their list of homes features many lovely restored houses dating back 100 years or more . . . and for something quite different, if you've ever wanted to stay at a working farm, here's your chance. This B&B agency boasts quite a few of them, also a mountaintop estate.

South Carolina

Historic Charleston Bed and Breakfast
43 LEGARE STREET, CHARLESTON, SC 29401

Offers B&B Homes In:
Historic District of Charleston, S.C. only

Reservations Phone: (803) 722-6606
Phone Hours: 24 hours a day   **Available:** 7 days a week
Price Range of Homes:
Single: $35 to $100   Double: $45 to $100
Breakfast Included in Price:
Continental (juice, roll/toast, coffee)
Brochure Available: Free
Reservations Should Be Made: 2 weeks in advance NOTE: March to June, 2-3 months in advance (last minute reservations accepted if possible)

Scenic Attractions Near the B&B Homes:
Historic homes, museums, harbor tours, famous gardens, beaches

Major Schools, Universities Near the B&B Homes:
The Citadel, College of Charleston

B&B Bonuses

There is a gazebo garden house, circa 1838, which was the original bath and card house for the Kerrison mansion. Another home has been created from the stables and kitchen building of a circa 1720 Georgian mansion, and a 1797 house is owned by the seventh generation of the same family that built it.

Guests are treated like "nonpaying friends" and have been invited for cocktails or elaborate brunches, or given gift mementos to take home.

Charleston Society Bed & Breakfast
84 MURRAY BLVD., CHARLESTON, SC 29401

Offers B&B Homes In:
Historic area of Charleston

Reservations Phone: (803) 723-4948
Phone Hours: 9 a.m. to 5 p.m.   **Available:** 7 days a week
Price Range of Homes:
Single: $45 to $60   Double: $60 to $100
Breakfast Included in Price:
Continental (juice, roll/toast, coffee)
Brochure Available: Free
Reservations Should Be Made: 2 or 3 weeks in advance (last minute reservations accepted if possible)

Scenic Attractions Near the B&B Homes:
All the Historic District Homes and other historic points of interest are within easy walking distance

Major Schools, Universities Near the B&B Homes:
The Citadel, the College at Charleston, Baptist College

B&B Bonuses
"Enjoy the gracious hospitality of a stay in America's most historic city. Eighteenth-century homes, handsome interiors, period furniture, and charming Charleston gardens characterize the life-style of the aristocrats who lived in these great houses during the pre-Revolutionary, post-Revolutionary and ante-bellum days, all within easy walking distance of shops, restaurants, and historic points of interest."

A licensed tour guide is available.

SOUTH CAROLINA / VIRGINIA • 165

Virginia

Princely Bed & Breakfast Ltd.
819 PRINCE STREET, ALEXANDRIA, VA 22314

Offers B&B Homes In:
Alexandria and nearby areas

Reservations Phone: (703) 683-2159
Phone Hours: 9 a.m. to 6 p.m.   **Available:** 6 days a week
Price Range of Homes:
Single: $32 to $44   Double: $45 to $60
Breakfast Included in Price:
Continental (juice, roll/toast, coffee)
Brochure Available: Free
Reservations Should Be Made: 2 weeks in advance (*no last minute reservations accepted*)

Scenic Attractions Near the B&B Homes:
Washington, D.C., Mt. Vernon

B&B Bonuses
"Our houses in Alexandria's famous 'Old Town' date from 1750 to 1830. Most are filled with museum-quality antiques."

Hosts frequently drive guests to Mt. Vernon (George Washington's Home and Estate), the Capitol, the White House, and all of the many places of interest in the District of Columbia.

There are at least seven major universities in the area.

Guesthouses Reservation Services Inc.
P.O. BOX 5737, CHARLOTTESVILLE, VA 22905

Offers B&B Homes In:
City of Charlottesville and others in Albemarle County, Shenandoah National Park (Luray, Virginia)

Reservations Phone: (804) 979-7264 or 979-8327
Phone Hours: 1 p.m. to 6 p.m.   **Available:** Monday to Friday
Price Range of Homes:
Single: $28 and up   Double: $36 and up
Breakfast Included in Price:
Continental or full American (small additional price for full breakfast—hostess specialties range from a "breakfast soufflé" to homemade breads and muffins)
Brochure Available: Free if inquirer sends stamped, self-addressed #10 envelope
Reservations Should Be Made: One months to 6 weeks in advance (last minute reservations accepted if possible)

Scenic Attractions Near the B&B Homes:
Monticello, Ash Lawn (James Madison's Home), Skyline Drive, Shenandoah National Park, Blue Ridge Parkway, Appalachian Trail, April Historic Garden Week

Major Schools, Universities Near the B&B Homes:
U. of Virginia (founded by Thomas Jefferson)

B&B Bonuses
Some of the interesting homes are a 150-year-old log cabin for guests with its own driveway, a private wing in a newly built Georgian home in horse country, a picturesque country cottage from a design by a renowned architect of the past, and an upstairs suite in old slave quarters, adjacent to the University of Virginia.

Sojourners Bed & Breakfast
3609 TANGLEWOOD LANE, LYNCHBURG, VA 24503

Offers B&B Homes In:
Lynchburg, Virginia

Reservations Phone: (804) 384-1655
Phone Hours: Before 10 a.m., after 6 p.m.

Available: Answer phone coverage— prompt reply by mail or collect call

Price Range of Homes:
Single: $28 to $32   Double: $36 and up
Breakfast Included in Price:
Many homes serve continental, but some serve full breakfasts, with homemade breads
Brochure Available: Free
Reservations Should Be Made: 3 weeks in advance (last minute reservations accepted if possible)

Scenic Attractions Near the B&B Homes:
Blue Ridge Parkway, Appomattox National Park, Jones Memorial Library, Virginia Ten Miler Road Race, Virginia House & Garden Tour, Patrick Henry home.

Major Businesses Near the B&B Homes:
Babcock Wilcox, GE, Lynchburg Foundry, C. B. Fleet, Meredith/Burda, International Circuit Technology, First Colony Life, Westminster-Canterbury

Major Schools, Universities Near the B&B Homes:
Lynchburg College, Randolph Macon Woman's College, Sweet Briar College, Virginia Episcopal School, Liberty Baptist College

B&B Bonuses

Available to guests are a wide current selection of brochures on Central Virginia, books and magazines of particular interest to history buffs, copies of menus from the best restaurants, guides to sightseeing, shopping, and nature trails.

Airport pickups can be arranged, given sufficient notice.

Bed & Breakfast of Tidewater Virginia
P.O. BOX 3343, NORFOLK, VA 23514

Offers B&B Homes In:
Norfolk, Virginia Beach, Portsmouth, Chesapeake, Eastern Shore of Virginia, Chincoteague, Hampton

Reservations Phone: (804) 627-1983 or 627-9409
Phone Hours: 8 a.m. to 8 p.m.   **Available:** 7 days a week (phone answering service)

Price Range of Homes:
Single: $25 to $40   Double: $30 to $60
Breakfast Included in Price:
"We leave it up to the hosts. Some serve elaborate breakfasts, and the rate is consequently higher than for Continental. A minimum of fruit, beverage, rolls or muffins, is required."
Brochure Available: Free
Reservations Should Be Made: At least 2 weeks in advance, but the more the better (last minute reservations accepted if possible)

Scenic Attractions Near the B&B Homes:
Norfolk Naval Base, Chrysler Museum, McArthur Memorial, Waterside Festival Marketplace, Chesapeake Bay fishing and water sports, Virginia Beach

Major Schools, Universities Near the B&B Homes:
Old Dominion U., Eastern Virginia Medical School, Norfolk Naval Base & Air Station

B&B Bonuses

A short walk over the sand dunes and you are on your own private beach on the Bay; the house is a traditional Eastern Shore design—big house, little house, colonnade and kitchen—attractively furnished with antiques. Or enjoy the working fireplace in your elegant guestroom a few minutes from downtown Norfolk and its most popular restaurants. The hosts are a psychologist and an artist who enjoy fixing breakfast for their guests, especially Irish oatmeal.

"We have a most genial and enthusiastic group of hosts who roll out the red carpet for their B&B guests."

VIRGINIA • 169

Bensonhouse of Richmond
P.O. BOX 15131, RICHMOND, VA 23227

Offers B&B Homes In:
Richmond, Charles City, and James River Plantation

Reservations Phone: (804) 648-7560 or 321-6277
Phone Hours: 9:30 a.m. to 5:30 p.m.   **Available:** Monday to Friday (weekend hours vary—24 hour-a-day phone recording service)

Price Range of Homes:
Single: $22 to $60   Double: $30 to $72 (estate homes at higher rate)
Breakfast Included in Price:
Continental or full American, depending on individual home. Many homes serve home-baked breads and muffins.
Brochure Available: Free if inquirer sends stamped, self-addressed #10 envelope
Reservations Should Be Made: 3 or more weeks in advance (last minute reservations accepted if possible)

Scenic Attractions Near the B&B Homes:
St. Johns Church, Edgar Allan Poe Museum, Museum of the Confederacy, John Marshall House, State Archives, Virginia Historical Society, Science Museum of Virginia, Virginia Museum and Virginia Theater for the Performing Arts . . . within short drive of Williamsburg, Busch Gardens, Kings Dominion, and James River Plantations

Major Businesses Near the B&B Homes:
Ethyl Corp., Virginia Electric and Power Co., Philip Morris, Reynolds Metals, Western Electric, Universal Leaf Tobacco, A. H. Robins, Peat, Marwick, Mitchell Co., Coopers and Lybrand Inc., C. T. Sauer Co., Figgic International, Inc., James River Corp. of Virginia

Major Schools, Universities Near the B&B Homes:
U. of Richmond, Medical College of Virginia, Virginia Commonwealth U., Randolph Macon College, Union Theological Seminary, St. Catherine's School, St. Christopher's School.

B&B Bonuses

The architectural style of a 1920's house is derived from the Cotswold District in England, and decorated with Italian Renaissance furniture and tapestries. Another interesting home is a renovated 1910 row house in the prestigious "FAN" district, which was shown in *Better Homes & Gardens* in 1982.

The Travel Tree
P.O. BOX 838, WILLIAMSBURG, VA 23187

Offers B&B Homes In:
Williamsburg

Reservations Phone: (804) 229-4037 or 565-2236
Phone Hours: 5 p.m. to 9 p.m.   **Available:** Monday to Friday evenings, and weekends

Price Range of Homes:
Single: $20 to $48   Double: $25 to $60
Breakfast Included in Price:
Continental (juice, roll/toast, coffee)
Brochure Available: Free
Reservations Should Be Made: Several weeks in advance

Scenic Attractions Near the B&B Homes:
Colonial Williamsburg, Busch Gardens, Yorktown, Jamestown

Major Businesses Near the B&B Homes:
Camp Peary, Ft. Eustis, Naval Weapons Station, Cheatham Annex, NASA, Anheuser-Busch, Ball Metal, Langley Air Force Base, Badische

Major Schools, Universities Near the B&B Homes:
College of William and Mary

B&B Bonuses
   Among their comfortable homes are a Colonial-style house overlooking a lake, with antiques, canopied beds, and a formal garden; a condominium townhouse with pool privileges; a newly furnished and decorated ranch house with private entrance; a cozy Cape Cod with a four-poster bed; and a twin-bedded room with a private entrance.

GREAT LAKES AREA

Illinois
Michigan
Ohio
Wisconsin

Illinois

Bed & Breakfast Chicago, Inc.
P.O. BOX 14088, CHICAGO, IL 60614

Offers B&B Homes In:
Chicago and nearby areas of Wisconsin, Michigan, and Indiana

Reservations Phone: (312) 951-0085 or 248-2555
Phone Hours: 9 a.m. to 5 p.m.   **Available:** Monday to Saturday
Price Range of Homes:
Single: $25 to $50   Double: $30 to $75
Breakfast Included in Price:
Continental or full American, depending on individual home
Brochure Available: Free
Reservations Should Be Made: 2 weeks in advance (last minute reservations accepted if possible)

Scenic Attractions Near the B&B Homes:
Lake Michigan, Lake Geneva, McCormick Place, Glencoe Botanic Garden, Bahai Temple, Galena, Ravinia Festival

Major Businesses Near the B&B Homes:
Sears, Abbott Labs, G. D. Searle, Motorola, Kraft, American Hospital, Rotary International, Avon

Major Schools, Universities Near the B&B Homes:
Northwestern U., Kendall College, National College of Education, Lake Forest College, Barret College, Loyola U., U. of Chicago, U. of Illinois at Chicago, Wheaton College, De Paul

B&B Bonuses

In Glencoe, a home overlooking a lake with private beach is filled with antiques, needlepoint, and quilts, and last but not least, charming hosts. The hostess of a remodeled, air-conditioned Victorian home is caterer, and will prepare meals.

Frequently offered are airport pickups, sightseeing tours, babysitting, driving back and forth to a hospital.

Michigan

Betsy Ross Bed & Breakfast
3057 BETSY ROSS DRIVE, BLOOMFIELD HILLS, MI 48013

Offers B&B Homes In:
All over the state of Michigan, including the lower peninsula

Reservations Phone: (313) 646-5357
Phone Hours: Days or evenings   **Available:** 7 days a week
Price Range of Homes:
Single: $25 to $55   Double: $30 to $60
Breakfast Included in Price:
Some homes serve Continental, but many offer a full breakfast, featuring dishes. . . . there is also a "Howell Festival" celebrating the Howell melons, and hand-blended coffee in one of the homes
Brochure Available: Free if inquirer sends stamped, self-addressed #10 envelope
Reservations Should Be Made: 2 weeks in advance (last minute reservations accepted if possible)

Scenic Attractions Near the B&B Homes:
Henry Ford Museum, Greenfield Village, Fisher Theater, Cranbrook Art Museum, Sleeping Bear Dunes National Park, Marshall Homes Tour, Meadow Brook Hall, Michigan Space Center, Ethnic Festivals Downtown Detroit, Grand Prix racing, Convention Center, Detroit Zoo, Irish Hills, resort areas

Major Businesses Near the B&B Homes:
General Motors Headquarters, General Motors Technical Center, Ford Motor Co., IBM, Burroughs, Chrysler

Major Schools, Universities Near the B&B Homes:
U. of Michigan, Michigan State U., Wayne State U., Albion College, Cranbrook Schools, Oakland U.

B&B Bonuses
   Homes of special interest include a Georgian Revival built by the famous architect Albert Kahn, a home with a golf practice room, a Spanish/English-speaking couple's residence, and a home on a peninsula overlooking East Travers Bay.
   Some of the hosts are gourmet cooks, many will make airport pickups, and some will even furnish transportation to football and baseball games!

MICHIGAN • 175

Bed & Breakfast of Grand Rapids
344 COLLEGE STREET, GRAND RAPIDS, MI 49503

Offers B&B Homes In:
Heritage Hill Historic District in downtown Grand Rapids, Michigan

Reservations Phone: (616) 456-7125
Phone Hours: 9 a.m. to 5 p.m.   **Available:** 7 days a week
Price Range of Homes:
Single: $30   Double: $40 to $45
Breakfast Included in Price:
Continental or full American, depending on individual home; some hosts provide family specialties
Brochure Available: Free
Reservations Should Be Made: 2 weeks in advance (last minute reservations accepted if possible)

Scenic Attractions Near the B&B Homes:
Gerald R. Ford Museum, Holland Tulip Festival, Lake Michigan, Heritage Hill District

Major Businesses Near the B&B Homes:
St. Mary's Hospital, Butterworth Hospital, downtown Grand Rapids business district

Major Schools, Universities Near the B&B Homes:
Grand Rapids Junior College, Davenport Business College, Grand Valley State College, Kendall School of Design, Calvin College

B&B Bonuses

All accommodations are in private, turn-of-the-century homes in the Heritage Hill Historic District

"We provide tourist packets, and can make arrangements for theater, ballet, opera, etc."

Ohio

Private Lodgings Inc.
P.O. BOX 18590, CLEVELAND, OH 44118

Offers B&B Homes In:
Greater Cleveland area, including outlying suburbs

Reservations Phone: (216) 321-3213
Phone Hours: 9 a.m. to 5 p.m.   **Available:** Monday to Friday (Saturday & Sunday 10 a.m. to 6 p.m. answering service)

Price Range of Homes:
Single: $20 to $50   Double: $25 to $65
Breakfast Included in Price:
Continental (juice, roll/toast, coffee) or full American in some host homes
Brochure Available: Free if inquirer sends stamped, self-addressed #10 envelope
Reservations Should Be Made: 1 to 2 weeks in advance (last minute reservations accepted if possible)

Scenic Attractions Near the B&B Homes:
Cleveland Museum of Art, Severance Hall, Cleveland Natural History Museum, Crawford Auto Museum, Cleveland Zoo, metropolitan parks

Major Businesses Near the B&B Homes:
Sohio, GE, Lincoln Electric, TRW, University Hospitals of Cleveland, Cleveland Clinic Foundation

Major Schools, Universities Near the B&B Homes:
Case Western Reserve U., Cleveland State U., John Carroll U., Cuyahoga Community College

B&B Bonuses
   A well-traveled couple (both sailors) offer you a B&B in a beautiful modern home set on a cliff, overlooking Rocky River and Lake Erie, with a watchtower and patio, the better to enjoy this spectacular view. A professional couple with a large Tudor home listed in the National Register enjoy helping visitors become acquainted with Cleveland.
   And there is a beautifully decorated duplex with cathedral ceiling and balcony overlooking the living room, within walking distance of transportation, shopping, and restaurants.

Columbus Bed & Breakfast
769 S. THIRD STREET, COLUMBUS, OH 43206

Offers B&B Homes In:
Columbus, Ohio area

Reservations Phone: (614) 443-3680/444-8888
Phone Hours: 8 a.m. to 11 p.m.   **Available:** 7 days a week (closed in January)

Price Range of Homes:
Single: $26 to $32   Double: $36 to $42
Breakfast Included in Price:
Continental (juice, roll/toast, coffee)
Brochure Available: Free
Reservations Should Be Made: 2 weeks in advance (last minute reservations accepted if possible)

Scenic Attractions Near the B&B Homes:
German Village, restored residential area listed in National Registry

Major Schools, Universities Near the B&B Homes:
Ohio State, Franklin U., Dennison College, Otterbein College, Kenyon College, Capital U.

B&B Bonuses
　A host home in German Village is close to downtown Columbus, but "a century away in character and ambiance." Small brick houses, brick paved streets and sidewalks, and wrought-iron fences combine to create an Old World atmosphere, with shops and restaurants within walking distance.

Buckeye Bed & Breakfast
P.O. BOX 130, POWELL (COLUMBUS), OH 43065

Offers B&B Homes In:
Columbus, Cincinnati, Delaware, Cambridge, Germantown, Spring Valley, Waynesville, Dublin, Muirfield, Westerville, Worthington, Marietta, Dayton, Logan, North Olmsted, and Seville, all in Ohio

Reservations Phone: (614) 548-4555
Phone Hours: 24 hours a day   **Available:** 7 days a week
Price Range of Homes:
Single: $17 to $25   Double: $28 to $50
Breakfast Included in Price:
Some homes serve Continental, others full American. Many hosts who are gardeners and "nutrition-oriented" serve organically grown specialties
Brochure Available: Free
Reservations Should Be Made: 10 days in advance (last minute reservations accepted if possible)

Scenic Attractions Near the B&B Homes:
Kings Island, Cincinnati Opera/Zoo, Ohio Historical Center, Muirfield Golf Course, Mound Builders' Sites, Little Brown Jug, Harness Classic, Vandalia Trap Shoot, Marietta River Festival

Major Businesses Near the B&B Homes:
Liebert Corp., Delco, TRW, Rockwell, Cincinnati Milling, Baldwin Piano, Proctor & Gamble, Lever Bros., Oasis Corp., Toledo Scale, Worthington Industries, Xerox, AccuRay, Borden's Mead Paper, Lancaster Colony, Wendy's Corp., RAX Corp.

Major Schools, Universities Near the B&B Homes:
Ohio State, Ohio U., Ohio Wesleyan, Otterbien, Capital, Kenyon, Muckingum, Marietta, Wilmington, Wright State, U. of Cincinnati, Wittenberg, Concordia College, Antioch, U. of Dayton, Columbus Tech, Ohio Dominican

B&B Bonuses

The Buell House in Marietta is a 147-year-old home which is listed on the National Historic Register. It is authentically furnished and has many special exhibits to delight the collector's heart, such as dolls and china, and boasts no less than seven porches.

"Aspen in Ohio" comes to mind at a cabin-style house nestled on Rockies-like slopes in Worthington. Your host is a well-traveled educator who likes to meet new people.

Wisconsin

Bed & Breakfast in Door County
ROUTE 2, ALGOMA, WI 54201

Offers B&B Homes In:
Door County, Wisconsin

Reservations Phone: (414) 743-9742
Phone Hours: 7 a.m. to 8 p.m.   **Available:** 7 days a week
Price Range of Homes:
Single: $30 to $55   Double: $35 to $65
Breakfast Included in Price:
"Practically all hosts serve a generous full breakfast"
Brochure Available: Free if inquirer sends stamped, self-addressed #10 envelope
Reservations Should Be Made: Preferably one or more weeks in advance (last minute reservations filled if possible)

Scenic Attractions Near the B&B Homes:
Seven state parks, fishing villages, cherry orchards

Major Businesses Near the B&B Homes:
Shipbuilders—Palmer Johnson, Bay Ship, Peterson Builders

B&B Bonuses

On seven acres of meadow overlooking Kangaroo Lake, a remodeled home boasts three guest bedrooms, each with a country motif. And how about a room in a home perched on the edge of Lake Michigan? This one's in a rural setting, too, with thousands of feet of shoreline available for exploring.

Many of their knowledgeable hosts are glad to accompany guests on sightseeing trips.

Bed & Breakfast of Milwaukee, Inc.
3017 N. DOWNER AVE. MILWAUKEE, WI 53211

Offers B&B Homes In:
Milwaukee, Wisconsin (lakeshore area)

Reservations Phone: (414) 342-5030
Phone Hours: 8 a.m. to 10 p.m.   **Available:** 7 days a week
Price Range of Homes:
Single: $30 to $50   Double: $35 to $55
Breakfast Included in Price:
Continental (juice, roll/toast, coffee) may include fresh fruit, croissant, cheese, yogurt, tea
Brochure Available: Free
Reservations Should Be Made: 2 weeks in advance (last minute reservations accepted if possible)

Scenic Attractions Near the B&B Homes:
Botanical Gardens, Zoo, Grand Avenue Mall, Audubon Center, Lake Michigan, museums, city parks, ethnic restaurants, major league baseball, symphony, ballet, repertory theater

Major Businesses Near the B&B Homes:
Koss, Oster, Miller, and Pabst Breweries, Masterlock, Harley-Davidson, Allis-Chalmers, Rexnord, Northwest Mutual, Usingers

Major Schools, Universities Near the B&B Homes:
U. of Wisconsin, Marquette U.

B&B Bonuses

A lovely 50-year old English Tudor home is located in a sophisticated urban setting, within walking distance of the park on Lake Michigan and the University area.

Extra meals, transportation, child care, and tours may be arranged with individual hosts.

NORTHWEST & GREAT PLAINS

Iowa
Minnesota
Montana
Nebraska
Oregon
South Dakota
Washington

Iowa

Bed & Breakfast in Iowa, Ltd.
7104 FRANKLIN AVE., DES MOINES, IA 50322

Offers B&B Homes In:
Throughout Iowa, and in Beresford, South Dakota

Reservations Phone: (515) 277-9018
Phone Hours: 9 a.m. to 5 p.m.   **Available:** 6 days a week
Price Range of Homes:
Single: $20 to $60   Double: $25 to $65
Breakfast Included in Price:
Full American, plus homemade breads and pastries, farm fresh eggs, Iowa pork
Brochure Available: Send $1.00 with stamped, self-addressed envelope for brochure and directory
Reservations Should Be Made: 2 weeks in advance (last minute reservations accepted if possible)

Scenic Attractions Near the B&B Homes:
Amana Colonies, Iowa Great Lakes, National Registry Homes, birthplaces of Mamie Eisenhower, John Wayne, and Herbert Hoover, Valley Junction Antiques, Danish Museum, State Fair, Living History Farms, Western Bluffs, Mesquakie Indian area

Major Businesses Near the B&B Homes:
Pioneer Hibred International, Meredith Publishing, Quaker Oats, John Deere, Bankers Life Insurance, Winnebago, Hy-Line International, Maytag, Amana Refrigeration, Rockwell Industries, Armstrong Rubber, Vermeer, Pella Windows, Vernon

Major Schools, Universities Near the B&B Homes:
U. of Iowa, Drake U., Coe College, U. of Northern Iowa, Grandview College, College of Osteopathic Medicine, Luther, Simpson College, Iowa State, Indian Hills, Northwestern

B&B Bonuses
One home boasts its own 9-hole golf course, and another a private lake. There are also five restored National Registry homes and a 100-year-old restored Victorian house furnished with antiques.
Many hosts will take guests sightseeing, hiking, boating, and fishing.

Minnesota

Bed & Breakfast Upper Midwest, Inc.
P.O. BOX 28036, MINNEAPOLIS, MN 55428

Offers B&B Homes In:
Minneapolis, New Hope, St. Louis Park, Richfield, Edina, Sturgeon Lake, Monticello, Old Frontenac, Stillwater, and Albert Lea (Minnesota), Canova (So. Dakota), Virogue, Bangor (Wisconsin)

Reservations Phone: (612) 535-7135
Phone Hours: 8 a.m. to 8 p.m.   **Available:** 7 days a week
Price Range of Homes:
Single: $20 to $39   Double: $25 to $54
Breakfast Included in Price:
Varies with individual homes, from Continental to full American
Brochure Available: Free if inquirer sends stamped, self-addressed #10 envelope
Reservations Should Be Made: 2 weeks in advance preferred (last minute reservations accepted if possible)

Scenic Attractions Near the B&B Homes:
Guthrie Theater, Walker Art Center, Minneapolis Art Institute, Northern States Nuclear Power Plant, Mayo Clinic

B&B Bonuses

For those who would like to explore Duluth, Mille Lacs, and the Iron Range, there is a house on 90 wooded acres, with a sandy beach. Here, "each morning your host will make a delicious full American breakfast using the fresh blueberries and rhubarb from their wooded acreage."

In the historic Lake District of Minneapolis, in a location convenient to transportation and many attractions, a home built by a local architect in 1897 has been beautifully preserved and furnished with antiques.

Montana

Western Bed & Breakfast Hosts
P.O. BOX 322, KALISPELL, MT 59901

Offers B&B Homes In:
Kalispell, Whitefish, St. Ignatius, Columbia Falls, Miles City, Lonepine, Helena, Ronan, Lewistown, Missoula, Glacier National Park Area

Reservations Phone: (406) 257-4476
Phone Hours: 8 a.m. to 6 p.m.   **Available:** 7 days a week
Price Range of Homes:
Single: $18 to $30   Double: $22 to $50
Breakfast Included in Price:
Continental or full American, which can include homemade blueberry or huckleberry muffins and bread.
Brochure Available: Free
Reservations Should Be Made: 2 weeks in advance (last minute reservations accepted if possible)

Scenic Attractions Near the B&B Homes:
Glacier National Park, National Bison Range, Whitefish Big Mountain Ski Area, Bob Marshall Wilderness Area, Yellowstone National Park, Charlie Russell Museum, State Capitol

Major Businesses Near the B&B Homes:
Big Mountain Ski Area

Major Schools, Universities Near the B&B Homes:
Montana State University

B&B Bonuses
   Many of the hosts delight in "showing off" their knowledge of this vast and beautiful mountainous area. They are often glad to make pickups at the airport when necessary.

Nebraska

Bed & Breakfast of Nebraska
1464 28TH AVENUE, COLUMBUS, NE 68601

Offers B&B Homes In:
Throughout Nebraska, primarily along Interstate 80

Reservations Phone: (402) 564-7591
Price Range of Homes:
Single: $20 and up   Double: $30 and up
Breakfast Included in Price:
Continental or full American . . . "a hospitable host will serve you a nourishing breakfast, with choices offered"
Brochure Available: Free
Reservations Should Be Made: 2 weeks in advance (no last minute reservations accepted)

Scenic Attractions Near the B&B Homes:
Blair, Nebraska (De Sota Bend Wildlife Refuge), Ft. Atkinson Museum, Bertrand Steamboat, SAC Air Base, Henry Doorly Zoo, Boys Town, Sheldon Art Gallery, horse racing

Major Businesses Near the B&B Homes:
NPPD Power Co., Dale Electronics, Lindsay Mfg. Co., BD Medical Supplies, Omaha meat-packing industry, Goodyear Tire, Snyder Industry, Sperry, Union-Pacific railroad yards

Major Schools, Universities Near the B&B Homes:
UNO, Creighton U., UNL, Wesleyan U., Kearney State College, Chadron State

B&B Bonuses

"Comfortable homes in a peaceful environment." One 92-year-old home is surrounded by nine acres of woods, and is decorated with antique woodwork and stained glass windows. Another home is in the chalet style, on a private lake.

Airport pickups can often be arranged.

Oregon

Gallucci Hosts Hostels, Bed & Breakfast
P.O. BOX 1303, LAKE OSWEGO, OR 97034

Offers B&B Homes In:
Oregon, parts of Washington, and in Vancouver

Reservations Phone: 1-503-636-6933
Phone Hours: 10 a.m. to 6 p.m.   **Available:** 7 days a week
Price Range of Homes:
Single: $12 to $35   Double: $15 to $50
Breakfast Included in Price:
Continental (juice, roll/toast, coffee)
Brochure Available: For a $1.00 fee, plus stamped, self-addressed envelope
Reservations Should Be Made: 3 days in advance (last minute reservations accepted if possible)

Scenic Attractions Near the B&B Homes:
Mt. St. Helens, Fort Vancouver, state parks, zoos, historic homes

B&B Bonuses

Hosts have a wide variety of special interests which may match yours, such as Oriental art, psychology, classical and country music and jazz, antiques, real estate, finance, travel, law, history, sports, cooking, drama, fishing, horseback riding, vegetarianism, sci-fi, puppeteering, painting, and you name it.

Homes are on the ocean, in the countryside, and in major cities. Hosts often make airport pickups and arrange sighseeing tours.

Bed & Breakfast Oregon
5733 S. W. DICKINSON STREET, PORTLAND, OR 97219

Offers B&B Homes In:
Portland, Bend, Roseburg, Eugene, Astoria, Seaside, Lincoln City, Newport, Florence, Coos Bay, Port Orford (all in Oregon), and in Long Beach in Washington

Reservations Phone: (503) 245-0642
Phone Hours: 9 a.m. to 9 p.m. **Available:** Monday to Friday, and some weekends

Price Range of Homes:
Single: $18 to $50   Double: $30 to $50

Breakfast Included in Price:
Full American which may include home-canned preserves, fresh goat yogurt, fresh-baked bread and hot muffins, "cheese eggs strata," and German egg and pancake specialties

Brochure Available: For a $2.00 fee

Reservations Should Be Made: One month or more in advance in summer (last minute reservations accepted if possible)

Scenic Attractions Near the B&B Homes:
Portland Zoo (with Elephant Herd), Pittock Mansion, Sternwheeler "Columbia Gorge," Rose Garden, Bonneville Dam Fish Hatchery, Mt. Hood National Forest, Pint Mt. Observatory, skiing on Mt. Bachelor, site of extinct volcanic activity, deep-sea fishing, whale migration in Spring and Fall

Major Businesses Near the B&B Homes:
White Stag, Jantzen Inc., Pendleton Woolen Mills, Omark Industries Inc., Intel Corp., Oregon Steel Mills, Reynolds Aluminum

Major Schools, Universities Near the B&B Homes:
U. of Portland, Portland State U., Oregon Health Sciences University, U. of Oregon

B&B Bonuses
View the sunsets from a two-story houseboat! Self-serve breakfast is provided by your hosts, enough to feed you and the ducks, too. Or see the stars at night through the sky-light over your king-size bed. In this "very artistic" home, your breakfast is served in the glass-enclosed garden room (champagne or Bloody Marys included), and you will have the use of a wet bar, fireplace, and video tape machine.

"Our hosts will pick up at the airport, train, or bus depot. They'll have special information on local events and directions to any place, maps, packets of sightseeing materials."

South Dakota

Bed & Breakfast of South Dakota
P.O. BOX 80137, SIOUX FALLS, SD 57116

Offers B&B Homes In:
The whole state of South Dakota, including the cities of Yankton, Sioux Falls, Salem, Howard, Armour, Academy, Buffalo, Volga, Rapid City, and Deadwood

Reservations Phone: (605) 339-0759 or 528-6571
Phone Hours: Any time before 10 p.m.   **Available:** 7 days a week
Price Range of Homes:
Single: $20 to $30   Double: $27.50 to $40
Breakfast Included in Price:
Full American (juice, eggs, bacon, toast, coffee)
Brochure Available: Free
Reservations Should Be Made: 2 weeks in advance (last minute reservations accepted if possible)

Scenic Attractions Near the B&B Homes:
Mount Rushmore, the Black Hills, Laura Ingalls Wilder Pageant, Missouri River fishing and hunting, Hutterite Colony

Major Businesses Near the B&B Homes:
Citibank, Eros, Gold Mines

Major Schools, Universities Near the B&B Homes:
South Dakota State U., U. of South Dakota, S. D. School of Mines, Augustana College, Sioux Falls College, Black Hills State

B&B Bonuses
  A three-story home built in 1904, with neo-classical features, is beautifully furnished with antiques. A screened summer porch and a "bicycle built for two" provide enjoyment for guests. Tennis, swimming pool, and golf course are nearby to this National Registry historic home.
  "Accommodations for hunters, tour of Hutterite Colony, and tips for touring the Black Hills" are offered.

Washington

R.S.V.P. Bed & Breakfast Reservation Service
P.O. BOX 778, FERNDALE, WA 98248

Offers B&B Homes In:
Washington from Canadian border to Everett, plus on the islands in Puget Sound

Reservations Phone: (206) 384-6586
Phone Hours: 8 a.m. to 1 p.m.   **Available:** Any time (answering service)
Price Range of Homes:
Single: $26 to $55   Double: $30 to $65
Breakfast Included in Price:
"More than a Continental, but sometimes less than a full breakfast, in some host homes"
Brochure Available: For a fee
Reservations Should Be Made: 3 weeks in advance (last minute reservations accepted if possible)

Scenic Attractions Near the B&B Homes:
Mount Baker Ski Resort, Gateway to North Cascades National Park, Puget Sound, Vancouver BC site of 1986 World's Fair, many lakes and mountains

Major Businesses Near the B&B Homes:
Intalco Alumnium, Mobil Oil Refinery, Arco Refinery, Bumble Bee Seafoods, many canneries

Major Schools, Universities Near the B&B Homes:
Western Washington U., Whatcom Community College, Huxley and Fairhaven College

B&B Bonuses

Enjoy family-style meals with "fresh milk from the cows and eggs from the hens" on a farm located on the shore of a Pacific Northwest island. Finnish sauna and bicycles available, too. Or, "would you like to sleep in a big brass bed, gaze at Whitehorse Mountain from your private balcony, relax in a huge claw-footed bathtub or Jacuzzi hot tub? All of this, plus a huge country breakfast, is what you can expect at this lovely home in a restful mountain valley." Plus hiking, rafting, mountain climbing, fishing and Blue Grass music fests!

For guests who stay at the home on Lummi Island, the hostess will pick them up at the ferry terminal.

Traveller's Bed & Breakfast (Seattle)
P.O. BOX 492, MERCER ISLAND, WA 98040

Offers B&B Homes In:
Seattle, Tacoma, Olympia, Port Angeles, Port Townsend, Bellevue, North Bend, Mt. Rainier, Bainbridge, Vashon, Mercer and Whidbey Islands, Washington; Portland and Seaside in Oregon; Victoria and Vancouver, BC, Canada

Reservations Phone: (206) 232-2345
Phone Hours: 7 a.m. to 7 p.m.   **Available:** 7 days a week
Price Range of Homes:
Single: $25 to $75   Double: same as single
Breakfast Included in Price:
Continental or full American, plus regional specialties such as Danish rolls and blueberry muffins
Brochure Available: For a $5.00 fee descriptive directory with maps and pictures
Reservations Should Be Made: As early as possible (last minute reservations accepted)

Scenic Attractions Near the B&B Homes:
Mt. Rainier National Park, Glencove Historic Hotel, Woodland Zoo, Seattle Center (World Fair '61), Salmon Locks, ferries to Washington islands, Mt. St. Helens tours, Stanley Park and Expo 86 in Vancouver, Provincial Museum, Empress Hotel, and Butchart Gardens in Victoria

Major Businesses Near the B&B Homes:
Boeing

Major Schools, Universities Near the B&B Homes:
U. of Washington, Seattle College, Seattle Pacific U., U. of British Columbia, U. of Puget Sound

B&B Bonuses

Stay at a home full of French Provincial antiques including a clock collection and canopied four-poster bed, or a house with two grand pianos and a harpsichord. Or how about a 60-foot sailboat in the San Juan Islands with queen-size bed? Homes range from "modest to luxurious with waterfront views."

Many hosts make airport pickups, arrange sightseeing tours, and a few offer facilities for family get-togethers and wedding parties of up to 75 people.

Pacific Bed & Breakfast
701 N. W. 60TH STREET, SEATTLE, WA 98107

Offers B&B Homes In:
Greater Metropolitan Seattle area and throughout the state of Washington, including Mt. Rainier and San Juan Islands; also, a few homes in Oregon, British Columbia, and Hawaii

Reservations Phone: (206) 784-0539
Phone Hours: 8 a.m. to 7 p.m.   **Available:** Monday to Friday
Price Range of Homes:
Single: $20 to $49   Double: $28 to $60
Breakfast Included in Price:
"Gourmet" Continental, or full American (homemade breads, muffins, and croissants are a specialty)
Brochure Available: Free if inquirer sends stamped, self-addressed #10 envelope (or $2.00 for Listing Directory)
Reservations Should Be Made: 3 weeks in advance (last minute reservations accepted if possible)

Scenic Attractions Near the B&B Homes:
City and national parks, museums, theaters, opera house, ferry rides, all kinds of sightseeing

Major Businesses Near the B&B Homes:
Boeing Company

Major Schools, Universities Near the B&B Homes:
U. of Washington and more than 8 other universities and colleges

B&B Bonuses

Sip your afternoon tea in a gazebo overlooking the lake, in a mansion with priceless stained glass windows, oak staircase, and a magnificent fireplace, or watch the ferries go by on Puget Sound from the private deck of a Queen Anne home built in the early 1900's.

"We offer lakefront homes, island rentals for long-term vacations, in the most undiscovered area of the Pacific Northwest. Languages spoken: German, French, Spanish, Scandinavian, Italian, and Dutch."

SOUTHEASTERN STATES

Alabama
Florida
Georgia
Kentucky
Mississippi
Tennessee

Alabama

Bed & Breakfast Birmingham, Inc.
P.O. BOX 31328, BIRMINGHAM, AL 35222

Offers B&B Homes In:
Greater Birmingham, with referral to other Alabama areas

Reservations Phone: (205) 591-6406
Phone Hours: 9:30 a.m. to 5:30 p.m.   **Available:** Any time on answering machine

Price Range of Homes:
Single: $25 to $40   Double: $28 to $55 (exceptional—$50 to $125)

Breakfast Included in Price:
Continental (fruit, juice, breads, beverage) although some hosts enjoy adding their Southern specialties

Brochure Available: Free (also sample description of homes)

Reservations Should Be Made: 2 weeks in advance (last minute reservations with deposit accepted if possible)

Scenic Attractions Near the B&B Homes:
Sloss Furnace Restoration, Victorian and Art Deco buildings, Red Mountain Museum, Farmers' Markets, Indian history, state parks

Major Businesses Near the B&B Homes:
In Birmingham 231 of the Fortune 500 businesses are represented; also headquarters for Harbert International, Vulcan Materials, Rust Engineering

Major Schools, Universities Near the B&B Homes:
U. of Alabama in Birmingham

B&B Bonuses
  Some of the interesting homes include a restored 1918 brick and shingle in a historic neighborhood, boasting a harpsichord and Murphy bed; a prize-winning contemporary white brick and glass with windows overlooking three wooded acres and swimming pool; and a suburban modern with oriental influence in its furnishings and its hillside garden paths.
  For those who require an apartment, there is a fully furnished one in an elegant suburban home with a lovely view.

Bed & Breakfast Mobile
P.O. BOX 66261, MOBILE, AL 36606

Offers B&B Homes In:
Mobile, Spanish Fort, Daphne

Reservations Phone: (205) 473-2939
Phone Hours: 8 a.m. to 12 p.m. **Available:** 7 days a week
Price Range of Homes:
Single: $30 to $80 Double: $35 to $80
Breakfast Included in Price:
Continental (juice, roll/toast, coffee)
Brochure Available: Free
Reservations Should Be Made: 2 weeks in advance (last minute reservations accepted if possible)

Scenic Attractions Near the B&B Homes:
Mardi Gras (February), Mobile Bay, Dauphin Islands, Gulf Shores, USS Alabama, USS Drum, Fort Conde, Oakleigh and other ante-bellum homes, Junior Miss Pageant, Bellingrath Gardens, Mobile Greyhound Park, Village of Fairhope

Major Businesses Near the B&B Homes:
Alabama State Docks, Scott Paper, International Paper, Quality Micro Systems, Alabama Drydock & Shipbuilding, Morrison Inc., De Gussa Corp., Stauffer Chemical, Union Carbide

Major Schools, Universities Near the B&B Homes:
U. of South Alabama, Springhill College, Mobile College

B&B Bonuses

Located in Old Springhill, a guest house offers complete privacy "among the azaleas." Or step back in time to 1867 in a barn-red Gothic home. Or hit the beaches in Gulf Shores, in accommodations perfect for several couples vacationing together.

Some of the special amenities provided are a package of brochures in each guest room, restaurant and sightseeing suggestions, and directions. "Each host will bend over backwards to make visits as enjoyable as possible."

Florida

Tropical Isles Bed & Breakfast
P. O. BOX 490382, KEY BISCAYNE, FL 33149

Offers B&B Homes In:
Key Biscayne, Key West, Miami Kendall area

Reservations Phone: (305) 361-2937
Phone Hours: Any time **Available:** 7 days a week
Price Range of Homes:
Single: $35 and up Double: $55 to $60 (deluxe, $65 and up)
Breakfast Included in Price:
Continental or full American, with most of the homes serving full breakfasts, that might include imported German ham served by a German hostess, and gourmet delights whipped up by another hostess who is a professional cook
Brochure Available: Free if inquirer sends a stamped, self-addressed #10 envelope
Reservations Should Be Made: 3 weeks in advance (last minute reservations accepted if possible)

Scenic Attractions Near the B&B Homes:
Planet Ocean, Miami Seaquarium, homes of Ernest Hemingway and Tennessee Williams, Vizcaya, Parrot Jungle, Metro Zoo, Sunrise Theater, Serpentarium, Monkey Jungle, Shark Valley, Coral Castle, Jai Alai

Major Schools, Universities Near the B&B Homes:
Barry College, Biscayne College, Florida International U., Florida Memorial College, Miami-Dade Community College, U. of Miami (Marine Laboratory)

B&B Bonuses

A "De Luxe Paradise Found" for $75 a day, offers a room in a very beautiful house with a screened-in oversize pool in a tropical setting, with private beach, only five minutes from the eight-mile-long Key Biscayne beach, and 15 minutes from exciting Miami. Breakfasts can be served at poolside or in a serene garden.

"Your host will treat you more as a friend than a casual guest, and will be a goldmine of information. Many foreign languages are spoken by our hosts."

Bed & Breakfast of The Florida Keys & The Palm Beaches, Inc.
5 MAN-O-WAR DRIVE (or P.O. Box 1373), MARATHON, FL 33050

Offers B&B Homes in:
The entire Florida Keys, from Key Largo to Key West, including Marathon Key and homes along the Florida East coast, Jupiter, Hobe Sound, Tequesta, West Palm Beach, Palm Beach, Sebastian, Boynton Beach and Pompano Beach

Reservations Phone: (305) 743-4118
Phone Hours: 8 a.m. to 5 p.m. **Available:** Monday to Friday, and weekends 9 a.m. to 1 p.m. (closed 3½ months from June 30 to October 15, 1985—call 201/223-5979

Price Range of Homes:
Single: $25 to $35 Double: $25 to $70 (rooms sleeping 6 to $100 per night)
Breakfast Included in Price:
Continental or full American, depending on individual home (bread from home-grown bananas is a specialty in some homes)
Brochure Available: Free if inquirer sends stamped, self-addressed #10 envelope.
Reservations Should Be Made: 3 weeks in advance (last minute reservations accepted if possible)

Scenic Attractions Near the B&B Homes:
John Pennekamp State Park, Bahia Honda State Park, Long Key State Park, Flipper's Sea School, Theater of the Sea, Ernest Hemingway Home, Florida White House, many historical homes in Key West, Seven Mile Bridge, and entire Southeast coast of mainland Florida, Burt Reynolds Theater

Major Schools, Universities Near the B&B Homes:
Florida Atlantic U. in Boca Raton

B&B Bonuses
Most homes have ocean front rooms for full enjoyment of the beautiful sunrises and sunsets and palm trees, with swimming, shelling, sunning, and fishing right outside your door. The agency's own home, the "Hopp-Inn Guest House" affords three guest rooms with private baths and entrances, a half-mile from Marathon's only beach. It's surrounded with palm and banana trees, hibiscus plants, and lush tropical foliage.

Your "Hopp-Inn" host, as well as some of the others, will pick you up at the airport.

Bed & Breakfast Co. Tropical Florida
P.O. BOX 262, MIAMI, FL 33243

Offers B&B Homes In:
Miami, Hallandale, Ft. Lauderdale, Pompano Beach, Jupiter, Lake Worth, Palm Beach, Delray Beach, Vero Beach, Tequestra, Coco, Tampa, St. Petersburg, Key West and the Florida Keys

Reservations Phone: (305) 661-3270
Phone Hours: 8:30 a.m. to 5 p.m. (answering service 24 hours)
Price Range of Homes:
Single: $20 to $54   Double: $24 to $65 (depending on season)
Breakfast Included in Price:
Continental (juice, roll/toast, coffee)
Brochure Available: Free, if inquirer sends stamped, self-addressed #10 envelope
Reservations Should Be Made: 2 weeks in advance (last minute service if possible)

Scenic Attractions Near the B&B Homes:
Everglades National Park, Coconut Grove Village, Hialeah Race Track, Monkey Jungle, Seaquarium, Planet Ocean, Parrot Jungle, Serpentarium, Vizcaya, Homes of Ernest Hemingway and Tennessee Williams, Burt Reynolds Dinner Theater, Dania Jai-Alai, Flagler Museum, Pennekamp Coral Reef

Major Businesses Near the B&B Homes:
Corporate offices of approximately 60 multinationals, also Eastern Airlines, Wachenhut Corp., Burger King, cruise ship industry, banking industry

Major Schools, Universities Near the B&B Homes:
U. of Miami (including medical and law schools), Florida International U., Miami Dade Community College, Nova U.

B&B Bonuses

Stay on a private residential island on Biscayne Bay, in an original Art Deco home, the former Hoover estate. Three guest rooms and private baths, and breakfast is served on the loggia next to the rose garden courtyard. Experience a tree house on one of the Florida keys. Explore the coral reefs, fish, swim, sail, and snorkel. Walk a block to the ocean from your bed-sitting room suite in a beautifully quiet residential area of Palm Beach.

Discount admission tickets are provided to many of the major attractions in their service area.

Florida Suncoast Bed & Breakfast (Soon to be "Florida & England Bed & Breakfast")
P.O. BOX 12, PALM HARBOR, FL 33563

Offers B&B Homes In:
Clearwater, St. Petersburg, Tampa, Sarasota, Bradenton, Venice, Ft. Myers, Sanibel, Winter Springs, Sanford, Kissimmee, Zephyr Hill, Englewood, Clearwater Beach, Redington Beach, Largo, Dunedin, Palm Harbor, Orlando, Tarpon Springs (all in Florida)

Reservations Phone: (813) 784-5118
Phone Hours: 8 a.m. to 8 p.m. **Available:** 7 days a week
Price Range of Homes:
Single: $22 to $35 Double: $28 to $60
Breakfast Included in Price:
Continental (juice, roll/toast, coffee), plus regional specialties available in some homes such as homegrown grapefruit and orange juice, and homemade bread and muffins
Brochure Available: Free. A Directory of Homes is $3.00.
Reservations Should Be Made: 3 weeks in advance (last minute reservations accepted if possible)

Scenic Attractions Near the B&B Homes:
Walt Disney World, Epcot, Sea World, Circus World, Cypress Gardens, Silver Springs, Gulf Beaches, Busch Gardens Tampa, Tampa Bay Football Stadium

Major Businesses Near the B&B Homes:
General Electric, Honeywell, Sperry-Rand, Paradyne Inc., Jim Walters Corp., U.S. Homes Corp.

Major Schools, Universities Near the B&B Homes:
South Florida U., U. of Tampa, St. Petersburg Jr. College

B&B Bonuses

One of the more interesting homes is the Bayboro House, the oldest house in the city, which has been beautifully restored, with fine antiques and a large veranda looking out to the bay.

Some hosts offer mini-tours of the area, with maps and brochures, and will pick up at the airport. They will also inform guests about special places known only to the locals, and the really good restaurants.

Suncoast Accommodations
8690 GULF BLVD., ST. PETE BEACH, FL 33706

Offers B&B Homes In:
Throughout Florida, specializing in the Gulf Coast and Orlando

Reservations Phone: (813) 360-1753
Phone Hours: 8 a.m. to noon, 5 p.m. to 10 p.m. **Available:** 7 days a week
Price Range of Homes:
Single: $34 to $85 Double: Winter 84-85 season, $40 to $100
Breakfast Included in Price:
Continental (juice, roll/toast, coffee), "But a few hosts are gourmet cooks and enjoy whipping up a full, delicious breakfast"
Brochure Available: Free for Florida ($3 for listings throughout U. S. and foreign countries)
Reservations Should Be Made: 2 weeks to 1 month in advance (last minute reservations accepted in St. Petersburg area)

Scenic Attractions Near the B&B Homes:
Walt Disney World, Sea World, Sunken Gardens, Busch Gardens, Dali Museum

Major Schools, Universities Near the B&B Homes:
St. Petersburg Jr. College, Eckard College, U. of Florida, Tampa College, Stetson Law School, Baypines VA Hospital

B&B Bonuses
From a stilt home on an island accessible only by boat to rooms and private efficiencies in waterfront homes to traditional Victorian homes, there is a B&B here for everyone. Some hosts will pick up from the airport, take guests on tours and boat rides, provide extra meals, and take care of laundry (small extra charge may be made for these).
"Ask about our 'Sunnymoon in Florida' package."

Tallahassee Bed & Breakfast, Inc.
3023 WINDY HILL LANE, TALLAHASSEE, FL 32308

Offers B&B Homes In:
Tallahassee, the Capitol of Florida in the panhandle of the state; some in Georgia and Alabama

Reservations Phone: (904) 385-3768 or 421-5220
Phone Hours: 6 a.m. to 11 p.m. **Available:** Any time
Price Range of Homes:
Single: $25 to $50 Double: $35 to $65
Breakfast Included in Price:
Usually Continental during the work week, and full breakfasts on weekends, with specialties like eggs mornay and hot popovers
Brochure Available: Free
Reservations Should Be Made: 2 weeks in advance (last minute reservations accepted if possible)

Scenic Attractions Near the B&B Homes:
Gulf Coast, St. Mark's Wildlife Preserve, Tall Timbers Research Station, St. George Island, antebellum homes, garden and plantation tours, Civic Center for North Florida, Alabama, and Georgia
Major Schools, Universities Near the B&B Homes:
Florida State U. (and Center for Professional Development), Florida Agricultural & Mechanical U.

B&B Bonuses
"The splendor of plantation life need not be a part of the past any longer. Relive a part of the great Southern tradition" . . . by staying at Water Oak Plantation. It sits high on a hill overlooking a sparkling lake and acres of rolling hills, mammoth oaks, and untouched woodland, with excellent fishing and hunting, and close to shopping and schools.

At the other end of the spectrum is an octagonal glass home in a bird sanctuary bordering Highway I-10, with schools and shopping just 10 minutes away. Attention, cat lovers: there are two in residence here.

Chauffeuring to early morning university conferences, airport pickups, invitations to dinner with the family, expert advice on restaurants and sightseeing; these are some of the extras that may be provided.

AAA Bed & Breakfast of Florida, Inc.
P.O. BOX 1316, WINTER PARK, FL 32790

Offers B&B Homes In:
Orlando, Central Florida area including Winter Park, Maitland, Altamonte Springs, Kissimmee, and Bay Hills, also Tallahassee, New Smyrna Beach, Sanford, Winter Haven, St. Petersburg, Tampa

Reservations Phone: (305) 628-3233
Phone Hours: 9 a.m. to 6 p.m. **Available:** 7 days a week
Price Range of Homes:
Single: $25 and up Double: $35 and up
Breakfast Included in Price:
Full American (juice, eggs, bacon, toast, coffee) generally includes homemade bread and rolls
Brochure Available: Free if inquirer sends stamped, self-addressed #10 envelope
Reservations Should Be Made: 2 weeks in advance (last minute reservations accepted if possible)

Scenic Attractions Near the B&B Homes:
Disney World, Sea World, Cape Kennedy, Winter Park Arts Festival

Major Businesses Near the B&B Homes:
Martin Marietta, Naval Training Center at Orlando

Major Schools, Universities Near the B&B Homes:
U. of Central Florida, Rollins College

B&B Bonuses
"History for the asking" is available in a charming Orlando home, where the hostess can give you the story behind each beautiful antique. A Jacuzzi and sunken marble Italian bath make a Maitland home special, and a lakeside Tudor home is filled with mementos of African, Australian, and South American duty stations and holidays.

When a deaf mute requested B&B accommodations rather than an impersonal motel, a search was made through religious organizations, with the result that a hostess was found who knew sign language!

Georgia

At Home in Athens
444 OLD EDWARDS ROAD, ARNOLDSVILLE, GA 30619

Offers B&B Homes In:
Athens and Watkinsville, in Georgia

Reservations Phone: (404) 546-1573
Phone Hours: 8 a.m. to 8 p.m. **Available:** 7 days a week
Price Range of Homes:
Single: $20 to $30 Double: $25 to $55
Breakfast Included in Price:
Mostly Continental although some homes provide specialties, like grits, hash browns
Brochure Available: Free
Reservations Should Be Made: 2 weeks in advance (last minute reservations accepted if possible)

Scenic Attractions Near the B&B Homes:
Stone Mountain, Cyclorama, Falcon-Braves Stadium, Botanical Gardens, Lake Burton, Alexander H. Stephens Home, Taylor Grady Home

Major Businesses Near the B&B Homes:
Westinghouse, General Time, DuPont, Curity, Fowler Products

Major Schools, Universities Near the B&B Homes:
University of Georgia

B&B Bonuses
  A home that is part of the historic Cobbham District offers guests a suite of rooms beautifully decorated with period antiques. It is conveniently close to the University of Georgia.
  Airport pickups, tours of historic Athens and the University of Georgia, and special dinners or picnic baskets are frequently provided.

Bed & Breakfast Atlanta
1221 FAIRVIEW RD. N.E., ATLANTA, GA 30306

Offers B&B Homes In:
Metropolitan Atlanta, Stone Mountain, Marietta, North Georgia

Reservations Phone: (404) 378-6026
Phone Hours: 10 to 12 a.m. and 2 to 5 p.m. **Available:** Monday to Friday
Price Range of Homes:
Single: $24 to $36   Double: $28 to $40 (some exceptional rooms, $40 to $60)
Breakfast Included in Price:
Continental or full American with Southern breakfasts occasionally served at the discretion of individual host
Brochure Available: Free if inquirer sends stamped, self-addressed #10 envelope
Reservations Should Be Made: 2 weeks or more in advance (last minute reservations accepted if possible)

Scenic Attractions Near the B&B Homes:
Stone Mountain, Cyclorama, Civil War Monuments, World Congress Center, Woodruff Art Center

Major Businesses Near the B&B Homes:
Scientific Atlanta, AT&T, National Service Industries, Georgia-Pacific, Hewlett-Packard, Cable Network News, IBM, Coca-Cola

Major Schools, Universities Near the B&B Homes:
Emory U., Georgia Tech, Atlanta U., Oglethorpe U., Devery Institute of Technology, Georgia State U.

B&B Bonuses

   A spacious old brick home with beautifully landscaped, tree-shaded yard, is located near Emory University, 10 minutes from downtown Atlanta. The neighborhood is a historically designated "exemplary development of the 1920's." Another home in the mountains affords a spectacular view.
   Recently, last-minute symphony tickets were obtained for guests through the efforts of their host. Another host has been particularly helpful to guests who were in the process of re-locating.

Atlanta Home Hospitality
2472 LAUDERDALE DRIVE N.E., ATLANTA, GA 30345

Offers B&B Homes In:
Atlanta, Georgia; Brooklyn, NY; Boston, Mass; Barbados, West Indies

Reservations Phone: (404) 493-1930
Phone Hours: 9 a.m. to 10 p.m. **Available:** 7 days a week
Price Range of Homes:
Single: $18 to $25 Double: $30 to $40
Breakfast Included in Price:
Mostly Continental, but may include grits and country ham, pecan rolls, redeye gravy
Brochure Available: Free
Reservations Should Be Made: 2 weeks in advance (last minute reservations accepted if possible)

Scenic Attractions Near the B&B Homes:
Martin Luther King Memorial Site, High Museum, Stone Mountain Park, largest shopping mall in the Southeast

Major Businesses Near the B&B Homes:
"Almost all of the Fortune 500 companies have a branch in Atlanta"

Major Schools, Universities Near the B&B Homes:
Emory U., Atlanta U.

B&B Bonuses

A hostess who knows all about Atlanta can entertain you in a beautiful five-bedroom home near the downtown area, with swimming pool and other recreational facilities nearby.

"Several host homes invite guests to special dinners, take them to church, pick them up at airports, train and bus stations, and take them on sightseeing tours."

Note: Prospective guests are required to join this organization for an annual fee of $10.00

Hideaway Bed & Breakfast
DIAL STAR ROUTE, BOX 76, BLUE RIDGE, GA 30513

Offers B&B Homes In:
North Georgia mountains, tri-state Copper Basin area of North Carolina, Georgia, Tennessee

Reservations Phone: (404) 632-3669 or 632-2411
Phone Hours: 9 a.m. to 9 p.m. **Available:** 7 days a week
Price Range of Homes:
Single: $30 Double: $35
Breakfast Included in Price:
Continental, which may include extras like sourdough bread, country butter, sausage and biscuits, apple cider, home-canned juices, jams, jellies, and local honey
Brochure Available: Free
Reservations Should Be Made: 2 weeks in advance (last minute reservations accepted if possible)

Scenic Attractions Near the B&B Homes:
Appalachian Trail, Cohutta Wilderness, Chattahoochie National Forest, Ocoee River Rafting, TVA, Lake Blue Ridge, wild-life management areas for hunting and fishing, tubing on wild Toccoa River

Major Businesses Near the B&B Homes:
Tennessee Chemical, Levi Strauss Co., large carpet mills

Major Schools, Universities Near the B&B Homes:
Young Harris College, Pickens Tech., Chattanooga and Atlanta area universities

B&B Bonuses
Three contemporary homes along the Toccoa River are furnished with antiques and local crafts, with fireplaces and fully equipped kitchens.
"We offer Southern mountain hospitality, can accommodate family reunions and small groups, arrange hiking, horseback riding, visits to local craft studios, antique shops, and fine country restaurants."

Savannah Historic Inns & Guest Houses—Reservations Service
1900 LINCOLN ST., SAVANNAH, GA 31401

Offers B&B Homes In:
The downtown historic district of Savannah

Reservations Phone: (912) 233-7666
Phone Hours: 9 a.m. to 9 p.m. **Available:** Monday to Saturday, Sunday 1 to 7 p.m.

Price Range of Homes:
Single: $30 to $78 Double: $38 to $88

Breakfast Included in Price:
Continental (may include croissants, corn cakes, homemade bread, pastries)

Brochure Available: Free

Reservations Should Be Made: 1 month in advance (last minute reservations accepted if possible)

Scenic Attractions Near the B&B Homes:
Owen-Thomas House, Davenport House, Telfair Academy, St. Simons Island, Jekyll Island, Cumberland National Seashore, Okefenokee Swamp

Major Businesses Near the B&B Homes:
Union Camp, Gulf Stream, Great Dane Trailers, Savannah Foods, Dixie Crystals Sugar

Major Schools, Universities Near the B&B Homes:
Armstrong State College, Savannah State College, Savannah College of Art & Design

B&B Bonuses

All the homes are circa 1850 and located in the 2½ square miles covering the largest historic district in the U. S. Many of them boast working fireplaces, ceiling fans, garden courtyards, four-poster beds, oriental rugs, English and American antiques, and for history buffs, libraries of books on Savannah and the coastal area.

From bicycles to baby-sitters to complimentary wine and cordials, hosts provide a variety of services. (As part of a special program, disabled persons in the area operate the centralized phone reservations service, thus helping the community and themselves).

Intimate Inns of Savannah
19 WEST PERRY STREET, SAVANNAH, GA 31401

Offers B&B Homes In:
All in historic district of Savannah, Georgia

Reservations Phone: (912) 233-6809
Phone Hours: 9 a.m. to 9 p.m. **Available:** 7 days a week
Price Range of Homes:
Single: $50 to $75 Double: $50 to $125
Breakfast Included in Price:
Continental (juice, roll/toast, coffee)—"Croissants our specialty"
Brochure Available: Free
Reservations Should Be Made: As far in advance as possible (last minute reservations accepted if possible)

Scenic Attractions Near the B&B Homes:
Beautiful restored homes, Jekyll Island, Sea Island, St. Simons Island, Hilton Head

Major Businesses Near the B&B Homes:
Dixie Sugar, Union Camp

Major Schools, Universities Near the B&B Homes:
Savannah College of Art & Design, Armstrong College, Savannah College

B&B Bonuses

B&B's are in such well-known historical homes as the Stoddard-Cooper House, the Remshart-Brooks House, and Mary Lee Guest Accommodations. All are beautifully restored town or carriage houses, with private entrances to complete apartments and lovely secluded gardens. "Yesteryear's hospitality lives today" in these grand pre-Civil War homes along the city's unique bay front.

Many hosts can provide babysitting, swimming and tennis, books and games, airport pickups, etc.

Quail Country Bed & Breakfast, Ltd.
1104 OLD MONTICELLO RD., THOMASVILLE, GA 31792

Offers B&B Homes In:
Thomasville, Georgia (city and country)

Reservations Phone: (912) 226-7218 or 226-6882
Phone Hours: 8 a.m. to 10 p.m. **Available:** Every day of the year
Price Range of the Homes:
Single: $30 to $40 Double: $35 to $50
Breakfast Included in Price:
Continental (juice, roll/toast, coffee)
Brochure Available: Free if inquirer sends stamped, self-addressed #10 envelope
Reservations Should Be Made: One week in advance (last minute reservations accepted if possible)

Scenic Attractions Near the B&B Homes:
Pebble Hill Plantation Museum, April Rose Festival, plantation tours, historic restorations, hunting preserves, 30 miles from Tallahassee attractions

Major Businesses Near the B&B Homes:
Flowers Industries, Sunnyland Meat Packing, TRW, Davis Water and Waste

Major Schools, Universities Near the B&B Homes:
Florida State U., Valdosta State U.

B&B Bonuses
   "Lovely neo-Classical house, circa 1903, is located in the Thomasville Historic District. Your hospitable hostess will fascinate you with stories of her extensive world travels. Guest wing with private entrance includes bedroom, full bath, and screened porch where guests may enjoy breakfast."
   "Any of our hosts will be happy to share their knowledge of Thomasville history and points of interest in the surrounding area."

Kentucky

Kentucky Homes Bed & Breakfast
1431 ST. JAMES COURT, LOUISVILLE, KY 40208

Offers B&B Homes In:
Throughout Kentucky

Reservations Phone: (502) 635-7341 or 452-6629
Phone Hours: 8:30 a.m. to 5:30 p.m. **Available:** 7 days a week
Price Range of Homes:
Single: $22 to $34 Double: $32 to $44
Breakfast Included in Price:
Continental (juice, roll/toast, coffee)—some hosts will serve full American, often featuring a regional specialty, country ham and grits
Brochure Available: Free if inquirer sends stamped, self-addressed #10 envelope
Reservations Should Be Made: As far in advance as possible

Scenic Attractions Near the B&B Homes:
National Historic Preservation, Old Louisville, Simpsonville (saddle-horse capital of world), Mammoth Cave, Lexington Bluegrass, Old Kentucky Home

Major Businesses Near the B&B Homes:
Brown Williamson, Glenmore Distilleries

Major Schools, Universities Near the B&B Homes:
Bellarmine, U. of Louisville, Spalding College, Western Kentucky U., Murray State U., Eastern Kentucky U.

B&B Bonuses
   Turn-of-the-century homes are numerous, with one of them being the original house on a "gentleman's farm." "All our hosts go out of their way, as recently when a guest became ill in the night, the hostess drove guest to the hospital and then stayed by guest's husband's side all night as he waited for diagnosis."

Mississippi

Lincoln Ltd. Bed & Breakfast
BOX 3479, MERIDIAN, MS 39303

Offers B&B Homes In:
The whole state of Mississippi, from Holly Springs in the north to Pass Christian in the south

Reservations Phone: (601) 482-5483
Phone Hours: From 8 a.m. **Available:** Monday to Friday, and also Saturday mornings.

Price Range of Homes:
Single: $45 to $95 Double: $45 to $107

Breakfast Included in Price:
Full American (juice, eggs, bacon, toast, coffee), served simply or elegantly according to guest's preference

Brochure Available: Free if inquirer sends stamped, self-addressed #10 envelope

Reservations Should Be Made: 1 or 2 weeks in advance (no last minute reservations accepted)

Scenic Attractions Near the B&B Homes:
National Civil War Park and historic homes in Vicksburg, Jackson State Capitol, Columbus Pilgrimage, Holly Springs Pilgrimage, William Faulkner home in Meridian, Jimmy Rodgers Festival, Miss. Gulf Coast

Major Businesses Near the B&B Homes:
Lockheed, Delco-Remy, GM, Owens-Corning, Burlington Mills, GE, Masonite, Weyerhauser

Major Schools, Universities Near the B&B Homes:
U. of Mississippi at Oxford, Mississippi State U., Starkville, Millsaps College, Mississippi College, Mississippi U. for Women, Columbus

B&B Bonuses

Step back in time in the oldest house in Columbus, built in 1828, or on a working plantation of 100 acres surrounding a home built in 1857, where you breakfast in formal elegance in the family dining room. In William Faulkner's home town there is a National Register ante-bellum home made entirely of native timber, in 1838. In this "perfect example of planter-type architecture" the hostess is a retired university professor and world traveler.

Natchez Pilgrimage Tours
410 S. COMMERCE—P.O. BOX 347, NATCHEZ, MS 39120

Offers B&B Homes In:
Natchez, Adams County, Mississippi

Reservations Phone: (601) 446-6631 or 800-647-6742
Phone Hours: 8:30 a.m. to 5:30 p.m.   **Available:** 7 days a week (except Christmas)

Price Range of Homes:
Single: $60 to $85   Double: $70 to $105
Breakfast Included in Price:
Continental or full American.
Brochure Available: Free
Reservations Should Be Made: 2 weeks in advance (last minute reservations accepted if possible)

Scenic Attractions Near the B&B Homes:
Natchez State Park, Natchez Bluffs (overlooking Mississippi River), Natchez Under the Hill (on river), 500 historic structures and 30 historic tour homes

Major Businesses Near the B&B Homes:
Armstrong Tire, International Paper Co., Johns-Manville, Natchez Port

Major Schools, Universities Near the B&B Homes:
Copiah-Lincoln Junior College, U. of Southern Mississippi Branch

B&B Bonuses
   All homes are historic and part of the famous "Natchez Pilgrimage." They are individually owned and furnished with private collections of antiques and family heirlooms.
   The "Southern hospitality" includes a tour of your host home, airport pickups, and other extras.

Tennessee

River Rendezvous
P.O. BOX 240001, MEMPHIS, TN 38124

Offers B&B Homes In:
Memphis, Tennessee, and New Orleans, Louisiana and expects to expand to the Mississippi River cities between Memphis and New Orleans

Reservations Phone: (901) 767-5296
Phone Hours: 24 hours a day **Available:** 7 days a week
Price Range of Homes:
Single: $20 to $32 Double: $25 to $40
Breakfast Included in Price:
Continental (juice, roll/toast, coffee)
Brochure Available: Free
Reservations Should Be Made: 2 weeks in advance (last minute reservations accepted if possible)

Scenic Attractions Near the B&B Homes:
Historic homes, French Quarter, Beale St., Graceland, Libertyland, Mud Island, site of 1983 World's Fair

Major Businesses Near the B&B Homes:
Sun Recording Studio, Sharp Electronics, Plough Inc., Schlitz Brewery, Federal Express

Major Schools, Universities Near the B&B Homes:
Southwestern, Memphis State, U. of Tennessee Medical School, Southern College of Optometry

B&B Bonuses
  Stay in a loft condo overlooking the Mississippi River, or enjoy downtown New Orleans with all its attractions outside your door. Many of the hosts are in the entertainment business!
  They will often pick up at airports and take guests to scenic areas.

Nashville Bed & Breakfast
P.O. BOX 150651, NASHVILLE, TN 37215

Offers B&B Homes In:
Middle Tennessee (Nashville, Hendersonville, Centerville, Brentwood, Franklin, Hermitage and environs)

Reservations Phone: (615) 298-5674
Phone Hours: 9 a.m. to 6 p.m. **Available:** 7 days a week
Price Range of Homes:
Single: $21 to $34 Double: $27 to $40
Breakfast Included in Price:
Continental (juice, roll/toast, coffee)
Brochure Available: Free
Reservations Should Be Made: 2 weeks in advance (prefer not to accept last minute reservations, but will try to accommodate)

Scenic Attractions Near the B&B Homes:
Opryland, Cheekwood Botanical Gardens & Fine Arts Center, Car Collectors' Hall of Fame, The Hermitage and Tulip Grove, Tennessee State Museum, Country Music Hall of Fame and Museum, Belle Carol Riverboat, Belle Mead mansion, House of Cash, Twitty City

Major Businesses Near the B&B Homes:
Northern Telecom, General Electric, Nissan, Genesco, Ford Glass Plant, Hospital Corp. of America, Service Merchandise, AVCO Aerospace, Dupont, NLT, plus all major record labels and music publishers

Major Schools, Universities Near the B&B Homes:
Vanderbilt U., Belmont College, David Lipscomb College

B&B Bonuses

Homes include a restored historic church, a 150-acre country estate, small farms, and a real Tennessee Walking Horse farm.

Besides frequently picking up at airports, providing babysitting and such, hosts have at times arranged for guests to attend tapings of TV shows, and to go behind the scenes in homes not yet open to the public.

SOUTHWEST & SOUTH CENTRAL AREA

Colorado
Kansas
Louisiana
Missouri
New Mexico
Texas

Colorado

Bed & Breakfast of Boulder Inc.
P.O. BOX 6061, BOULDER, CO 80302

Offers B&B Homes In:
Boulder County and nearby mountain area

Reservations Phone: (303) 442-6664
Phone Hours: 8 a.m. to 8 p.m. **Available:** 6 days a week (closed Sundays)
Price Range of Homes:
Single: $19 to $32 Double: $27 to $40
Breakfast Included in Price:
Continental or full American (juice, eggs, bacon, toast, coffee). Breakfasts vary with each home. Some may offer continental during week, with full breakfast on weekends.
Brochure Available: Free
Reservations Should Be Made: 2 weeks in advance (last minute reservations accepted if possible, but no placements after sundown)

Scenic Attractions Near the B&B Homes:
Rocky Mt. National Park, Coors International Bicycle Race, Shakespeare Festival, World Affairs Conference, skiing

Major Businesses Near the B&B Homes:
IBM, Storage Tech, National Center for Atmospheric Research, Bureau of Standards, Celestial Seasonings, Ball Corp., Rockwell, NBI, Beech Aircraft, AMF Head Division, Neodata, Valley Lab

Major Schools, Universities Near the B&B Homes
U. of Colorado, Naropa Institute

B&B Bonuses
If you need more than one or two B&B rooms, ask about the fully furnished homes which are available at this agency, when owners go on vacation or sabbaticals.

Hosts are friendly and obliging, as one certainly was to a guest with a broken leg. The host drove this guest to and from the University daily during a three-week period.

Bed & Breakfast Rocky Mountains
P.O. BOX 804, COLORADO SPRINGS, CO 80901

Offers B&B Homes In:
Colorado, Montana, Wyoming, and New Mexico

Reservations Phone: (303) 630-3433
Phone Hours: 9 a.m. to 6 p.m.   **Available:** Monday to Friday
Price Range of Homes:
Single: $17 to $75   Double: $20 to $95
Breakfast Included in Price:
"Over 50% of our hosts serve a full breakfast—often homemade delicacies are part of the bargain, even for the less than 50% who serve Continental"
Brochure Available: Free if inquirer sends stamped, self-addressed #10 envelope; for special directory of hosts send $2 plus business-size with 37¢ stamps
Reservations Should Be Made: 3 weeks in advance (last minute reservations accepted if possible)

Scenic Attractions Near the B&B Homes:
National forests, 30 state parks, skiing, hiking, gold panning, white water rafting, ballooning, snowmobiling, horseback riding, jeep tours, sleigh rides, hay rides, fishing; 53 mountain peaks over 14,000 feet high

Major Businesses Near the B&B Homes:
IBM, Hewlett-Packard, Digital, NORAD, Denver oil companies, Space Command, Air Force, Army

Major Schools, Universities Near the B&B Homes:
Colorado State U., Colorado College, Colorado School of Mines, U. of Colorado, U. of Denver, Colorado Mountain College, U.S. Air Force Academy

B&B Bonuses

Over 100 host homes and inns in a four-state area include a charming house on a Denver lake overlooking snow-capped mountains, near the Coors Brewery, Buffalo Bill Museum, Heritage Square and Melodrama, and Railroad Museum, and another home where business people can enjoy the host's secretarial and phone-answering services.

Ski area listings are their specialty, like Aspen, Vail, Copper Mountain, Breckenridge, Winter Park, Steamboat, etc.

Bed & Breakfast Colorado
P.O. BOX 20596, DENVER, CO 80220

Offers B&B Homes In:
Denver, Colorado Springs, Evergreen, Manitou Springs, Aspen, Pueblo, Beulah, Durango, Carbondale, Steamboat Springs, Loveland, Mancos, La Veta, Vail, Glenwood Springs, Dillon, Crested Butte, Greeley, Boulder, Eaton, Gypsum, Idledale, Englewood, Breckenridge, Aurora, Central City

Reservations Phone: (303) 333-3340
Phone Hours: 1 p.m. to 6 p.m. (Mountain time)   **Available:** Monday to Friday

Price Range of Homes:
Single: $20 to $35   Double: $25 to $40 (Inns: $40 to $80)
Breakfast Included in Price:
Continental or full American (juice, eggs, bacon, toast, coffee). Type of breakfast up to individual host. Many are gourmet cooks. Farm-fresh eggs and whole wheat cinnamon rolls are a few of the specialties offered.
Brochure Available: Free—1985 Directory of Homes costs $3.00
Reservations Should Be Made: 2 weeks in advance *Note:* Suggest a month or two for winter sports months (last minute reservations accepted if possible)

Scenic Attractions Near the B&B Homes:
Rocky Mountain National Park, Mesa Verde National Park, Denver Zoo, Broadmoor Zoo, Central City Opera House, Air Force Academy, Garden of the Gods, Hot Sulphur Springs, famous mining towns, Molly Brown House (Denver), U.S. Mint, Denver Art Museum, Pike's Peak, Red Rocks, major ski areas

Major Businesses Near the B&B Homes:
Martin Marietta, Kodak, IBM, Xerox, Motorola, all major companies in the Denver Technological Center, and most major oil companies

Major Schools, Universities Near the B&B Homes:
U. of Denver, U. of Southern Colorado, U. of Northern Colorado (Greeley), Colorado State U. (Boulder), Colorado School of Mines (Golden), Metro State College, Colorado Mountain College (Glenwood Springs), Colorado College

B&B Bonuses

Host homes in Denver are near all major hospitals. A home in Beulah, Colorado, is an 1870 homestead on 67 acres, run by a 60-year-old lady. She restores antique carriages and sleighs, which she uses to take guests riding through the countryside.

Most homes pick up from airports, and there are a few gourmet cooks who furnish menus for guests who wish to have supper with them.

222 • THE SOUTHWEST & SOUTH CENTRAL AREA

Victorian Inn-Bed & Breakfast of Durango
2117 WEST 2D AVENUE, DURANGO, CO 81301

Offers B&B Homes In:
City limits of Durango

Reservations Phone: (303) 247-2223
Phone Hours: 9 a.m. to 5 p.m.   **Available:** 7 days a week
Price Range of Homes:
Single: $30 to $45   Double: $40 to $55
Breakfast Included in Price:
Continental or full American, some homes serving coffee cake with apple butter and local honey
Brochure Available: Free
Reservations Should Be Made: 2 weeks in advance off season, otherwise 3 weeks (last minute reservations accepted if possible)

Scenic Attractions Near the B&B Homes:
Mesa Verde National Park, Durango Silverton Narrow-Gauge Railroad, Purgatory Ski Area, Valleoto Lake, Lemon Dam

Major Schools, Universities Near the B&B Homes:
Fort Lewis College

B&B Bonuses

   A Victorian home built in 1878 is filled with antiques and boasts a large, well-landscaped yard. Lawn games are available. Convenient, too—just within walking distance to downtown.
   Given notice, guest pickups can be made, and guests have been treated to complimentary wine at a local restaurant.

Bed & Breakfast, Vail

P.O. BOX 491, VAIL, CO 81658

Offers B&B Homes In:
Vail ski area, Beaver Creek, Avon, Carbondale—all in Colorado

Reservations Phone: (303) 476-1225
Phone Hours: 9 a.m. to 9 p.m.   **Available:** 7 days a week
Price Range of Homes:
Single: $40 to $55   Double: $45 to $65
Breakfast Included in Price:
Continental or full American, depending on individual home
Brochure Available: Free
Reservations Should Be Made: 2 weeks in advance (last minute reservations accepted if possible)

Scenic Attractions Near the B&B Homes:
Vail skiing and winter events, summer Jerry Ford Invitational Golf Tournament, American Tennis Classic, Jimmy Connors Tennis, rafting, hiking, swimming

B&B Bonuses

Spacious mountain homes with spectacular views are to be found here. Some offer tours of the Vail and Beaver Creek area.

Some other extras offered are pickups from terminals, garage parking, and ski storage.

Kansas

Kansas City Bed & Breakfast
P.O. BOX 14781, LENEXA, KS 66215

Offers B&B Homes In:
Liberty, Kansas City, Parkville, Lee's Summit, and Warrensburg in Missouri; Lenexa, Shawnee, Overland Park, Merriam, Leawood, Prairie Village, Lake Quivira, and Modoc in Kansas

Reservations Phone: (913) 268-4214
Phone Hours: 8 a.m. to 9 p.m.   **Available:** 7 days a week
Price Range of Homes:
Single: $25 to $48   Double: $30 to $50
Breakfast Included in Price:
Some Continental, but most of the homes serve a full breakfast
Brochure Available: "Homes Directory" available free if inquirer sends stamped, self-addressed #10 envelope
Reservations Should Be Made: 2 weeks in advance (last minute reservations usually accepted)

Scenic Attractions Near the B&B Homes:
Truman Library, Worlds of Fun, Crown Center, Plaza, Kansas City Zoo, Nelson Art Gallery, American Royal

Major Businesses Near the B&B Homes:
Hallmark, GM, Ford, Board of Trade

Major Schools, Universities Near the B&B Homes:
William Jewell College, U. of Missouri, Avila College, U. of Kansas

B&B Bonuses

An ante-bellum home in Liberty is furnished with antiques and boasts an unusually beautiful staircase. In a farm home resembling a Swiss chalet, the hostess serves a ham-and-egg casserole with homemade cinnamon rolls for breakfast, on a glassed-in patio. Condominiums with swimming and tennis are also available.

"Some hosts will pick up at points where the airport bus leaves travelers."

Louisiana

Southern Comfort Bed & Breakfast Reservation Service
2856 HUNDRED OAKS, BATON ROUGE, LA 70808

Offers B&B Homes In:
20 cities in Louisiana and Mississippi, and southern New Mexico

Reservations Phone: (504) 346-1928 or 926-9784
Phone Hours: 8 a.m. to 8 p.m.   **Available:** 7 days a week (no collect calls)

Price Range of Homes:
Single: $25 to $95   Double: $30 to $150 a day depending on number of people

Breakfast Included in Price:
Continental or full American (some homes serve "plantation breakfasts" which can include various meats, grits and gravy, hot breads, and native preserves)

Brochure Available: For a fee, which is $1.00

Reservations Should Be Made: 2 weeks in advance (last minute reservations accepted if possible)

Scenic Attractions Near the B&B Homes:
In New Orleans, Audubon Park and Zoo, French Quarter, famous restaurants and museums, 1984 World's Fair (May to November). In Baton Rouge, old and new State Capitols, historic sites. In Mississippi, ante-bellum homes, plantations, Civil War battle sites, museums, Gulf Coast; in New Mexico desert, mountains, and art colonies.

Major Businesses Near the B&B Homes:
54 major industries in industrial corridor of Mississippi River

Major Schools, Universities Near the B&B Homes:
Louisiana State U., Southern U., Tulane, Loyola, Xavier, Dillard, U. of Mississippi, Mississippi Southern, U. of New Mexico

B&B Bonuses
  "An elegant 150-year-old Vicksburg town house with slave quarters also has modern amenities such as a pool, hot tub, and Jacuzzi. The gracious hosts greet you with a mint julep and bid you farewell with a lavish Southern breakfast. In New Mexico, an equally old hacienda has the traditional adobe construction, with thick walls and lots of fireplaces. It's situated on a running stream and surrounded by mountains."

Bed & Breakfast Inc.
1236 DECATUR STREET, NEW ORLEANS, LA 70116

Offers B&B Homes In:
New Orleans and surrounding areas

Reservations Phone: (504) 525-4640
Phone Hours: 24 hour service   **Available:** 7 days a week
Price Range of Homes:
Single: $25 to $110   Double: $25 to $110 (some rates may go up seasonally)
Breakfast Included in Price:
Continental (juice, roll/toast, coffee)
Brochure Available: Free
Reservations Should Be Made: Any time (last minute reservations accepted if possible)

Scenic Attractions Near the B&B Homes:
French Quarter, Mississippi River, Superdome, Audubon Zoo, New Orleans Museum of Art, Jazz Halls, world-famous restaurants, antique stores, historic St. Charles Ave. streetcar, Jackson Square Artists, World's Fair May-November

Major Scenic Schools, Universities Near the B&B Homes:
Tulane U., Loyola U., U. of New Orleans, Dominican College

B&B Bonuses
   Homes include a historic Bourbon Street house, and another luxury 19th-century mansion with a hot tub amid landscaped surroundings. Some hosts offer babysitting, assistance to the blind and handicapped, and accommodation of pets.

New Orleans Bed & Breakfast
3658 GENTILLY BLVD. - P.O. BOX 8163, NEW ORLEANS, LA 70182

Offers B&B Homes In:
New Orleans, Baton Rouge, Shreveport, Ruston, Lake Charles, Sulphur, Natchitoches, Opelousas, and Wakefield in Louisiana; Ocean Springs, Natchez, Waveland in Mississippi; Ft. Walton Beach and Milton in Florida

Reservations Phone: (504) 949-6705 or (800) 541-9852
Phone Hours: 7 a.m. to 10 p.m.   **Available:** 7 days a week
Price Range of Homes (and apts.)
Single: $20 to $50   Double: $25 to $150
Breakfast Included in Price:
Continental (juice, roll/toast, coffee) . . . some homes serve French toast
Brochure Available: Free if inquirer sends stamped, self-addressed envelope (#10)
Reservations Should Be Made: As early as possible, especially for 1984 World's Fair (last minute reservations accepted if possible)

Scenic Attractions Near the B&B Homes:
Historic homes, Audubon Park Zoo, plantation tours and river cruises, Cajun bayou tours, Gulf Coast, Acadian country, French Quarter, New Orleans night life, '84 World's Fair, Longvue Gardens, Magazine Street antique shops

Major Schools, Universities Near the B&B Homes:
Tulane U., Loyola U., U. of New Orleans, Dominican College, Dillard, New Orleans Baptist Seminary

B&B Bonuses

Listings include an "artsy-eclectic" home in the French Quarter, a large 1920's home in an area of great live oak trees, homes in a lovely garden district, and many more, from hostel-type to deluxe rooms and apartments.

Special needs of guests are usually met, such as tourist information and occasional transportation. Past extra services have included nursing a guest who was ill, and providing clothes for special occasions and emergencies.

Missouri

Ozark Mountain Country Bed & Breakfast
BOX 295, BRANSON, MO 65726

Offers B&B Homes In:
Ozark Mountain country surrounding Branson

Reservations Phone: (417) 334-4720 or 334-5077
Phone Hours: Any time   **Available:** 7 days a week
Price Range of Homes:
Single: $20 to $31   Double: $25 to $38
Breakfast Included in Price:
Continental (juice, roll/toast, coffee), some homes serving a regional specialty called "funnel cakes"
Brochure Available: Free if inquirer sends stamped, self-addressed #10 envelope
Reservations Should Be Made: 2 weeks in advance (last minute reservations accepted if possible)

Scenic Attractions Near the B&B Homes:
Mountain Music Shows, Silver Dollar City, White Water Fun Park, trout fishing in Taneycomo and Table Rock lakes

B&B Bonuses
  Several host homes are located on beautiful Table Rock Lake. All homes are located close to the great trout fishing for which the area is famous, and to other outstanding tourist attractions.
  "The traveler is treated more like a guest than a source of income."

Truman Country B&B
P.O. BOX 14, INDEPENDENCE, MO 64051

Offers B&B Homes In:
Independence, Missouri

Reservations Phone: (816) 254-6657
Phone Hours: 10 a.m. to 5 p.m.   **Available:** 7 days a week
Price Range of Homes:
Single: $20 to $37.50   Double: $25 to $40
Breakfast Included in Price:
Full American (juice, eggs, bacon, toast, coffee)
Brochure Available: Free
Reservations Should Be Made: 2 weeks in advance (last minute reservations accepted if possible)

Scenic Attractions Near the B&B Homes:
Kansas City Zoo, Harry S. Truman home, many historical homes and sites, antique and handcraft shops

Major Businesses Near the B&B Homes:
Allis-Chalmers

Major Schools, Universities Near the B&B Homes:
U. of Missouri/Kansas City Extension Center

B&B Bonuses

In an 1850's Victorian home near the Harry Truman house, the hostess will give you a tour of the furnishings of the period. Another home, in the suburbs, features Early American decor, including a featherbed. There is a patio and picnic area, and this gracious hostess also gives tours.

One hostess picks up guests at the local train stop, known as the Harry Truman Whistle Stop.

Midwest Host B&B and Southwest Host
P.O. BOX 27, SAGINAW, MO 64864

Offers B&B Homes In:
St. Louis, Kansas City, Blue Eye, Joplin, in Missouri; Houston, New Braunfels, San Marcos, Galveston, Bryan, San Antonio, Kerrville, and Georgetown in Texas; also Fort Wayne in Indiana, Fayetteville in Arkansas, and Albuquerque in New Mexico

Reservations Phone: (417) 782-9112
Phone Hours: 8 a.m. to 10 p.m.   **Available:** 7 days a week
Price Range of Homes:
Single: $8 to $18   Double: $15 to $35
Breakfast Included in Price:
Full American (juice, eggs, bacon, toast, coffee), although in some areas huevos rancheros and Mexican breakfasts are available
Brochure Available: Free if inquirer sends stamped, self-addressed #10 envelope
Reservations Should Be Made: 3 weeks in advance (no last minute reservations accepted)

Scenic Attractions Near the B&B Homes:
Lakes, creeks, Gulf of Mexico, Indian dances and craft centers in Oklahoma, Texas, New Mexico, Mexican border and beyond

Major Businesses Near the B&B Homes:
Oil refineries in Tulsa, Oklahoma

Major Schools, Universities Near the B&B Homes:
U. of Texas in Austin, U. of Arkansas in Fayetteville, and many colleges in all towns listed above

B&B Bonuses

Many homes cater to those interested in Indian and Mexican culture. A home in Galveston has a boat dock for water-skiing and ocean cruising, and another in Hannibal, Missouri, offers Mark Twain history.

"Most hosts have agreed to meet flights and buses and provide service to special sites although in small towns there's an added charge of $10 round trip to the airport."

Bed & Breakfast of St. Louis, River Country of Missouri, and Illinois
#1 GRANDVIEW HEIGHTS, ST. LOUIS, MO 63131

Offers B&B Homes In:
Throughout Missouri, including St. Louis, and many cities in Southern Illinois

Reservations Phone: (314) 965-4328
Phone Hours: 9 a.m. to 11 p.m.   **Available:** 7 days a week
Price Range of Homes:
Single: $15 to $35   Double: $30 to $60
Breakfast Included in Price:
Continental or full American, depending on individual home . . . a working cattle farm lets guests share farmhands' breakfast of home-grown eggs, vegetables, and beef
Brochure Available: For a fee, which is $3.00 and covers Directory and newsletter
Reservations Should Be Made: 2 weeks in advance (last minute reservations accepted if possible)

Scenic Attractions Near the B&B Homes:
Repertory Theater of St. Louis, St. Louis Art Museum, St. Louis Zoo, Clemens Amphitheater, Civil War Fort, Dillard Mill, Onondaga Cave, Mark Twain National Forest, the Great River Road attractions, Mark Twain's boyhood home

Major Businesses Near the B&B Homes:
Ralston, McDonnell Douglas, Monsanto, Anheuser-Busch

Major Schools, Universities Near the B&B Homes:
Webster College, Washington U., Fontbonne College, Columbia U.

B&B Bonuses

Enjoy a candlelight dinner in a log cabin, featuring chicken breast wrapped in ham, with grape sauce, or watch geese and ducks on a lake from your window, just 20 minutes from Lambert Airport. Another home, called "B 'n' Bale" has a stable for a horse, which you can ride and see the country. Ever hear of "his and hers" bathtubs? Well, one home has two claw-footed tubs, side by side!

In a river town on Mississippi, the hostess will arrange for a guest's boat to be kept overnight in the marina, and she will return it for them the next day.

St. Louis Bed & Breakfast
16 GREEN ACRES, ST. LOUIS, MO 63137

Offers B&B Homes In:
City and suburbs of St. Louis

Reservations Phone: (314) 868-2335
Phone Hours: 7 a.m. to 10 p.m.   **Available:** 7 days a week
Price Range of Homes:
Single: $20 to $40   Double: $25 to $50
Breakfast Included in Price:
Continental or full American (often including home-baked rolls, coffee cakes, buttermilk waffles, and regional specialties like sausage strata and huevos rancheros)
Brochure Available: Free if inquirer sends stamped, self-addressed #10 envelope
Reservations Should Be Made: 2 weeks in advance (last minute reservations accepted if possible)

Scenic Attractions Near the B&B Homes:
River front with famous Arch, Busch Stadium, Forest Park Zoo, Muny Outdoor Opera Theater, restored Fox Theater, brewery and winery tours, steamboat excursions, Laclede's Landing

Major Businesses Near the B&B Homes:
Anheuser-Busch, Monsanto, Emerson Electric, General Dynamics, McDonnell Douglas, General Motors, Ford Motors, AT&T, Interco

Major Schools, Universities Near the B&B Homes:
St. Louis U., Washington U., Webster U., U. of Missouri SL, Fontbonne College, Kenrick Seminary, Covenant Presbyterian Seminary, Logan Chiropractic College

B&B Bonuses

An energetic retired teacher who "loves having the world come to her door through her guests" welcomes them to a refurbished turn-of-the-century Gothic-style residence, centrally located. If you prefer rustic pleasures, there is a barn-style home "nestled in a 3-acre hideaway in rolling wooded hills" with a park nearby that offers horse-back riding, trails, and swimming.

Many hosts are glad to provide local and airport transportation and interesting historical information about the area.

New Mexico

Bed & Breakfast of Santa Fe
218 E. BUENA VISTA, SANTA FE, NM 87501

Offers B&B Homes In:
Santa Fe only

Reservations Phone: (505) 982-3332
Phone Hours: 9 a.m. to 5 p.m.   **Available:** 5 days a week September to April
7 days a week May to August

Price Range of Homes:
Single: $25 to $30   Double: $35 to $60
Breakfast Included in Price:
Continental; in some homes food is left for guests to prepare and enjoy at their leisure
Brochure Available: Free if inquirer sends stamped, self-addressed #10 envelope
Reservations Should Be Made: 2 weeks in advance (last minute reservations accepted if possible)

Scenic Attractions Near the B&B Homes:
Annual Indian Market (third weekend of Aug.), cliff dwellings, pueblo and Spanish church ruins, colorful adobe architecture, major art center, ski basin, opera, Chamber Music Festival, Arts Festival

B&B Bonuses

  Several accommodations are in typical Santa Fe style, with adobe walls, walled yards, shady patios, ceiling "vigas," and tiled baths with Mexican decor.
  Host families have driven guests to local festivities, served cool drinks, made restaurant reservations. Many close friendships have been formed, with continuing correspondence!

Texas

The Bed & Breakfast Society of Houston
4432 HOLT, BELLAIRE, TX 77401

Offers B&B Homes In:
Houston and surrounding suburbs

Reservations Phone: (713) 666-6372
Phone Hours: 8 a.m. to 5 p.m.   **Available:** 7 days a week
Price Range of Homes:
Single: $25 to $50   Double: $35 to $50 (some discounts for long-term stays)
Breakfast Included in Price:
Continental or full American (juice, eggs, bacon, toast, coffee). Some homes offer full breakfast plus regional specialties, such as huevos rancheros, jalapeno cornbread, taquitos, etc., and some will accommodate special diets.
Brochure Available: Free (local special-events brochure also available)
Reservations Should Be Made: 2 weeks in advance (last minute reservations accepted if possible)

Scenic Attractions Near the B&B Homes:
NASA Space Center, Astrodome, Texas Medical Center, San Jacinto Monument, Herman Park, Miller Outdoor Theater

Major Businesses Near the B&B Homes:
Texas Instruments, The Galleria, and all Texas oil companies

Major Schools, Universities Near the B&B Homes:
U. of Houston, U. of St. Thomas, Rice U., Baylor College of Medicine

B&B Bonuses
   One home is an exact replica of a Louisiana plantation house, beautifully and authentically decorated, but with all modern conveniences, including a gazebo and pool. Hospitality and flexibility can include anything from airport pickups in a Cadillac and sightseeing tours, to washing guests' clothes and introducing them to the wild life in Houston "just like a Western movie!"

Sand Dollar Hospitality/Bed & Breakfast
3605 MENDENHALL, CORPUS CHRISTI, TX 78415

Offers B&B Homes In:
Texas Coastal Bend, primarily Corpus Christi

Reservations Phone: (512) 853-1222 or 992-4497
Phone Hours: 8 a.m. to 8 p.m.   **Available:** 7 days a week
Price Range of Homes:
Single: $20 to $35   Double: $25 to $40
Breakfast Included in Price:
Continental or full American, depending on individual home—plus some Mexican specialties, such as breakfast taquitos and Mexican sweetbreads
Brochure Available: Free
Reservations Should Be Made: 10 days in advance preferred (last minute reservations accepted if possible)

Scenic Attractions Near the B&B Homes:
Padre Island, King Ranch, Aransas Wildlife Refuge (home of the whooping crane), Rockport Art Colony, Japanese Art Museum, Corpus Christi Art Museum

Major Businesses Near the B&B Homes:
Coastal States Refinery, Reynolds Aluminum, Celanese, DuPont, Exxon, Texaco, Naval Air Station

Major Schools, Universities Near the B&B Homes:
Corpus Christi State U., Del Mar Junior College

B&B Bonuses

Corpus Christi is sometimes called the "Texas Riviera." Dine on freshly caught fish and shrimp at fine restaurants overlooking the ocean, dress up for an evening at the Symphony or down for country and western dancing, or experience a different facet of Southwestern living, at the famous King Ranch.

Several homes have three or four bedrooms available, making them ideal for groups traveling together.

Bed & Breakfast Texas Style

4224 W. RED BIRD LANE, DALLAS, TX 75237

Offers B&B Homes In:
Dallas, Houston, Austin, San Antonio, Fort Worth, Arlington, Jefferson, Carthage, Garland, University Park, Hurst, Waxahachie, Waco, Clifton, Rockwell, Amarillo

Reservations Phone: (214) 298-8586 or 298-5433
Phone Hours: 8 a.m. to 6 p.m.   **Available:** Monday to Saturday
Price Range of Homes:
Single: $20 to $35   Double: $25 to $50
Breakfast Included in Price:
Continental or full American which may include regional specialties such as jalapena muffins, JR pancakes, sourdough biscuits and gravy, grits, crêpes, omelettes
Brochure Available: Free; for full directory, send $2 plus stamped, self-addressed envelope
Reservations Should Be Made: 2 weeks in advance (last minute reservations accepted if possible)

Scenic Attractions Near the B&B Homes:
Texas Stadium, Texas Hill Country, Japanese Botanical Gardens, Carthage Home, Azalea Trails, Gulf of Mexico, Galveston Bay, Texas Safari Wild Game Park, lakes

Major Businesses Near the B&B Homes:
Texas Instruments, General Dynamics, IBM, Houston Port City and Oil City, Cowtown, stockyards, Finance Center of Southwest in Fort Worth

Major Schools, Universities Near the B&B Homes:
Southern Methodist U., Rice, U. of Houston, Texas U., TCU Fort Worth, Trinity U., Our Lady of the Lake in San Antonio

B&B Bonuses

A large, comfortable home in North Dallas has three upstairs bedrooms decorated with country charm, and boasting two heirloom spool beds. Overlooks a pool, too.

The "Sam Rayburn Lake Guesthouse" is excellent for a group or family, with a lake for water skiing or fishing. "Hosts are nearby and will stock the new refrigerator with breakfast food for weekend visitors."

Gasthaus Bed & Breakfast Lodging Services
330 W. MAIN STREET, FREDERICKSBURG, TX 78624

Offers B&B Homes In:
Fredericksburg and Gillespie County (hill country of Texas)

Reservations Phone: (512) 997-4712
Phone Hours: 10 a.m. to 5 p.m.   **Available:** Monday to Saturday
Price Range of Homes:
Single: $25 to $50   Double: $35 to $125
Breakfast Included in Price:
Continental (juice, roll/toast, coffee)
Brochure Available: Free
Reservations Should Be Made: "Any time—last minute reservations accepted and bookings based on availability"

Scenic Attractions Near the B&B Homes:
"Alt Friedrichsburg" (German historic district), Lyndon B. Johnson State and National Historic Park, Enchanted Rock Natural Park, pioneer architecture

B&B Bonuses

There are some 22 homes in the town of Fredericksburg. Also available nearby is a game ranch of 10,000 acres, and "Wilhelmina's Host Home." Wilhelmina speaks fluent German, is an antique collector, and serves "blumengarten" breakfasts under pecan shade trees. She loves to plan scenic drives and "volksmarching" walks.

Fredericksburg is the birthplace of "volksmarching" in the U.S. and is famous for its walkways. Visitors are given souvenir medallions for taking the Fredericksburg Pilgrimage Walk, a trek through historic and scenic areas. Walkers receive a guidebook and map, and they can walk at their own pace.

Bed & Breakfast Hosts of San Antonio (Home Lodging Services)
166 ROCKHILL, SAN ANTONIO, TX 78209

Offers B&B Homes In:
San Antonio, Kerrville, Grapevine, New Braunfels, Moore

Reservations Phone: (512) 824-8036
Phone Hours: 9 a.m. to 5 p.m.   **Available:** 7 days a week
Price Range of Homes:
Single: $37.75 to $53   Double: $53 to $80
Breakfast Included in Price:
Continental or full American, depending on home (regional specialties available in some homes, with advance notice)
Brochure Available: Free
Reservations Should Be Made: 2 weeks in advance (last minute reservations accepted if possible)

Scenic Attractions Near the B&B Homes:
San Antonio River attractions, The Alamo, Spanish Governor's Palace, Mission Trail, San Antonio Zoo, Breckenridge Park, Sunken Gardens Mexican Market

Major Schools, Universities Near the B&B Homes:
U. of Texas at San Antonio, Trinity U., Incarnate Word U., St. Mary's Law School, Our Lady of the Lake U., U. of Texas Medical, Dental, Nursing Schools

B&B Bonuses
Some of their "extras" can be fresh fruit and flowers in the guestroom, invitations to dinner, and guidance in sightseeing.

Bed & Breakfast of Wimberley, Texas

P.O. BOX 589, WIMBERLEY, TX 78676

Offers B&B Homes In:
The Hill Country near Austin, San Marcos, San Antonio

Reservations Phone: (512) 847-9666 or 847-2837
Phone Hours: 9 a.m. to 5:30 p.m.   **Available:** 7 days a week
Price Range of Homes:
   Single: $25 to $40   Double: $30 to $50
Breakfast Included in Price:
Continental (juice, roll/toast, coffee)
Brochure Available: No
Reservations Should Be Made: 3 days to 2 weeks in advance (last minute reservations accepted if possible)

Scenic Attractions Near the B&B Homes:
Pioneer Town, LBJ Park, German town of Fredericksburg, Austin State Capitol

Major Businesses Near the B&B Homes:
IBM, Texas Instruments, Motorola, Lockheed, 3M, Micro Electronic Research, many smaller hi-tech companies

Major Schools, Universities Near the B&B Homes:
Southwest Texas State U., U. of Texas, Austin and San Antonio, and 10 smaller colleges in Austin and San Antonio

B&B Bonuses

   A guest house on a private estate is called "The Golden Pavilion." It features Japanese architecture, and while having access to the Blanco River for sunning and swimming, it is also only two miles from the center of town. Has a grand piano and pool table, too. Accommodations are also available on a small ranch, with horses and swimming pool.
   If you call this B&B, they will pick you up and conduct you to the host home.

CALIFORNIA & THE WEST

Arizona
California
Utah

Arizona

Bed & Breakfast in Arizona, Inc.

8433 N. BLACK CANYON HIWAY, SUITE 160, PHOENIX, AZ 85021

Offers B&B Homes In:
Throughout Arizona (240 homes, ranches, and guesthouses)

Reservations Phone: (602) 995-2831
Phone Hours: 9 a.m. to 5 p.m.   **Available:** Monday thru Saturday (no holidays)

Price Range of Homes:
Single: $20 to $60   Double: $30 to $110

Breakfast Included in Price:
Full American, many hosts are gourmet cooks, serving quiches, homemade breads, and an "Arizona" breakfast featuring Spanish omelette

Brochure Available: Free if inquirer sends stamped, self-addressed #10 envelope

Reservations Should Be Made: 2 weeks in advance (last minute reservations accepted if possible)

Scenic Attractions Near the B&B Homes:
Grand Canyon, Indian Monuments, Phoenix and Tucson Zoos, Zane Grey home, national forests, 19 state parks, Lake Havasu, Lake Powell, Lowell Observatory

Major Business Near the B&B Homes:
IBM, Motorola, GE, American Express, Sperry

Major Schools, Universities Near the B&B Homes:
American Graduate School of Business, U. of Arizona at Tucson, Northern Arizona U. at Flagstaff, Arizona State U. at Tempe, Orme and Judson private schools

B&B Bonuses

Stays of 2 nights or longer are preferred by this B&B, and for a week's stay in the same home, the seventh night is **free**. You can ride on a host's houseboat on Lake Powell, or relax in a movie star's guest suite while she fixes you an omelette, or enjoy ranch, Spanish contemporary, or restored older homes.

Hosts often meet guests at the airport, make restaurant reservations, plan sightseeing, reserve tickets to sports events or concerts, take guests shopping, backpacking, bird-watching, etc., and even plan menus for special diets.

Mi Casa—Su Casa Bed & Breakfast
BOX 950, TEMPE, AZ 85281

Offers B&B Homes in :
Throughout Arizona

Reservations Phone: (602) 990-0682
Phone Hours: 8 a.m. to 8 p.m.   **Available:** 7 days a week
Price Range of Homes:
Single: $20 to $50   Double: $25 to $50
Breakfast Included in Price:
Continental or full American; Southern-style or Swedish-style or hash browns and sausages may be served, according to individual hostess
Brochure Available: For a fee; send $1.00 for full descriptive directory of homes
Reservations Should Be Made: 2 weeks in advance (last minute reservations accepted if possible)

Scenic Attractions Near the B&B Homes:
Grand Canyon, Monument Valley, Hopi and Navajo villages, prehistoric cliff dwellings, national forests, missions, horse shows, Kitt and Lowell Observatories, Petrified Forest, Taliesin West, sports and fine art galleries in metropolitan areas

Major Businesses Near the B&B Homes:
Armour Dial, Greyhound Corp., Best Western Motels, Circle K, Del Webb Recreational Properties, Cudahy, Kaibab Industries, Ramada Inns, Sperry Flight Systems

Major Schools, Universities Near the B&B Homes:
Arizona State U., U. of Arizona at Tucson, Northern Arizona U., American Graduate School of Int'l Management, Orme School, Village Oasis School, Verde Valley School, Judson School, Phoenix Country Day School

B&B Bonuses

Homes vary from luxury mountainside metropolitan houses to National Register homes and ranches, from rambling homes with guest wings or guests houses, to small, cozy ones. "All take pride in sharing the magnificent Western scenery and unique life style."

Airport pickups and mini-tours can often be arranged, and some outlying ranches far from restaurants offer dinner with the family for a modest charge.

California

Eye Openers Bed & Breakfast Reservations
P.O. BOX 694, ALTADENA, CA 91001

Offers B&B Homes In:
Southern California, primarily Los Angeles/Pasadena area and adjacent suburbs and cities

Reservations Phone: (213) 684-4428
Phone Hours: 24 hours a day   **Available:** 7 days a week
Price Range of Homes:
Single: $30 to $55   Double: $35 to $60
Breakfast Included in Price:
Continental or full American (juice, eggs, bacon, toast, coffee) and regional specialties
Brochure Available: Free if inquirer sends stamped, self-addressed #10 envelope
Reservations Should Be Made: 2 weeks in advance (last minute reservations accepted if possible)

Scenic Attractions Near the B&B Homes:
Angeles National Forest, Huntington Library & Gardens, Los Angeles Zoo, Universal Studios, Rose Bowl, Norton Simon Museum, Asia Pacific Museum, Dodger Stadium, Santa Anita Race Track, NBC-TV Studios, L. A. County Arboretum, Gamble House, Tournament of Roses Mansion

Major Businesses Near the B&B Homes:
Parsons, Avery Label, Jet Propulsion Lab, Bank Americard, Pacific Telephone, Jacobs Engineering

Major Schools, Universities Near the B&B Homes:
California Institute of Technology, Pasadena City College, Ambassador College, Pasadena College of Chiropractic, Art Center College of Design, Sawyer College of Business, Fuller Theological Seminary, UCLA, U. of Southern California, Claremont Colleges, Occidental College, Cal. State L. A., Cal State Northridge

B&B Bonuses

Adjacent to scenic Angeles National Park sites a spacious home with swimming pool and wine cellar, close to hiking and equestrian trails. Have breakfast by the garden-fountain in another, old Spanish-style, home. Interested in astronomy? Ask for the host has a telescope and observatory area!

Airport and bus depot pickups are frequently made in the Pasadena area, and one host offers free transportation every weekday, from the San Gabriel mountain foothills to downtown Los Angeles.

Digs West

8191 CROWLEY CIRCLE, BUENA PARK, CA 90621

Offers B&B Homes In:
Approximately 35 cities and towns throughout California

Reservations Phone: (714) 739-1669
Phone Hours: Any time   **Available:** 7 days a week
Price Range of Homes:
Single: $30 to $45   Double: $36 to $55 (luxury accommodations $55 to $110)
Breakfast Included in Price:
Continental or full American, depending on individual home (homemade muffins and other specialties often served)
Brochure Available: Free if inquirer sends stamped, self-addressed #10 envelope; also a complete directory will soon be available for $2.00
Reservations Should Be Made: No fixed requirements, the earlier the better (last minute reservations accepted if possible)

Scenic Attractions Near the B&B Homes:
The many tourist and natural attractions throughout California

Major Businesses Near the B&B Homes:
Hughes, Rockwell, Beckman Instruments, Hunt Foods, Fluor Corp.

Major Schools, Universities Near the B&B Homes:
Cal State at Fullerton and Long Beach, UC Irvine, UC Santa Barbara, UC San Diego, U. of Southern California, UCLA

B&B Bonuses

"Most of our homes offer a warm family feeling. One with a real country flavor is situated conveniently near Disneyland. Several hosts are artists and offer individualistic atmosphere and decor."

Recently, a couple from England were escorted by their hosts on a tour all over Southern California, and were served dinner to boot!

Homestay

P.O. BOX 326, CAMBRIA, CA 93428

Offers B&B Homes In:
Cambria, Cayucos, Morro Bay, Los Osos, San Luis Obispo, Paso Robles, San Simeon, Santa Barbara, Monterey

Reservations Phone: (805) 927-4613
Phone Hours: Any time   **Available:** 7 days a week
Price Range of Homes:
Single: $25 to $40   Double: $30 to $50
Breakfast Included in Price:
Continental or full American, depending on individual home (some with no breakfast)—a specialty in one home is a vegetarian open-face omelet
Brochure Available: Free
Reservations Should Be Made: up to 90 days in advance (last minute reservations accepted if possible)

Scenic Attractions Near the B&B Homes:
Hearst Castle, Santa Barbara Missions

Major Schools, Universities Near the B&B Homes:
U. of San Luis Obispo and U. of Santa Barbara

B&B Bonuses

 Residents believe that "Cambria is synonymous with Camelot." A "castle" called "Treehouse" sits atop a hill overlooking rocky beaches and crashing surf, affording a view of magnificent sunsets. An atrium decorated with plants and ferns, hand-hewn driftwood furniture, private deck, fireplace, and a queen-size waterbed are to be found in some of the homes.
 Certain hosts allow kitchen privileges for extended stays, or even occupancy of the entire home, if privacy is desired.

Hospitality Plus

P.O. BOX 336, DANA POINT, CA 92629

Offers B&B Homes In:
80 cities throughout California
Reservations Phone: (714) 496-6953
Phone Hours: 9 a.m. to 5 p.m.   **Available:** Mon. to Fri.—& Sat. & Sun. evenings

Price Range of Homes:
Single: $15 to $40   Double: $20 to $55

Breakfast Included in Price:
About 20% of homes serve Continental, others serve full breakfasts with specialties such as Swedish round pancakes, Ortega Omelettes, and cinnamon rolls

Brochure Available: For a fee, which is 50¢

Reservations Should Be Made: 2 weeks in advance (last minute reservations accepted if possible)

Scenic Attractions Near the B&B Homes:
Disneyland, Sequoia National Park, Yosemite, San Diego Zoo, Wild Animal Park, Lion Country Safari, Amtrak to Missions of California

Major Businesses Near the B&B Homes:
Silicon Valley computer firms

B&B Bonuses

A house on what is said to be "the most romantic spot on the California coast" is totally separate from the main house, its deck overlooking a white water view of Capistrano Bay. Relax in the garden with a tiled Jacuzzi under towering eucalyptus trees, and enjoy peaches and cream for breakfast from the host's own peach trees.

Another bluffside location affords the pleasure of watching and listening to the surf from the garden.

Bed & Breakfast of Southern California
P.O. BOX 218, FULLERTON, CA 92632

Offers B&B Homes In:
Southern California, primarily Orange County

Reservations Phone: (714) 879-2568
Phone Hours: 8 a.m. to 9 p.m.   **Available:** 7 days a week
Price Range of Homes:
Single: $22 to $42   Double: $28 to $49
Breakfast Included in Price:
Continental (juice, roll/toast, coffee)
Brochure Available: Free
Reservations Should Be Made: 3 weeks in advance (last minute reservations accepted if possible)

Scenic Attractions Near the B&B Homes:
Disneyland, Knott's Berry Farm, Movieland Wax Museum, Kingdom of Dancing Stallions, Pageant of the Masters, Irvine Meadows, all Los Angeles attractions a short drive away

Major Businesses Near the B&B Homes:
Fluor Corporation, Hughes Aircraft, Hunt-Wesson, Kimberley-Clark, Ford, Northrop, Philco, Anaheim Convention Center, Anaheim Stadium, Beckman Instruments, Rockwell International

Major Schools, Universities Near the B&B Homes:
California State U., U. of California, Western State College of Law, Fullerton College, Cypress College, Orange Coast College

B&B Bonuses

 A typical host is "Tom," who has traveled through the Orient collecting rugs, furniture, and pieces of art for "The Pink Home." Tom believes that making a guest feel at home and yet free to come and go is part of "the art of being a B&B host."

 Airport pickups, sightseeing tours, and tips on how to get the most for your vacation dollar, are frequently provided.

Bed & Breakfast Rent-A-Room
11531 VARNA STREET, GARDEN GROVE, CA 92640

Offers B&B Homes In:
Los Angeles, Disneyland, San Diego, and along the coast

Reservations Phone: (714) 638-1406
Phone Hours: 8 a.m. to 10 p.m.   **Available:** 7 days a week
Price Range of Homes:
Single: $25 to $35   Double: $30 to $50
Breakfast Included in Price:
Continental (some hosts serve a different continental breakfast every day, with crêpes, French toast, etc.), and some full American
Brochure Available: Free if inquirer sends stamped, self-addressed #10 envelope
Reservations Should Be Made: 2 weeks in advance (last minute reservations accepted if possible)

Scenic Attractions Near the B&B Homes:
Hollywood, Universal City, Marineland, Ports O' Call, Queen Mary, Disneyland, Knott's Berry Farm, Lion Country Safari, San Diego Zoo, Wild Animal Park, Sea World, Tijuana, Mexico missions in San Diego, San Juan Capistrano

Major Businesses Near the B&B Homes:
Hughes Aircraft, McDonnell Douglas, Fluor Corp, Angels and Rams organizations

Major Schools, Universities Near the B&B Homes:
UCLA, U. of Southern California, Long Beach State, Fullerton State, Irvine, U. of California at San Diego, San Diego State

B&B Bonuses

A large home with four bedrooms with private baths boasts an inside fountain, Jacuzzi, swimming pool, tennis courts, and breakfast served in a gazebo. You will be close to beaches, Disneyland, and Knott's Berry Farm, too.

Airport pickups are frequently made, and some hosts offer full or half-day tours, use of private beach, and local golfing privileges.

Seaview Reservations Bed & Breakfast
P.O. BOX 1355, LAGUNA BEACH, CA 92652

Offers B&B Homes In:
From San Diego to the San Francisco Bay area, particularly in Laguna Beach

Reservations Phone: (714) 494-8878
Phone Hours: 9 a.m. to 5 p.m.   **Available:** Monday through Friday
(24-hour answering service)
Price Range of Homes:
Single: $35 and up   Double: $40 and up
Breakfast Included in Price:
Continental or full American, depending on individual home
Brochure Available: No
Reservations Should Be Made: 2 weeks in advance (last minute reservations accepted if possible)

Scenic Attractions Near the B&B Homes:
Laguna Beach Arts Festival, Disneyland, San Diego Sea World and Zoo, Del Mar Racetrack

Major Businesses Near the B&B Homes:
Greater Irvine Industrial Complex, Fluor Corp., Newport Center, Orange City

Major Schools, Universities Near the B&B Homes:
San Diego State U., Scripps Clinic

B&B Bonuses
   There are several ocean-front homes available, and a historic inn among listings in Laguna Beach. "Many hosts will pick up at airport, cook dinner, act as tourist guides."

Sacramento Innkeepers' Ass'n.
2209 CAPITOL AVE., SACRAMENTO, CA 95816

Offers B&B Homes In:
Sacramento

Reservations Phone: (916) 441-3214
Phone Hours: 8 a.m. to 9 p.m.   **Available:** 7 days a week
Price Range of Homes:
Double: $45 to $75
Breakfast Included in Price:
Full American (juice, eggs, bacon, toast, coffee); may include homemade breads and fresh fruit
Brochure Available: Free
Reservations Should Be Made: 2 weeks in advance (last minute reservations accepted if possible)

Scenic Attractions Near the B&B Homes:
State Capitol, Sutter's Fort, Governor's Mansion, Railroad Museum, Oldtown, Crocker Art Museum, Convention Center

Major Businesses Near the B&B Homes:
Diamond Almond Factory, Sacramento Tomato Co., IBM

Major Schools, Universities Near the B&B Homes:
American River College, Sacramento City College

B&B Bonuses

The famous "Briggs House" is a 1901 Colonial Revival home furnished with period antiques, elegant and comfortable, with a spa and a sauna in the shaded garden. At the "Amber House" you can partake of wine with the hosts and other guests every afternoon, and the Continental breakfast will be served in your room, on Limoges china with silver service.

The "Morning Glory" house hosts will pick up guests at the airport, with a surprise bubble bath prepared for them! Other hosts will often assist with dinner reservations, babysitting, and guidance on points of interest.

Carolyn's Bed & Breakfast Homes in San Diego
P.O. BOX 84776, SAN DIEGO, CA 92138

Offers B&B Homes In:
San Diego city and county

Reservations Phone: (619) 435-5009 or 481-7662
Phone Hours: 9 a.m. to 8 p.m.   **Available:** 7 days a week
Price Range of Homes:
Single: $20 to $60   Double: $30 to $85 (cottages $55 to $125)
Breakfast Included in Price:
Continental or full American, depending on individual home (fresh-baked muffins often served)
Brochure Available: Free if inquirer sends stamped, self-addressed #10 envelope
Reservations Should Be Made: 2 weeks in advance (last minute reservations accepted if possible, with $5 extra charge)

Scenic Attractions Near the B&B Homes:
Pacific Ocean, Torrey Pines Golf Course, Sea World, San Diego Zoo, Scripps Aquarium, Scripps Institute of Oceanography, Del Coronado Hotel, Disneyland, 1984 Olympics, Tijuana, Mexico

Major Businesses Near the B&B Homes:
Solar, 3 major naval bases

Major Schools, Universities Near the B&B Homes:
U. of Southern California, California State College

B&B Bonuses

There are modern homes and Victorian homes with beautiful antiques, ranch homes in the mountains with horseback riding available, and homes on the beach and ocean.

Airport, train and bus pick-ups are frequent, and some hosts offer laundry facilities and sightseeing tours.

American Family Inn/Bed & Breakfast San Francisco
P.O. BOX 349, SAN FRANCISCO, CA 94101

Offers B&B Homes In:
San Francisco, Marin County, Carmel, Monterey, wine country, gold country of California

Reservations Phone: (415) 931-3083
Phone Hours: 8 a.m. to 10 p.m.   **Available:** 7 days a week
Price Range of Homes:
Single: $35 to $45   Double: $45 to $75 (family accommodations $65 to $80)
Breakfast Included in Price:
Full American, with many of the hosts making their own breads and jams
Brochure Available: Free
Reservations Should Be Made: 2 weeks in advance (last minute reservations accepted if possible)

Scenic Attractions Near the B&B Homes:
San Francisco cable cars, Fishermen's Wharf, Chinatown, new Moscone Convention Center

Major Businesses Near the B&B Homes:
"Wall Street of the West" in San Francisco, computer companies in Silicon Valley, Bechtel, Levi Strauss

Major Schools, Universities Near the B&B Homes:
U.S. Medical Center in San Francisco

B&B Bonuses

   A list of over 100 accommodations includes romantic Victorian homes as well as modern houses with decks and hot tubs. For real luxury, you can live on a yacht on San Francisco Bay, either at Fishermen's Wharf or Sausalito.
   Some hosts will pick up at the airport, or give sightseeing tours, and all of them are experts on San Francisco sights and restaurants. "Newest listings include houseboats in the price range of $100 to $115 per night."

Wine Country Bed & Breakfast
P.O. BOX 3211, SANTA ROSA, CA 95403

Offers B&B Homes In:
Santa Rosa and approximately 35 mile radius, including Healdsburg, Sebastopol, Sonoma, St. Helena, Calistoga

Reservations Phone: (707) 578-1661
Phone Hours: 10 a.m. to 8 p.m.   **Available:** 7 days a week
Price Range of Homes:
Single: $35 to $60   Double: $40 to $65
Breakfast Included in Price:
Full American (juice, eggs, bacon, toast, coffee)
Brochure Available: Free if inquirer sends stamped, self-addressed #10 envelope
Reservations Should Be Made: 2 weeks in advance (no last minute reservations, but will accept one week ahead, if deposit is sent)

Scenic Attractions Near the B&B Homes:
Over 24 world-famous wineries and vineyards, Redwood Forest in Armstrong State Park, Bodega Bay, Sonoma Old Spanish Mission, Jack London House and Museum, Russian River Resorts, Historic Russian Settlement at Fort Ross

Major Businesses Near the B&B Homes:
Hewlett-Packard, State Farm Insurance, Optical Coating

Major Schools, Universities Near the B&B Homes:
Sonoma State U., Santa Rosa Junior College

B&B Bonuses
   You can breakfast on the terrace of a beautifully restored Victorian home, or enjoy the pool and sundeck of a house in the Valley of the Moon, or relax in the hot tub at many of the homes. Quite a few of the hosts are originally Europeans who chose this area of California as *the* place to live!

Bed & Breakfast Exchange
P.O. BOX 88, ST. HELENA, CA 94574

Offers B&B Homes In:
Napa County and Sonoma County, Mendocino County and the Gold Country

Reservations Phone: (707) 963-7756
Phone Hours: 9 a.m. to 4 p.m.   **Available:** Monday to Friday
Price Range of Homes:
Single: $25 to $85   Double: $35 to $300
Breakfast Included in Price:
Continental (juice, roll/toast, coffee)
Brochure Available: Free
Reservations Should Be Made: 3 weeks in advance (last minute reservations accepted if possible)

Scenic Attractions Near the B&B Homes:
State parks, Russian River rafting and beaches, famous wineries and restaurants, mineral and hot springs in Calistoga, hot air balloons and glider rides, horse-drawn carriage rides

Major Businesses Near the B&B Homes:
Wineries and vineyards

Major Schools, Universities Near the B&B Homes:
Napa Junior College, Pacific Union College, Sonoma State U.

B&B Bonuses

A host home surrounded by vineyards features a "bed that came around the Cape," pool, spa, unusual birds, masseuse available, and catered dinners on request.

Hosts can arrange for private winery tours in an antique car, dinner reservations, and even "mud bath" reservations!

Bed & Breakfast of Los Angeles
32074 WATERSIDE LANE, WESTLAKE VILLAGE, CA 91361

Offers B&B Homes In:
Los Angeles, Ventura, Orange counties

Reservations Phone: (818) 889-8870 or 889-7325
Phone Hours: 7 a.m. to 10 p.m.   **Available:** 7 days a week
Price Range of Homes:
Single: $24 to $50   Double: $30 to $65
Breakfast Included in Price:
Continental or full American (juice, eggs, bacon toast, coffee), with some homes serving regional specialties
Brochure Available: Free with legal-size stamped, self-addressed envelope with 40¢ postage
Reservations Should Be Made: one month in advance (last minute reservations accepted if possible)

Scenic Attractions Near the B&B Homes:
All Southern California tourist attractions

Major Businesses Near the B&B Homes:
Home offices of many major business firms are located in the area, including film, TV, and recording industries.

Major Schools, Universities Near the B&B Homes:
U. of Southern California, UCLA, Occidental, Pepperdine, Marymont, Loyola, Whittier, State College at Long Beach, Northridge, Saddleback, Domingas Hills, Los Angeles, Fullerton, Cal Poly at Pomona, and University System at Riverside

B&B Bonuses

Host homes range from exclusive Beverly Hills and Westlake Village, to Marina del Rey, Hollywood, Huntington Beach, and many other desirable areas. One host speaks four languages and will prepare gourmet dinners at additional cost.

Picnic lunches, babysitting, airport pickups, use of TV, golf clubs, patio and barbecue, pools, bicycles are some of the extra services available in certain homes.

Bed & Breakfast—California Sunshine
22704 VENTURA BLVD.—SUITE 1984, WOODLAND HILLS, CA 91364

Offers B&B Homes In:
Southern California from Santa Barbara south to San Diego, and from the ocean, inland

Reservations Phone: (213) 274-4494 or (818) 992-1984
Phone Hours: 8 a.m. to 10 p.m. · **Available:** 7 days a week
Price Range of Homes:
Single: $24 to $48   Double: $30 to $78
Breakfast Included in Price:
Continental, may include fresh fruit; many hosts offer gourmet breakfasts, dinners and picnic lunches for a nominal fee, to be arranged for in advance
Brochure Available: Free
Reservations Should Be Made: 2 weeks in advance (last minute reservations accepted if possible)

Scenic Attractions Near the B&B Homes:
Hollywood Bowl, Greek Theater, Griffith Park Observatory, Equestrian Center, Zoo, Dodger Stadium, L.A. Art Museum, Disneyland, Knott's Berry Farm, Universal City and Studios, NBC Studios, Santa Ana and Hollywood Park race tracks, Farmers Market, Olivera Street, Coliseum, Forum, Sports Arena

Major Businesses Near the B&B Homes:
Financial center of L.A., all major corporations represented in the L.A. and San Fernando Valley area

Major Schools, Universities Near the B&B Homes:
UCLA, U. of Southern California, Occidental College, Loyola, Marymont, U.C. at Santa Barbara, Claremont Colleges, Pasadena City College, Cal State Northridge, Cal Tech, U.C. at San Diego, Pieree College, Valley College

B&B Bonuses

Homes can be quiet and secluded, or right in the heart of the city. "Indescribable ocean views in contractors' ocean homes." One home has extensive facilities for pets, and will only accept guests with a pet! Multilingual homes abound.

Host homes offer all sports facilities, hot tubs and spas, horseback riding and equipment, complimentary use of health clubs and golf privileges. "Most hosts wish to communicate before arrival so that a pleasurable exchange between people of similar background and interests can be experienced."

Napa Valley B&B Reservations (Bed & Breakfast Association of Napa Valley)

P.O. BOX 2147, YOUNTVILLE, CA 94599

Offers B&B Homes In:
Throughout Napa Valley

Reservations Phone: Phone currently not in operation—contact by writing to address above
Price Range of Homes:
Single: $45 to $125   Double: $45 to $125
Breakfast Included in Price:
Continental (juice, roll/toast, coffee), which may include muffins, fruit, cheese, coffee, teas, and juices
Brochure Available: For a fee, which is $1.00
Reservations Should Be Made: 2 weeks in advance (last minute reservations accepted if possible)

Scenic Attractions Near the B&B Homes:
150 premium wineries, ballooning, hiking, bike trails, Calistoga mud and mineral baths, walking tours of old homes

Major Schools, Universities Near the B&B Homes:
Napa Junior College, Pacific Union College

B&B Bonuses

A 100-acre ranch in a peaceful valley features a game room, fireplace, pool, Jacuzzi, and "heartwarming hospitality." For Swiss chalet fanciers, this one overlooks acres of vineyards, with French doors opening onto balconies. Another home includes an art gallery, with complimentary wine! Pickups and private winery tours can be arranged.

This B&B also operates an inn, "The Ambrose Bierce House", which is the former residence of the celebrated author, humorist, and man of mystery, Ambrose Bierce.

Utah

Bed 'n Breakfast Association of Utah
P.O. BOX 81062, SALT LAKE CITY, UT 84108

Offers B&B Homes In:
Throughout Utah

Reservations Phone: (801) 532-7076
Phone Hours: 9 a.m. to 5 p.m. **Available:** 7 days a week
Price Range of Homes:
Single: $15 to $55 Double: $25 to $65
Breakfast Included in Price:
Full American, which may include omelets, wheatcakes, homemade breads and jams
Brochure Available: Free (prefer that inquirer send stamped, self-addressed #10 envelope, please)
Reservations Should Be Made: 2 weeks in advance, minimum (last minute reservations accepted if possible)

Scenic Attractions Near the B&B Homes:
Zion National Park, Bryce National Park, Annual Utah Shakespeare Festival, St. George Resort Area, Mormon Temple Square, "Days of '47" Rodeo, Indian reservations and ancient ruins, skiing, snowmobiling, river running

Major Businesses Near the B&B Homes:
American Express International Headquarters in Salt Lake City

Major Schools, Universities Near the B&B Homes:
U. of Utah, Brigham Young U., Utah State College at Logan, Southwestern Utah State

B&B Bonuses
A historic mansion previously owned by an eccentric, wealthy spinster, is known for the cat cemetery in the front yard. Some of the more than 800 cats she had over the years, are buried with their own little headstones.

ALASKA & HAWAII

Alaska

Alaska Private Lodgings
P.O. BOX 110135, ANCHORAGE, AK 99511

Offers B&B Homes In:
Anchorage, Girdwood, Kenai, Soldotna, Eagle River, Willow, Talkeetna

Reservations Phone: (907) 345-2222
Phone Hours: 8 a.m. to 7 p.m. **Available:** 7 days a week
Price Range of Homes:
Single: $25 to $40 Double: $35 to $60
Breakfast Included in Price:
"Breakfasts are as varied as our homes and hosts, ranging from Continental to full sourdough Alaska can be found"
Brochure Available: Free if inquirer sends stamped, self-addressed #10 envelope
Reservations Should Be Made: 2 weeks in advance (last minute reservations accepted if possible)

Scenic Attractions Near the B&B Homes:
Alaska Oil Pipeline, Alaska Railroad, glaciers, gold mines, salmon-spawning waters, mountain ranges, native wildlife, city, state, and national parks

Major Businesses Near the B&B Homes:
Elmendorf Air Base, Port of Anchorage, Alyeska Oil Pipeline Co., State Government offices

Major Schools, Universities Near the B&B Homes:
U. of Alaska at Anchorage, Alaska Pacific U.

B&B Bonuses
Pan for gold at Crow Creek Gold Mine in summer, ski downhill at Alyeska in winter, take a chairlift up the mountain to Turnagain Arm, all within a few minutes from a luxurious home with heated indoor pool and sauna. If sourdough waffles, a duck pond, and moose in the back yard appeal to you, they can be enjoyed in a home 20 minutes from Anchorage.

Obliging hosts have outfitted children with mittens and sleds for fun in the snow, and have loaned golf clubs and 10-speed bikes to guests.

Stay With A Friend—B&B "Alaskan Style"
BOX 173—3605 ARCTIC BLVD., ANCHORAGE, AK 99503

Offers B&B Homes In:
Anchorage, Hatcher Pass, Palmer-Wasilla, Kenai-Soldotna

Reservations Phone: (907) 274-6445
Phone Hours: 9:30 a.m. to 5:30 p.m. **Available:** Daily during June, July, & August
Price Range of Homes:
Single: $25 to $40 Double: $35 to $60 (Apts. $59 and up)
Breakfast Included in Price:
Continental or full American (many homes will specify full breakfast)
Brochure Available: Free if inquirer sends stamped, self-addressed #10 envelope
Reservations Should Be Made: A month in advance for summer season, 2 weeks in advance other times.

Scenic Attractions Near the B&B Homes:
Mt. McKinley, wilderness areas, hiking, wildlife, fishing and hunting, glaciers, ballooning, clamming, gateway to Kenai Penn

Major Businesses Near the B&B Homes:
Most of the major oil companies

Major Schools, Universities Near the B&B Homes:
University of Alaska

B&B Bonuses

"Accommodations as varied as the traveler's that seek them," such as a home with a library and game room where you can pick raspberries in the garden, or perhaps, the highest lodge in the state, rising 3,000 feet into the sky. Here you can have a breakfast of your choice, and enjoy the sauna after berry-picking.

As for extras, "the long dark Alaskan winter seems to breed a type of hospitality that is unequalled. People will accommodate in any way that seems necessary."

Fairbanks Bed & Breakfast
BOX 74573, FAIRBANKS, AK 99707

Offers B&B Homes In:
Throughout Fairbanks

Reservations Phone: (907) 452-4967
Phone Hours: 8 a.m. to 8 p.m.   **Available:** 7 days a week (operational from May 1 to Sept. 15 only)
Price Range of Homes:
Single: $36 and up   Double: $48
Breakfast Included in Price:
Continental (juice, roll/toast, coffee)
Brochure Available: Free
Reservations Should Be Made: Reservations accepted any time if guaranteed, with $25 deposit

Scenic Attractions Near the B&B Homes:
Cruises on sternwheeler "Discovery," Alaska Salmon Bake, Mining Valley at Alaskaland

Major Schools, Universities Near the B&B Homes:
U. of Alaska, at Fairbanks

B&B Bonuses
"We are a family-run reservations and referral service. We book travelers into English-style lodgings. Many extras are offered. We meet the express train from Denali Park and Anchorage; all guests receive a free map and Visitors' Guide; we can book your cruise on the 'Discovery' and arrange tickets for the Alaska Salmon Bake."
  This B&B may soon be open all-year-round, on a limited basis.

Alaska Bed & Breakfast
526 SEWARD ST., JUNEAU, AK 99801

Offers B&B Homes In:
Southeast Alaska, communities of Juneau, Ketchikan, Wrangell, Petersburg, Sitka, Haines and in the small villages of Angoon, Pelican, and Elfin Cove

Reservations Phone: (907) 586-2959
Phone Hours: 9 a.m. to 5 p.m. **Available:** 7 days a week
Price Range of Homes:
Single: $32 to $40   Double: $40 to $48
Breakfast Included in Price:
Continental or full American—sourdough hot cakes, Highbush cranberry jam, and "Dutch babies" are some of the specialties served
Brochure Available: Free
Reservations Should Be Made: One month in advance (last minute reservations accepted if possible)

Scenic Attractions Near the B&B Homes:
Spectacular mountain climbing, glaciers, salmon fishing, hiking

B&B Bonuses
You can really get away from it all here, whether in an old miner's home or in a log cabin on an isolated beach. Hosts often arrange for transportation, fishing, and hiking expeditions.

Ketchikan Bed & Breakfast
BOX 7814, KETCHIKAN, AK 99901

Offers B&B Homes In:
Ketchikan

Reservations Phone: (907) 247-8444 or 225-6044
Phone Hours: 8:30 a.m. to 9 p.m. **Available:** 7 days a week
Price Range of Homes:
Single: $35 Double: $45
Breakfast Included in Price:
Continental or full American, according to individual home
Brochure Available: Free
Reservations Should Be Made: One month in advance (last minute reservations accepted if possible)

Scenic Attractions Near the B&B Homes:
Misty Fjords National Monument

Major Businesses Near the B&B Homes:
Large fish-processing facilities

B&B Bonuses

Guest homes offer economical rates and good locations, many being located within easy walking distance of downtown. Breakfast options range from hot coffee and rolls to hearty, home-cooked meals.

"Meet interesting hosts who will make you feel welcome in a new town, and enjoy a home-away-from-home atmosphere."

Hawaii

Bed & Breakfast Hawaii
BOX 449, KAPAA, HI 96746

Offers B&B Homes In:
State of Hawaii, all islands except Lanai

Reservations Phone: (808) 822-7771
Phone Hours: 8:30 a.m. to 4:30 p.m. **Available:** 6 days a week (closed Sundays)

Price Range of Homes:
Single: $15 to $30 Double: $20 to $60 (some large condos are more)

Breakfast Included in Price:
Continental (juice, roll/toast, coffee), plus regional specialties at some homes, such as banana pancakes, papaya and mango breads, Hawaiian French toast with coconut syrup, fresh fruit

Brochure Available: Free

Reservations Should Be Made: 3 weeks in advance (last minute reservations accepted if possible)

Scenic Attractions Near the B&B Homes:
All national and state parks, famous zoos, historic homes, all the beauty and romance of the tropics

Major Businesses Near the B&B Homes:
Sugarcane mills, coffee mills, macadamian orchards, papaya and guava groves, pineapple fields

Major Schools, Universities Near the B&B Homes:
U. of Hawaii and branches on outer islands

B&B Bonuses

Many homes feature ocean views, private pools and tennis, lanais, and nearby shopping. There is even a Japanese teahouse, and a home which serves organically grown vegetables. Many hosts will give sightseeing tours, and all will gladly give information as to restaurants, best buys, discount coupons, etc.

CANADA

Alberta
British Columbia
Nova Scotia
Ontario
Quebec

Alberta

Alberta Bed & Breakfast
4327—86 STREET, EDMONTON, AB T6K 1A9 CANADA
(also at 1619—14 Ave. S. W. Calgary, AB T3C 0W6)

Offers B&B Homes In:
Edmonton, Calgary, Canmore (13 miles from Banff), Harvey Heights (between Canmore and Banff), Cochrane and Westerose (Acreage), Redwood Meadows (between Calgary and Banff), and Duchess (Alberta)

Reservations Phone: (403) 462-8885
Phone Hours: 7 a.m. to 11 p.m.   **Available:** 7 days a week
Price Range of Homes:
Single: $15 to $25   Double: $20 to $35
Breakfast Included in Price:
Some Continental (juice, roll/toast, coffee), but most hosts serve more, frequently including homemade breads
Brochure Available: For a fee, which is $1.00
Reservations Should Be Made: More than a month in advance; mail from U.S. to Canada can take two weeks (last minute reservations accepted if possible)

Scenic Attractions Near the B&B Homes:
Calgary Exhibition and Calgary Stampede, Devonian Gardens, Calgary Zoo, Klondike Jet Boats, Edmonton Wildlife Park, Queen Elizabeth Planetarium, Edmonton Art Gallery

B&B Bonuses
   A short distance from Banff National Park, an interesting young couple own a bungalow-style duplex home with spectacular views of Three Sisters Mountain and Rundle Mountain Range. They both work in the restaurant business and "enjoy meeting people over good food." They are also certified downhill ski instructors, experienced hikers, cyclers, windsurfers, and runners. "You're invited to join them for a morning jog before breakfast."

British Columbia

V.I.P. Bed & Breakfast Ltd.
1786 TEAKWOOD RD., VICTORIA, BC V8N 1E2 CANADA

Offers B&B Homes In:
Victoria, Sidney, Nanaimo, Galiano Island

Reservations Phone: (604) 477-5604
Phone Hours: 7 a.m. to 10 p.m.   **Available:** 7 days a week
Price Range of Homes:
Single: $25 to $30   Double: $35 to $45
Breakfast Included in Price:
Full American (juice, eggs, bacon, toast, coffee)
Brochure Available: Free
Reservations Should be Made: 2 weeks in advance (last minute reservations accepted if possible)

Scenic Attractions Near the B&B Homes
Butchart Gardens, Provincial Museum, Craigdarroch Castle, Beacon Hill Park

Major Schools, Universities Near the B&B Homes:
U. of Victoria

B&B Bonuses

An Edwardian mansion boasts canopy beds, antiques, and stained glass; the host of a contemporary sea-view home conducts fishing trips; a country home is near the famed Butchart Gardens. They are proud of their muffins and waffles and their philosophy regarding breakfast is "enough to eliminate the need for lunch!"

One hostess received a rave letter for her "heartwarming friendship and special touches, like flowers in the room, turning on the light for homecoming . . . and I can still taste those muffins, fresh fruits and jams."

Nova Scotia

Nova Scotia Farm & Country Vacation Association
R. R. #3, CENTREVILLE, KINGS COUNTY, NS B0P 1J0 CANADA

Offers B&B Homes In:
Throughout rural Nova Scotia

Reservations Phone: (902) 678-2329 (October 15 to May 15: 538-8284)
Phone Hours: 24 hours a day   **Available:** 7 days a week
Price Range of Homes:
Single: $12 to $15   Double: $25 to $30
Breakfast Included in Price:
Continental or full American—in some homes, all meals can be provided if guest so wishes
Brochure Available: Free
Reservations Should be Made: Accepts last minute reservations

B&B Bonuses
   The homes are located in rural areas; farm vacations are their specialty. "In our program, guests are invited into our home and they become part of the family. They eat with us, participate in our activities if they so desire, etc. They do not have to stay in their rooms, but have the general use of the house."

Cape Breton Bed & Breakfast
P.O. BOX 1750, SYDNEY, NS B1P 6T7 CANADA

Offers B&B Homes In:
Cape Breton and surrounding area

Reservations Phone: Each B&B home must be phoned direct—send for brochure

Price Range of Homes:
Single: $18   Double: $24

Breakfast Included in Price:
Continental or full American . . . regional specialties of Cape Breton may be served, such as Bras d'Or trout, Scottish oat cakes, marrigan, oatmeal porridge, and homemade breads and preserves

Brochure Available: Free

Reservations Should Be Made: Advance reservations are welcome, but not necessary

Scenic Attractions Near the B&B Homes:
Cabot Trail, Miner's Museum, Savoy Theater, Heavy Water Plant, Fortress Louisborg, Newfoundland Ferry, Seal Island Bridge, Bell Museum, beaches, golf courses, Bras D'Or lakes

B&B Bonuses

One enthusiastic guest wrote, "Following a night of sleeping in a squeaky-clean room with embroidered pillow cases on the bed, and enjoying a breakfast of bacon, eggs, juice, milk, doughnuts, muffins, and two kinds of toast, my colleague and I left really feeling that we had been part of a Nova Scotia family for a day."

The hosts are "Cape Breton's best goodwill ambassadors—they frequently prepare picnic lunches, late night snacks, and meals other than breakfast, and drive guests to the airport and ferry."

Bed & Breakfast, Kingston Area
10 WESTVIEW ROAD, KINGSTON, K7M 2C3 CANADA

Offers B&B Homes In:
City of Kingston, and several in the country within 50-mile radius

Reservations Phone: (613) 542-0214
Phone Hours: 8 a.m. to 10 p.m.   **Available:** 7 days a week
Price Range of Homes:
Single: $23 to $27   Double: $31 to $35 ($ Canada)
Breakfast Included in Price:
Full American (guests are offered choices of hot or cold cereal, pancakes, coffee or tea, homemade breads and jams, and always either muffins or scones)
Brochure Available: Free (additional booklet describing each home costs $1.00)
Reservations Should Be Made: 2 weeks in advance, or more in busy summer season (last minute reservations accepted if possible)

Scenic Attractions Near the B&B Homes:
Bellevue House National Historic Site, Old Fort Henry, Thousand Islands, Marine Museum, Pump House Museum, MacLachlan Woodworking Museum, Murney Tower, sailing events in Kingston Harbor

Major Businesses Near the B&B Homes:
Alcan, Du Pont of Canada, Sears in major shopping mall

Major Schools, Universities Near the B&B Homes:
Queens U., Royal Military College, St. Lawrence College

B&B Bonuses
Their 25 host homes range from a beautiful early 19th-century limestone house, elegantly renovated, to a self-contained apartment with double beds and double-bed sofa, close to Grass Creek Park and the St. Lawrence River.
Tourist literature, advice, and pickups, are frequently offered.

Ontario

London Area Bed & Breakfast Association
720 HEADLEY DRIVE, LONDON, ON N6H 3V6 CANADA

Offers B&B Homes In:
City of London and surrounding countryside

Reservations Phone: (519) 471-6228
Phone Hours: 7 a.m. to 11 p.m.   **Available:** 7 days a week
Price Range of Homes:
Single: $20 to $25   Double: $25 to $35
Breakfast Included in Price:
Full breakfasts—varying menus
Brochure Available: Free if inquirer sends stamped, self-addressed #10 envelope
Reservations Should Be Made: 3 weeks in advance preferred—no strict rules (last minute reservations accepted if possible)

Scenic Attractions Near the B&B Homes:
Grand Theater, historic homes, parks

Major Businesses Near the B&B Homes:
GM, Diesel, 3M, University Hospital (Surgery and Research)

Major Schools, Universities Near the B&B Homes:
U. of Western Ontario

B&B Bonuses
  An air-conditioned home in the prestigious residential area of West London has a sun-room for relaxation. It is near Springbank Park and London theatre. Bus service is at the door. In a turn-of-the-century mood, a house with a turret and fireplace is conveniently located off Highway 401.
  Tour information, highway instruction, bus, train and plane pickups, and early morning breakfast service are some of the extra considerations often extended.

Ottawa Area Bed & Breakfast
P. O. BOX 4848 STATION E, OTTAWA, ON K1S 5J1 CANADA

Offers B&B Homes In:
Ottawa, Nepean, Kanata, Gloucester in Ontario; Hull, Aylmer, Gatineau in Quebec

Reservations Phone: (613) 563-0161
Phone Hours: 24 hours a day   **Available:** 7 days a week
Price Range of Homes:
Single: $18 to $25   Double: $25 to $35
Breakfast Included in Price:
Full American (juice, eggs, bacon, toast, coffee)
Brochure Available: Free
Reservations Should be Made: 2 weeks in advance (last minute reservations accepted if possible)

Scenic Attractions Near the B&B Homes:
Parliament Buildings of Canada, Rideau Canal, museums and art galleries

Major Schools, Universities Near the B&B Homes:
U. of Ottawa, Carleton U., Algonquin College, St. Paul's U.

B&B Bonuses
"We can offer you older homes situated right in the heart of our city, suburban homes with amenities such as pools and air-conditioning, or lovely country properties with farm animals or private beaches."

Country Host
R. R. #1, PALGRAVE, ON LON IPO CANADA

Offers B&B Homes In:
Ontario, from Toronto, North and West over 200 miles as far as Georgian Bay at Tobermory and also at Point Pelee National Park area on Lake Erie (where thousands of birds migrate Spring and Fall)

Reservations Phone: (519) 941-7633
Phone Hours: 8 a.m. to midnight   **Available:** 7 days a week (no collect calls)
Price Range of Homes:
Single: $28 to $30   Double: $35 to $40
Breakfast Included in Price:
Full American—juice or fruit in season, bacon or sausage, toast, coffee, real maple syrup and Canadian bacon often served
(lunches and dinners available in some homes if requested in advance)
Brochure Available: No—send for personal answer, including stamped, self-addressed envelope
Reservations Should Be Made: At least one week in advance (last minute reservations accepted if possible)

Scenic Attractions Near the B&B Homes:
Bruce Trail, conservation areas, swimming, fishing, golfing, skiing, ice-fishing, snowmobiling, antiques and craft shops, wild flowers and hundreds of bird species

B&B Bonuses
A really unique service of this B&B is "car jockey service"—when a guest is hiking on the trail, the first host will drive the guest's car to the second host home with the guest's overnight gear, change of clothing, bandaids for his blisters, "maybe even a bottle of wine for evening relaxation." On Day 2, the second host will likewise move the car to the third host home, etc. Women in particular like this service, which, for a very nominal fee, saves carrying anything other than a compass, lunch, binoculars, and camera, while on the famous Bruce Trail.

The Bruce Trail, where many birds are found, is on the Niagara Escarpment and stretches from Niagara to Tobermory on the tip of Bruce Peninsula, a distance of 430 miles, or 712.7 kilometers.

Bed & Breakfast Prince Edward County
BOX 1500, PICTON, ON K0K 2T0 CANADA

Offers B&B Homes In:
Prince Edward County on the north shore of Lake Ontario

Reservations Phone: (613) 476-6798
Phone Hours: 9 a.m. to 8 p.m.   **Available:** 7 days a week
Price Range of Homes:
Single: $25 to $30   Double: $30 to $40
Breakfast Included in Price:
Full American, including homemade muffins, breads, tea biscuits, jams, jellies, etc.
Brochure Available: For a fee, which is $1.00
Reservations Should Be Made: One month in advance in July and August (last minute reservations accepted if possible)

Scenic Attractions Near the B&B Homes:
Famous sand dunes, beaches, sailing, wind-surfing, bird-watching, museums, "Bird City," bicycling, the White Chapel Meeting House, Macaulay House

Major Businesses Near the B&B Homes:
Black River Cheese Company

B&B Bonuses

   An 1846 stone house is on the Bay of Quinte, 300 yards from a fully equipped marina with docking facilities, and near a Conservation area. "In the winter the blazing kitchen fireplace beckons cross-country skiers. The hosts are warm and welcoming and enthusiastic to share their interests in travel, horticulture, genealogy and crafts. Meals on request."
   "Hosts will offer to meet guests without a car, pack a picnic lunch, babysit, and provide information in any way to help a guest."

"Ambassador" B&B Guest House & Reservation Service
266 ONTARIO ST., STRATFORD, ON N5A 3H5 CANADA

Offers B&B Homes In:
Stratford and surrounding area

Reservations Phone: (519) 271-5385
Phone Hours: 8 a.m. to 10 p.m.   **Available:** 7 days a week
Price Range of Homes:
Single: $22 to $35   Double: $30 to $50
Breakfast Included in Price:
Continental (juice, roll/toast, coffee), which also may include homemade bran muffins, whole grain cooked cereal
Brochure Available: Free
Reservations Should Be Made: 2 months in advance in July and August, otherwise 2 weeks (last minute reservations accepted if possible)

Scenic Attractions Near the B&B Homes:
Stratford Shakespeare Theater, Rothman's Art Gallery, fresh water lakes and beaches

Major Businesses Near the B&B Homes:
Fisher Bearings, Canada Fab, Cooper Bessemer

Major Schools, Universities Near the B&B Homes:
Conestoga College of Continuing Education

B&B Bonuses
   "River Garden" is a spacious Victorian home filled with furnishings of the era. It was built on the shores of Lake Victoria, where a saw mill once stood. In another home, Reflexology and Deep muscle Therapy are available for a fee.
   Hosts will often make dinner reservations, arrange for babysitting, provide kitchen facilities, picnic facilities in back yard, and have tea and coffee available at all times.

Stratford & Area Bed & Breakfast
C/O 30 SHREWSBURY STREET, STRATFORD, ON N5A 2V5 CANADA

Offers B&B Homes In:
City and rural Stratford area (easy day trip to Toronto and Niagara Falls)

Reservations Phone: (519) 271-8520
Phone Hours: 9 a.m. to 10 p.m.   **Available:** 7 days a week
Price Range of Homes:
Single: $18 to $35   Double: $25 to $50
Breakfast Included in Price:
Continental (juice, roll/toast, coffee)—many homes give fresh fruit in season, and scones or muffins
Brochure Available: Free
Reservations Should Be Made: As soon as possible (last minute reservations accepted if possible)

Scenic Attractions Near the B&B Homes:
Wildwood Conservation Park, Avon Valley Hiking Trail, Stratford Shakespearean Theater, Stratford Summer Music, sandy beaches of Lake Huron

Major Schools, Universities Near the B&B Homes:
U. of Western Ontario (at London), U. of Waterloo, Sir Wilfred Laurier U., (Kitchener)

B&B Bonuses
One spacious, century-old home, with grounds gently sloping to the water, is filled with art and antiques. A stone farmhouse offers homegrown fruit and vegetables, fresh eggs, and homemade smoked hams, breads, and jams.

Toronto Bed & Breakfast

P.O. BOX 74—STATION M, TORONTO, ON M6S 4T2 CANADA

Offers B&B Homes In:
Metropolitan Toronto

Reservations Phone: (416) 233-3887 or 233-4041
Phone Hours: Evening hours   **Available:** Evenings and weekends
Price Range of Homes:
Single: $25 to $35   Double: $35 to $50
Breakfast Included in Price:
Full American (juice, eggs, bacon, toast, coffee)
Reservations Should Be Made: 2 weeks in advance (last minute reservations accepted if possible)

Scenic Attractions Near the B&B Homes:
CN Tower, Ontario Science Center, Eaton Centre, Canadian National Exhibition, Royal Ontario Museum, Metro Toronto Zoo, Canada's Wonderland, many historic homes

Major Schools, Universities Near the B&B Homes:
U. of Toronto, York U., Ryerson Polytech

B&B Bonuses

Located on the highest point in Toronto, an air-conditioned penthouse apartment commands a unique view of the City, and offers complete sports facilities. A large, antique-filled Victorian home offers guest rooms with hand-stitched quilts, fresh flowers, books and magazines. "A variety of breakfasts are served with linen, crystal, and silver in the homey kitchen/dining room."

Quebec

Montreal Bed & Breakfast
5020 ST. KEVIN, SUITE 8, MONTREAL, PQ H3W 1P4 CANADA

Offers B&B Homes In:
Montreal and nearby communities (Dorval, where Dorval airport is located) Lorraine Quebec with good access to Mirabel Airport, the Eastern Townships, Laurentian Mountains area

Reservations Phone: (514) 735-7493 or 738-3859
Phone Hours: 9 a.m. to 9 p.m.   **Available:** 7 days a week
Price Range of Homes:
Single: $25 to $35   Double: $35 to $50
Breakfast Included in Price:
Full American (juice, eggs, bacon, toast, coffee), plus regional specialties
Brochure Available: For a fee, which is $1.00
Reservations Should Be Made: 3 weeks in advance, if by mail (last minute reservations accepted if possible)

Scenic Attractions Near the B&B Homes:
Mt. Royal Park, Olympic Stadium, St. Joseph Oratory, Botanical Gardens, Place des Arts, Old Montreal, Museum of Fine Arts

Major Schools, Universities Near the B&B Homes:
McGill U., Université de Montreal

B&B Bonuses

Homes range from an apartment in the Olympic Village complex, built to house the athletes in the 1976 games, to a 19th-century stone mansion in Mount Royal Park. There are also duplexes, cottages, and Victorian row houses.

Some hosts give personalized city tours and drive guests to train station or airport, at no charge. Dinner meals can be arranged at certain homes, and when hosts can arrange meetings with people in the same field as the guests, they often do so.

Gite Quebec Bed & Breakfast
3729 AVE. LE CORBUSIER, STE-FOY, PQ G1W 4R8, CANADA

Offers B&B Homes In:
Quebec City

Reservations Phone: (418) 651-1860
Phone Hours: 8 a.m. to 9 p.m.   **Available:** 7 days a week
Price Range of Homes:
Single: $25 to $30   Double: $50 (Canadian money)
Breakfast Included in Price:
Full American (juice, eggs, bacon, toast, coffee)
Brochure Available: Free
Reservations Should Be Made: 2 weeks in advance (last minute reservations accepted if possible)

Scenic Attractions Near the B&B Homes:
Chateau Frontenac, The Citadel and Governors' Promenade, Dufferin Terrace, The Plains of Abraham, Ste. Anne de Beaupre, Winter Carnival, Montmorency Falls, Ile d'Orleans, Fort Museum Artillery Park, Chevalier House, Place d'Armes, Ursuline Convent and Museum

B&B Bonuses

Tour Quebec City, the nearest thing to Europe in our hemisphere, staying at accommodations in private homes offering comfortable rooms, a complete breakfast, and warm hospitality.

"All of our listings have been personally inspected for their comfort and cleanliness. All are convenient to the city's attractions via excellent public transportation."

B&B PHONE BOOKING FORM

Complete this section <u>before</u> you call the reservation service organization.

_____

NUMBER OF NIGHTS YOU WILL NEED THE B&B_____
DATES OF YOUR VISIT TO THE B&B_____
MEMBERS OF YOUR PARTY _____
NO. OF ___ADULTS
         ___CHILDREN
         ___PETS (KIND) _____

LOCATION DESIRED
- ☐ PARTICULAR AREA/NEIGHBORHOOD—NAME_____
- OR ☐ NEAR COLLEGE/UNIVERSITY—NAME_____
- OR ☐ NEAR SCENIC ATTRACTION—NAME_____
- OR ☐ NEAR COMPANY—NAME_____
- ☐ ?_____

SETTING OF HOME
- ☐ CITY
- OR ☐ SUBURBAN
- OR ☐ RURAL

TYPE OF HOME DESIRED
- ☐ MODERN
- ☐ HISTORIC/COLONIAL

BEDS PREFERRED
- ☐ TWIN BEDS
- ☐ DOUBLE
- ☐ QUEEN
- ☐ KING

COTS FOR CHILDREN IN ROOM—NO. _____

TYPE OF BREAKFAST PREFERRED
- ☐ CONTINENTAL (JUICE/ROLL/COFFEE)
- ☐ FULL AMERICAN—IF AVAILABLE (JUICE, EGGS, BACON, TOAST, COFFEE/TEA/SANKA)

PERSONAL PREFERENCES
- ☐ SMOKING PERMITTED
- ☐ NON-SMOKING HOUSEHOLD
- ☐ ANY ALLERGIES/CONCERNS ABOUT HOUSEHOLD PETS

SPECIAL INTERESTS OF TRIP
- ☐ BUSINESS
- OR ☐ VISITING FRIENDS/RELATIVES
- OR ☐ SIGHTSEEING
- OR ☐ ATTEND SPECIAL EVENT_____
- OR ☐ SPORTS—SKIING, HIKING, FISHING, ETC._____
- OR ☐ ?_____

WILL YOU BE:
- ☐ DRIVING IN FAMILY CAR
- ☐ ARRIVING BY
  - ___PLANE—AIRPORT_____
  - ___BUS—STATION_____
  - ___TRAIN—STATION_____

NEED TO BE PICKED UP BY HOST AT AIRPORT OR STATION?
- ☐ YES
- ☐ NO

NIGHTLY RATE PREFERRED
RANGE FROM $_____ TO A MAXIMUM OF $_____

Write down this information <u>during</u> your call to the reservation service organization

FULL NAME OF HOST_____

HOST PHONE NUMBER   AREA CODE (   ) _____

ADDRESS_____

DIRECTIONS TO B&B HOME (It may be necessary to call host for these)

_____

_____

_____

_____

NIGHTLY RATE—$_____

IS THERE AN EXTRA CHARGE IF WE ONLY STAY ONE NIGHT? IF SO, HOW MUCH? _____

PAYMENT
- ☐ DEPOSIT TO BE PAID TO RESERVATION SERVICE ORGANIZATION
  AMOUNT $_____
  HOW PAID:
  - ☐ TRAVELERS CHECKS
  - ☐ PERSONAL CHECK
  - ☐ CREDIT CARD
    - ___AMERICAN EXPRESS
    - ___MASTER CARD
    - ___VISA

MAILING ADDRESS OR RESERVATION SERVICE ORGANIZATION

NAME_____

CITY_____ STATE_____ ZIP_____

BALANCE TO BE PAID TO HOST ON ARRIVAL BY:
- ☐ TRAVELERS CHECKS
- ☐ CASH
- ☐ PERSONAL CHECK
- ☐ CREDIT CARD
  - ___AMERICAN EXPRESS
  - ___MASTER CARD
  - ___VISA

CANCELLATION POLICY OF RESERVATION SERVICE ORGANIZATION—

_____

_____

Write down this information <u>during</u> your call to the reservation service organization

FULL NAME OF HOST_____

HOST PHONE NUMBER   AREA CODE (   ) _____

ADDRESS_____

DIRECTIONS TO B&B HOME (It may be necessary to call host for these)

_____

_____

_____

_____

NIGHTLY RATE—$_____

IS THERE AN EXTRA CHARGE IF WE ONLY STAY ONE NIGHT? IF SO, HOW MUCH? _____

PAYMENT
- ☐ DEPOSIT TO BE PAID TO RESERVATION SERVICE ORGANIZATION
  AMOUNT $_____
  HOW PAID:
  - ☐ TRAVELERS CHECKS
  - ☐ PERSONAL CHECK
  - ☐ CREDIT CARD
    - ___AMERICAN EXPRESS
    - ___MASTER CARD
    - ___VISA

MAILING ADDRESS OR RESERVATION SERVICE ORGANIZATION

NAME_____

CITY_____STATE_____ZIP_____

BALANCE TO BE PAID TO HOST ON ARRIVAL BY:
- ☐ TRAVELERS CHECKS
- ☐ CASH
- ☐ PERSONAL CHECK
- ☐ CREDIT CARD
  - ___AMERICAN EXPRESS
  - ___MASTER CARD
  - ___VISA

CANCELLATION POLICY OF RESERVATION SERVICE ORGANIZATION—

_____

B&B PHONE BOOKING FORM

Complete this section <u>before</u> you call the reservation service organization.

NUMBER OF NIGHTS YOU WILL NEED THE B&B _____
DATES OF YOUR VISIT TO THE B&B _____
MEMBERS OF YOUR PARTY _____
NO. OF   ___ADULTS
         ___CHILDREN
         ___PETS (KIND) _____

LOCATION DESIRED
- ☐ PARTICULAR AREA/NEIGHBORHOOD—NAME _____
- OR ☐ NEAR COLLEGE/UNIVERSITY—NAME _____
- OR ☐ NEAR SCENIC ATTRACTION—NAME _____
- OR ☐ NEAR COMPANY—NAME _____
- ☐ ? _____

SETTING OF HOME
- ☐ CITY
- OR ☐ SUBURBAN
- OR ☐ RURAL

TYPE OF HOME DESIRED
- ☐ MODERN
- ☐ HISTORIC/COLONIAL

BEDS PREFERRED
- ☐ TWIN BEDS
- ☐ DOUBLE
- ☐ QUEEN
- ☐ KING
- COTS FOR CHILDREN IN ROOM—NO. _____

TYPE OF BREAKFAST PREFERRED
- ☐ CONTINENTAL (JUICE/ROLL/COFFEE)
- ☐ FULL AMERICAN—IF AVAILABLE (JUICE, EGGS, BACON, TOAST, COFFEE/TEA/SANKA)

PERSONAL PREFERENCES
- ☐ SMOKING PERMITTED
- ☐ NON-SMOKING HOUSEHOLD
- ☐ ANY ALLERGIES/CONCERNS ABOUT HOUSEHOLD PETS

SPECIAL INTERESTS OF TRIP
- ☐ BUSINESS
- OR ☐ VISITING FRIENDS/RELATIVES
- OR ☐ SIGHTSEEING
- OR ☐ ATTEND SPECIAL EVENT_____
- OR ☐ SPORTS—SKIING, HIKING, FISHING, ETC._____
- OR ☐ ?_____

WILL YOU BE:
- ☐ DRIVING IN FAMILY CAR
- ☐ ARRIVING BY
  - ___PLANE—AIRPORT_____
  - ___BUS—STATION_____
  - ___TRAIN—STATION_____

NEED TO BE PICKED UP BY HOST AT AIRPORT OR STATION?
- ☐ YES
- ☐ NO

NIGHTLY RATE PREFERRED
RANGE FROM $_____ TO A MAXIMUM OF $_____

Write down this information <u>during</u> your call to the reservation service organization

FULL NAME OF HOST_____

HOST PHONE NUMBER   AREA CODE (   ) _____

ADDRESS_____

DIRECTIONS TO B&B HOME (It may be necessary to call host for these)

_____

_____

_____

_____

NIGHTLY RATE—$_____

IS THERE AN EXTRA CHARGE IF WE ONLY STAY ONE NIGHT? IF SO, HOW MUCH? _____

PAYMENT
- ☐ DEPOSIT TO BE PAID TO RESERVATION SERVICE ORGANIZATION
  AMOUNT $_____
  HOW PAID:
  - ☐ TRAVELERS CHECKS
  - ☐ PERSONAL CHECK
  - ☐ CREDIT CARD
    - ___AMERICAN EXPRESS
    - ___MASTER CARD
    - ___VISA

  MAILING ADDRESS OR RESERVATION SERVICE ORGANIZATION

  NAME_____

  CITY_____STATE_____ZIP_____

  BALANCE TO BE PAID TO HOST ON ARRIVAL BY:
  - ☐ TRAVELERS CHECKS
  - ☐ CASH
  - ☐ PERSONAL CHECK
  - ☐ CREDIT CARD
    - ___AMERICAN EXPRESS
    - ___MASTER CARD
    - ___VISA

CANCELLATION POLICY OF RESERVATION SERVICE ORGANIZATION—
_____
_____

Write down this information <u>during</u> your call to the reservation service organization

FULL NAME OF HOST_____

HOST PHONE NUMBER   AREA CODE (   ) _____

ADDRESS_____

DIRECTIONS TO B&B HOME (It may be necessary to call host for these)

_____

_____

_____

_____

NIGHTLY RATE—$_____

IS THERE AN EXTRA CHARGE IF WE ONLY STAY ONE NIGHT? IF SO, HOW MUCH? _____

PAYMENT
- ☐ DEPOSIT TO BE PAID TO RESERVATION SERVICE ORGANIZATION
  AMOUNT $_____
  HOW PAID:
  - ☐ TRAVELERS CHECKS
  - ☐ PERSONAL CHECK
  - ☐ CREDIT CARD
    - ___AMERICAN EXPRESS
    - ___MASTER CARD
    - ___VISA

  MAILING ADDRESS OR RESERVATION SERVICE ORGANIZATION

  NAME_____

  CITY_____STATE_____ZIP_____

- **BALANCE TO BE PAID TO HOST ON ARRIVAL BY:**
  - ☐ TRAVELERS CHECKS
  - ☐ CASH
  - ☐ PERSONAL CHECK
  - ☐ CREDIT CARD
    - ___AMERICAN EXPRESS
    - ___MASTER CARD
    - ___VISA

CANCELLATION POLICY OF RESERVATION SERVICE ORGANIZATION—

B&B PHONE BOOKING FORM

Complete this section <u>before</u> you call the reservation service organization.

NUMBER OF NIGHTS YOU WILL NEED THE B&B_____
DATES OF YOUR VISIT TO THE B&B_____
MEMBERS OF YOUR PARTY _____
NO. OF ___ADULTS
       ___CHILDREN
       ___PETS (KIND) _____

LOCATION DESIRED
- ☐ PARTICULAR AREA/NEIGHBORHOOD—NAME_____

OR ☐ NEAR COLLEGE/UNIVERSITY—NAME_____
OR ☐ NEAR SCENIC ATTRACTION—NAME_____
OR ☐ NEAR COMPANY—NAME_____
    ☐ ?_____

SETTING OF HOME
- ☐ CITY

OR ☐ SUBURBAN
OR ☐ RURAL

TYPE OF HOME DESIRED
- ☐ MODERN
- ☐ HISTORIC/COLONIAL

BEDS PREFERRED
- ☐ TWIN BEDS
- ☐ DOUBLE
- ☐ QUEEN
- ☐ KING

    COTS FOR CHILDREN IN ROOM—NO. _____

TYPE OF BREAKFAST PREFERRED
- ☐ CONTINENTAL (JUICE/ROLL/COFFEE)
- ☐ FULL AMERICAN—IF AVAILABLE (JUICE, EGGS, BACON, TOAST, COFFEE/TEA/SANKA)

PERSONAL PREFERENCES
- ☐ SMOKING PERMITTED
- ☐ NON-SMOKING HOUSEHOLD
- ☐ ANY ALLERGIES/CONCERNS ABOUT HOUSEHOLD PETS

SPECIAL INTERESTS OF TRIP
- ☐ BUSINESS
- OR ☐ VISITING FRIENDS/RELATIVES
- OR ☐ SIGHTSEEING
- OR ☐ ATTEND SPECIAL EVENT_____
- OR ☐ SPORTS—SKIING, HIKING, FISHING, ETC._____
- OR ☐ ?_____

WILL YOU BE:
- ☐ DRIVING IN FAMILY CAR
- ☐ ARRIVING BY
  - ___PLANE—AIRPORT_____
  - ___BUS—STATION_____
  - ___TRAIN—STATION_____

NEED TO BE PICKED UP BY HOST AT AIRPORT OR STATION?
- ☐ YES
- ☐ NO

NIGHTLY RATE PREFERRED
RANGE FROM $_____ TO A MAXIMUM OF $_____

Write down this information <u>during</u> your call to the reservation service organization

FULL NAME OF HOST_____

HOST PHONE NUMBER   AREA CODE (   ) _____

ADDRESS_____

DIRECTIONS TO B&B HOME (It may be necessary to call host for these)

_____

_____

_____

_____

NIGHTLY RATE—$_____

IS THERE AN EXTRA CHARGE IF WE ONLY STAY ONE NIGHT? IF SO, HOW MUCH? _____

PAYMENT
- [ ] DEPOSIT TO BE PAID TO RESERVATION SERVICE ORGANIZATION
  AMOUNT $_____
  HOW PAID:
  - [ ] TRAVELERS CHECKS
  - [ ] PERSONAL CHECK
  - [ ] CREDIT CARD
    - ___AMERICAN EXPRESS
    - ___MASTER CARD
    - ___VISA

MAILING ADDRESS OR RESERVATION SERVICE ORGANIZATION

NAME_____

CITY_____ STATE_____ ZIP_____

BALANCE TO BE PAID TO HOST ON ARRIVAL BY:
- [ ] TRAVELERS CHECKS
- [ ] CASH
- [ ] PERSONAL CHECK
- [ ] CREDIT CARD
  - ___AMERICAN EXPRESS
  - ___MASTER CARD
  - ___VISA

CANCELLATION POLICY OF RESERVATION SERVICE ORGANIZATION—
_____
_____

Write down this information <u>during</u> your call to the reservation service organization

FULL NAME OF HOST_____

HOST PHONE NUMBER   AREA CODE (   )_____

ADDRESS_____

DIRECTIONS TO B&B HOME (It may be necessary to call host for these)
_____
_____
_____
_____

NIGHTLY RATE—$_____

IS THERE AN EXTRA CHARGE IF WE ONLY STAY ONE NIGHT? IF SO, HOW MUCH? _____

PAYMENT
- ☐ DEPOSIT TO BE PAID TO RESERVATION SERVICE ORGANIZATION
   AMOUNT $_____
   HOW PAID:
   - ☐ TRAVELERS CHECKS
   - ☐ PERSONAL CHECK
   - ☐ CREDIT CARD
      ___AMERICAN EXPRESS
      ___MASTER CARD
      ___VISA

MAILING ADDRESS OR RESERVATION SERVICE ORGANIZATION

NAME_____

CITY_____STATE_____ZIP_____

BALANCE TO BE PAID TO HOST ON ARRIVAL BY:
- ☐ TRAVELERS CHECKS
- ☐ CASH
- ☐ PERSONAL CHECK
- ☐ CREDIT CARD
   ___AMERICAN EXPRESS
   ___MASTER CARD
   ___VISA

CANCELLATION POLICY OF RESERVATION SERVICE ORGANIZATION—

Index

Alabama, 27, 38, 195-196
Alaska, 38
American Automobile Association (AAA), 26
American Samoa, 41
Andorra, 86
Antigua, 86
Arizona, 38
Arkansas, 38
Aruba, 86
Australia, 74-75, 86
Austria, 75-76, 87

Bahamas, 87
Barbados, 87
B & B directories, 43-45
B & B guests, 65-67
B & B hosts, 93-105
B & B referral agencies, 42-45
B & B reservation service organizations
   national and international, 46-64
   by state, *see* specific state
B & Bs abroad, 68-92
Bed & Breakfast, *see* B & B
Belgium, 87
Bermuda, 76-77, 87
Bhutan, 87
Bolivia, 87
Bonaire, 87
Brazil, 87
British Virgin Islands, 87
Bulgaria, 77, 87
Business travel, 22

California, 14, 27, 38
Canada, 87, 282-284
Caribbean, 91
Cayman Islands, 87
Ceylon, 85, 87
Chile, 88

China, Republic of, 88
Colombia, 88
Colorado, 38
Connecticut, 38, 111-114
Costa Rica, 88
Curaçao, 88
Cyprus, 77-78, 88
Czechoslovakia, 78-79, 88

Delaware, 28, 38, 149
Denmark, 79, 88
Directories, 43-45
Dominican Republic, 88

Egypt, 72, 72, 79, 88
England, *see* Great Britain

Finland, 88
Florida, 38, 197-203
Foreign tourist offices, 73-86
France, 68-71, 88
French West Indies, 79-80, 88

Georgia, 17-18, 28, 38, 204-210
Germany, 80-81, 88
Ghana, 89
Great Britain, 71, 81, 87
Greece, 72, 89
Guadeloupe, 79-80
Guam, 41
Guatemala, 89
Guests, 95-97

Haiti, 89
Hawaii, 38
Hong Kong, 89
Hosts, 93-105
Hungary, 89

Idaho, 38
Illinois, 38, 173
India, 82, 89
Indiana, 28, 38
Indonesia, 89
Iowa, 28-29, 38, 183
Ireland, 82, 89, 90
Israel, 82-83, 89
Italy, 72, 89

Jamaica, 89
Japan, 73, 83, 89, 73
Jordan, 89

Kansas, 39
Kentucky, 39, 211
Kenya, 89
Korea, 90

Laos, 90
Liberia, 90
Louisiana, 16-17, 29-30, 39
Luxembourg, 90

Maine, 29, 39, 115-116
Malaysia, 90
Mariana Islands, 41
Martinique, 80
Maryland, 39, 152
Massachusetts, 17, 30, 39, 117-129
Mauritius, 90
Mexico, 90
Michigan, 39, 174-175
Middle East, 72
    see also specific country
Minnesota, 31, 39, 184
Mississippi, 39, 212-213
Missouri, 30, 39
Monaco, 90
Montana, 39, 185
Morocco, 90

Nebraska, 31, 39, 186
Netherlands, 90
Nevada, 39

New Hampshire, 39, 130
New Jersey, 40, 153
New Mexico, 31-32, 40
New York, 19, 40, 131-143
New Zealand, 72-73, 83-84, 90
Nigeria, 90
North Carolina, 32, 40, 154-155
North Dakota, 40
Norway, 82, 84, 90

Ohio, 40, 176-178
Oklahoma, 40
Oregon, 32, 40, 187-188

Pakistan, 91
Panama, 91
Pennsylvania, 18, 40, 156-162
Pensions, 72
Peru, 91
Pets, 22
Philippines, 84-85, 91
Poland, 91
Portugal, 91
Puerto Rico, 41

Referral agencies, 42-45
Reservation service organizations
    national and international, 46-64
    by state, see specific state
    working with, 21-22
Rhode Island, 32-33, 40, 144-146
Romania, 91

St. Lucia, 91
St. Maarten, 91
St. Thomas, 41
St. Vincent and the Grenadines, 91
Scandinavia, 91
Senegal, 91
Singapore, 91
South Africa, 85, 91
South Carolina, 33, 40, 163-164
South Dakota, 40, 189
Spain, 91
Sri Lanka, 85, 87

State tourist offices, 27-41
Suriname, 92
Sweden, 92
Switzerland, 92

Tanzania, 92
Tennessee, 40, 214-215
Texas, 33, 40
Thailand, 92
Tobago, 92
Togo, 92
Tourist information booths, 25-26
Tourist Offices
 foreign, 73-86
 in the U.S. and territories of, 27-41
Trinidad, 92
Turkey, 92

U.S.S.R., 92
Uruguay, 92
Utah, 41

Venezuela, 92
Vermont, 34, 41
Virginia, 34-36, 41, 165-170

Washington, 36, 41, 190-192
Washington, D.C., 150-151
West Virginia, 36-37, 41
Wisconsin, 16, 37, 41, 179-180
Wyoming, 37, 41

Yugoslavia, 85-86, 92

Zambia, 92

SCHOOLS AND COLLEGES

Adelphi, 133, 141, 142
Albertus Magnus, 113
Albion, 174
Albright, 156
Alfred, 135
Algonquin, 275
Allentown, 156
Alvernia, 156
Ambassador, 245
American College of Physicians, 157
American Graduate School of Business 243
American Graduate School of International Management, 244
American River, 252
Amherst, 129
Antioch, 178
Arizona State, 243, 244
Arizona University, 243
Armstrong State, 208, 209
Art Center College of Design, 245
Atlanta University, 205-207
Augustana, 189
Avila, 224

Babson, 117, 120
Baptist College, 164
Barret, 173
Barry, 197
Baruch, 137
Bates, 115, 116
Baylor College of Medicine, 234
Baypines VA Hospital, 201
Beaver, 157
Bellarmine, 211
Belmont, 215
Belmont Hill, 117
Bennington, 114
Bentley, 125, 126
Berkeley School of Music, 126
Berkshire, 114
Biscayne, 197

Black Hills State, 189
Boston College, 118, 120, 124-126
Boston University, 118-121, 123, 125, 126, 146
Bowdoin, 115
Bowling, 141
Brandeis, 120, 125, 126
Brewster Head, 130
Bridgewater, 127
Brigham Young, 260
Brockport, 134
Brown, 124, 146
Bryn Mawr, 157
Buckingham Nichols, 117
Bucknell, 161
Buffalo State, 140

Cabrini, 157
California Institute of Technology, 245, 258
California State, 245, 246, 249, 253, 257, 258
Calvin, 175
Cambridge, 123
Canisius, 140
Cape Code Community College, 122, 128
Cape Cod Conservatory of Music and Art, 128
Capital, 177, 178
Carleton, 277
Case Western Reserve, 176
Catholic University, 150, 151
Cazenovia, 135, 143
Cedar Crest, 156
Central Piedmont, 154
Chadron State, 186
Chattanooga, 207
Choate, 112, 113
Citadel, The, 163, 164
City College (N.Y.), 139
Claremont, 245, 258

Clarkson, 136
Cleveland State, 176
Coast Guard Academy, 111-113
Coe, 183
Colby, 115
Colby-Sawyer, 130
Colgate, 131, 135
College of Charleston, 163, 164
College of Osteopathic Medicine, 183
Colorado College, 220, 221
Colorado Mountain, 220, 221
Colorado School of Mines, 220, 221
Colorado State, 220, 221
Columbia, 137-139, 231
Columbus Tech, 178
Concordia, 178
Concord, 130
Conestoga College of Continuing Education, 278
Connecticut College, 111
Copiah-Lincoln, 213
Cornell, 131, 135
Corpus Christi State, 235
Covenant Presbyterian Seminary, 232
Cranbrook, 174
Creighton, 186
Cuyahoga, 176
C. W. Post, 141, 142
Cypress, 249

Dartmouth, 124, 130
Davenport Business College, 175
David Lipscomb, 215
Deerfield Academy, 129
Delaware Law School, 149
Del Mar, 235
Dennison, 177
De Paul, 173
Devery Institute of Technology, 205
Dickinson, 162
Dillard, 255, 227
Dominican, 226, 227
Drake, 183
Drexel, 157, 160
Dufreye Medical Center, 157

Eaglebrook Prep, 129
Eastern College, 157
Eastern Kentucky, 211
Eastern Virginia Medical School, 168
Eckard, 201
Elizabethwoen, 158
Elmira, 131
Emmanuel, 120
Emory, 205, 206

Fairhaven, 190
Fairleigh Dickinson, 153
Florida Agricultural & Mechanical, 202
Florida Atlantic, 198
Florida International, 197, 199
Florida Memorial, 197
Florida State, 202, 210
Fontbonne, 231, 232
Fordham, 137
Fort Lewis, 222
Franklin, 177
Franklin & Marshal, 158
Fuller Theological Seminary, 245
Fullerton, 249
Fullerton State, 250

Geneseo, 134
Georgetown, 150, 151
George Washington, 150, 151
Georgia State, 205
Georgia Tech, 205
Gettysburg, 162
Gorham, 115
Goucher, 152
Grand Rapids, 175
Grand Valley State, 175
Grandview, 183

Hamilton, 131, 135
Hampden Hall, 113
Hampshire, 129
Harrisburg, 158
Harvard, 117-121, 123-126, 146
Haverford, 157
Hobart, 135

Hofstra, 133, 141, 142
Holderness, 130
Hopkins, 113
Hotchkiss, 112, 114
Howard, 150, 151
Hunter, 137
Huxley, 190

Incarnate Word, 238
Indian Hills, 183
Indian Mountain Gunnery, 114
Iona, 131
Irvine, 250
Iowa State, 183
Ithaca, 131, 135

Jefferson Medical School, 157
John Carroll, 176
John Jay, 137
Johns Hopkins, 150, 152
Judson, 243
Jones, W. Alton, Cell Science Center, 136
Judson, 244

Kearney State, 186
Keene State, 130
Kendall College, 173
Kendall School of Design, 175
Kenrick Seminary, 232
Kent, 112, 114
Kenyon, 177, 178
Kings Point Marine Academy, 141
Kutztown, 156

Lafayette, 156
Lake Forest, 173
Lake Placid Center for the Arts, 136
Lakeville, 112
La Salle, 126, 157
Lebanon Valley, 158
Lehigh, 156
Lemoyne, 135, 143
Lesley, 117, 120, 121, 126

Lewiston, 115
Liberty Baptist, 167
Lincoln, 159
Logan Chiropractic, 232
Long Beach State, 250
Louisiana State, 225
Loyola (Ca.), 257, 258; (Ill.), 173; (La.), 225-227
Luther, 183
Lynchburg, 167

McGill, 283
Maine Maritime, 116
Manhattanville, 131
Maria Regina, 143
Marietta, 178
Marymont, 257, 258
Marquette, 180
Massachusetts College of Art, 120
Massachusetts Institute of Technology, 117-121, 123, 146
Medical College of Virginia, 169
Memphis State, 214
Mercersburg Academy, 162
Metro State, 221
Miami Dade, 197, 199
Michigan State, 174
Milford Academy, 113
Millersville, 158
Millsaps, 212
Mississippi College, 212
Mississippi Southern, 225
Mississippi State, 212
Miss Porter's Farmington prep school, 112
MIT, 117-121, 123, 146
Montana State, 185
Moore College of Art, 160
Moravian, 156
Mt. Holyoke, 129
Mt. Vernon, 165
Muckingum, 178
Muhlenberg, 156
Murray State, 211

Napa, 256, 259
Naropa Institute, 219
National College of Education, 173
Naval War College, 145
Nazareth, 134
New England College, 116
New England Conservatory, 120
New Hampton, 130
New Orleans Baptist Seminary, 227
New School, The, 139
New York State Alpine Training Center, 136
New York University, 137-139
Niagara, 140
Norfolk, Naval Base & Air Station, 168
North Country, 136
Northeastern, 118, 120, 126
Northern Arizona, 243, 244
Northwestern, 173, 183
Northwood, 136
Nova, 199

Oakland, 174
Occidental, 245, 257, 258
Oglethorpe, 205
Ohio Dominican, 178
Ohio State, 177, 178
Ohio University, 178
Ohio Wesleyan, 178
Old Dominion, 168
Onondaga, 143
Orange Coast, 249
Oregon Health Sciences, 188
Orme, 243, 244
Otterbein, 177, 178
Our Lady of the Lake, 236, 238

Pace, 131, 138
Pacific Union, 256, 259
Pasadena City, 245, 258
Pasadena College of Chiropractic, 245
Paul Smith's, 136
Penn State, 158-162

Pepperdine, 257
Perkiomen, 156
Philadelphia Textile, 157
Phillips Academy in Andover, 124
Phoenix Country Day, 244
Pickens Tech, 207
Pieree, 258
Pine Manor, 120
Plymouth State, 130
Pomfret, 112
Portland (Me.), 115
Portland State (Ore.), 188
Portsmouth Abbey, 144, 145
Presbyterian Hospital, 157
Princeton, 153

Queens (N.C.), 154
Queens (Nova Scotia), 273

Randolph Macon, 167, 169
Rensselaer Polytechnic Institute, 131
Rhode Island School of Design, 124
Rice, 234, 236
Rochester Institute of Technology, 134, 135
Roger Williams, 144
Rollins, 203
Rosemary Hall, 112
Rosemont, 157
Royal Military, 275
Russell Sage, 131
Rutgers, 153
Ryerson Polytech, 282

Sacramento City, 252
St. Catherine's, 169
St. Christopher's, 169
St. George's, 144, 145
St. John Fisher, 134
St. John's, 151, 152
St. Josephs, 133, 157
St. Lawrence, 275, 136
St. Louis, 232

St. Mary's Law School, 238
St. Michael's, 145
St. Paul's, 277, 130
St. Petersburg, 200,201
Salisbury, 114
Salve Regina, 144, 145
San Diego State, 250, 251
Santa Rosa, 255
Sarah Lawrence, 131
Savannah College of Art & Design, 208, 209
Savannah State, 208, 209
Sawyer College of Business, 245
Scripps Clinic, 251
Seattle, 191
Seattle Pacific, 191
Shippensburg, 162
Simmons, 118-120, 125
Simon's Rock at Bard, 114
Simpson, 183
Sioux Falls, 189
Sir Wilfred Laurier, 281
Skidmore, 131
Smith, 129
Sonoma State, 255, 256
Southampton, 132, 133, 141
South Dakota School of Mines, 189
South Dakota State, 189
Southern College of Optometry, 214
Southern Connecticut State, 113
Southern Methodist, 236
Southern University, 225
South Florida, 200
Southwestern (Tenn.), 214
Southwestern Utah State, 260
Southwest Texas State, 239
Spalding, 211
Starkville, 212
Stetson Law School, 201
Suffolk, 125
SUNY (Buffalo), 140; (New Paltz), 131; (Oneonta), 135; (Pittsburgh), 136; (Potsdam), 136; (Stony Brook), 141, 142
Swarthmore, 157

Sweet Briar, 167
Syracuse, 135, 143

Tampa, 201
TCU Fort Worth, 236
Temple, 157, 160
Texas University, 236
Tilton Academy, 130
Trinity, 112, 150, 236, 238
Trudeau Institute, 136
Tufts, 118-120
Tulane, 225-227

Union Theological Seminary, 169
U.S. Air Force Academy, 220
U.S. Army War College, 162
U.S. Coast Guard Academy, 146
U.S. Medical Center, 254
U.S. Naval Academy, 151, 152
U.S. Olympic Training Center, 136
Universite de Montreal, 283
University of Alabama, 195
University of Alaska (Anchorage), 263, 264; (Fairbanks), 265
University of Arizona, 243, 244
University of Arkansas, 230
University of British Columbia, 191
University of Buffalo, 135, 140
University of California (Irvine), 246, 249; (Los Angeles), 245, 246, 250, 257, 258; (San Diego), 246, 250, 258; (Santa Barbara), 246, 258
University of Central Florida, 203
University of Chicago, 173
University of Cincinnati, 178
University of Colorado, 219, 220
University of Dayton, 178
University of Delaware, 149, 159
University of Denver, 220, 221
University of District of Columbia, 151
University of Florida, 201
University of Georgia, 204
University of Hawaii, 268

University of Houston, 234, 236
University of Illinois, 173
University of Iowa, 183
University of Kansas, 224
University of Louisville, 211
University of Maine, 116
University of Maryland, 152
University of Massachusetts, 129
University of Miami, 197, 199
University of Michigan, 174
University of Mississippi, 212, 225
University of Missouri, 224, 232
University of Missouri/Kansas City Extension Center, 229
University of Nebraska (Omaha), 186; (Lincoln), 186
University of New Hampshire, 146
University of New Mexico, 225
University of New Orleans, 226, 227
University of North Carolina, 154, 155
University of Northern Colorado, 221
University of Northern Iowa, 183
University of Oregon, 188
University of Ottawa, 277
University of Pennsylvania, 157, 160
University of Portland, 188
University of Puget Sound, 191
University of Rhode Island, 146
University of Richmond, 169
University of Rochester, 134
University of San Luis Obispo, 247
University of Santa Barbara, 247
University of South Alabama, 196
University of South Dakota, 189
University of Southern California, 245, 246, 253, 257, 258
University of Southern Colorado, 221
University of Southern Maine, 115
University of Southern Mississippi, 213
University of Tampa, 200
University of Tennessee, 214
University of Texas, 230, 238, 239
University of Toronto, 282
University of Utah, 260
University of Victoria, 272

University of Virginia, 166
University of Washington, 191, 192
University of Waterloo, 281
University of Western Ontario, 276, 281
University of Wisconsin, 180
Utah State, 260

Valdosta, 210
Valley, 258
Vanderbilt, 215
Vassar, 131
Verde Valley, 244
Village Oasis, 244
Villanova, 157
Virginia Commonwealth, 169
Virginia Episcopal, 167

Wallingford, 112
W. Alton Jones Cell Science Center, 136
Washington College (Md.), 152
Washington University (Mo.), 231, 232
Waterville, 115
Wayne State, 174
Webster, 231, 232
Wellesley, 118, 120
Wesleyan, 112, 113
Wesleyan, (Ne.), 186
Westbrook, 116
West Chester, 149, 159
Westchester Community College, 131
Western Kentucky, 211
Western State College of Law, 249
Western Washington, 190
Whatcom, 190
Wheaton, 173
Wheelock, 119
Whittier, 257
Widener, 159
William and Mary, 170
William Jewell, 224
Williams, 114
William Smith, 135

Wills Eye Hospital, 157
Wilmington, 178
Wilson, 162
Wittenberg, 178
Woods Hole Oceanographic Institute, 128
Wright State, 178

Xavier, 225

Yale, 112, 113, 124, 146
York (Canada), 280
York (Pa.), 162

MAJOR BUSINESSES

Abbott Labs, 173
AccuRay, 178
Aetna, 112, 113
Air Products, 156
Alabama Drydock & Shipbuilding, 196
Alabama State Docks, 196
Alcan, 275
Allied Chemical, 143
Allis-Chalmers (Mo.), 229; (Wis.), 180
Alyeska Oil Pipeline Co., 263
Amana Refrigeration, 183
American Express (Ariz.), 243; (Utah), 260
American Hospital, 173
AMF Head Division, 219
Anaheim Convention Center, 249
Anaheim Stadium, 249
Ancillary Software, 144
Anheuser-Busch (Mo.), 231, 232; (Va.), 170
Arco Refinery, 190
Armour Dial, 244
Armstrong (Iowa), 183; (Miss.), 213; (Pa.), 158
Arthur D. Little, 120, 121
AT&T (Ga.), 205; (Mo.), 232
AVCO Aerospace, 215
Avery Label, 245
Avis Car Rental, 141
Avon (Del.), 149; (Ill.), 173

Babcock Wilcox, 167
Badische, 170
Baldwin Piano, 178
Ball Corp., 219
Ball Metal, 170
Bally Block, 156
Bally Case & Cooler, 156
Bank Americard, 245
Bankers Life Insurance, 183
Bay Ship, 179
BD Medical Supplies, 186

Bechtel, 254
Beckman Instruments (Ca.), 246; 249; (Pa.), 160
Beech Aircraft, 219
Bell Aero systems, 140
Bell Telephone, 160
Beneficial Finance, 149
Best Western Motels, 244
Bethlehem Steel, 156, 158
Bic Pen, 113
Black & Decker, 152
Black River Cheese Co., 279
Bloomingdale's, 137
Blue Cross/Blue Shield (Mass.), 121
Boeing, 191, 192
Borden's Mead Paper, 178
Boyertown Casket, 156
Brookhaven Laboratories, 133, 141, 142
Brown Printing East, 156
Brown Williamson, 211
Bucksport Bath Iron Works, 115
Bumble Bee Seafoods, 190
Bureau of Standards, 219
Burger King, 199
Burlington Mills, 212
Burroughs (Mich.), 174; (Pa.), 159
Butterworth Hospital, 175

Cable Network News, 205
Camp Peary, 170
Canada Fab, 286
Carborundum, 140
Carpenter Technology, 156
Carrier, 135, 143
C-Cor Electronics, 161
Celanese (N.C.), 154; (Tex.), 235
Celestial Seasonings, 219
Chase Manhattan Bank (Del.), 149
Cheatham Annex, 170
Chrysler (Mich.), 174; (N.Y.), 135
Cigna Insurance (Del.), 149; (Pa.), 160

308 • INDEX

Cincinnati Milling, 178
Circle K, 244
Citibank (S.D.), 189
Cleveland Clinic Foundation, 176
Coastal States Refinery, 235
Coca-Cola, 205
Commonwealth Electric, 127
Cooper Bessemer, 280
Coopers and Lybrand (Va.), 169
Corning Glass (N.Y.), 134; (Pa.), 161
Cowtown, 236
Crouse & Hinds, 135, 143
Crown Petroleum, 152
Crucible Steel, 135
Cudahy, 244
Curity, 204

Dale Electronics, 186
Davis Water and Waste, 210
De Gussa, 196
Delco-Remy (Miss.), 212; (Ohio), 178
Del Webb Recreational Properties, 244
Diamond Almond Factory, 252
Diesel, 276
Digital (Col.), 220; (Mass.), 117-121, 123; (N.C.), 154
Dixie Crystals Sugar, 208, 209
Doubleday, 141
Dover Air Force Base, 149
Drug Plastics, 156
DuPont (Del.), 149; (Ga.), 204; (Tenn.), 215; (Tex.), 235
DuPont of Canada, 275

Eastern Airlines, 199
Eastman Kodak (Col.), 221; (N.Y.), 134, 135
Electric Boat, 111
Elmendorf Air Base, 263
Emerson Electric, 232
Eros, 189
Ethyl, 169
Exxon, 235

Fairchild, 162
Federal Express, 214
Figgic International, 169
First Colony Life, 167
Fisher Bearings, 280
Fleet, C. B., 167
Flowers Industries, 210
Fluor, 246, 249-251
Ford Glass Plant, 215
Ford Motors (Ca.), 249; (Kan.), 224; (Mich.), 174; (Mo.), 232
Fort Eustis, 170
Fort Ritchie, 162
Fowler Products, 204
Franklin Mint, 149
Frick, 162

Galleria, The, 234
General Dynamics, 232, 236
General Electric (Ariz.), 243; (Conn.), 112; (Fla.), 200; (Mass.), 120; (Miss.), 212; (N.Y.), 131, 135, 137, 143; (Ohio), 176; (Pa.), 160; (Tenn.), 215; (Va.), 167
General Electric Space Labs (Pa.), 157
General Foods, 131
General Motors (Canada), 276; (Kan.), 224; (Mich.), 174; (Miss.), 212; (Mo.), 232
General Time, 204
Genesco, 215
Genrad, 117, 120
Georgia-Pacific, 205
Gilbert Commonwealth, 156
Gillette, 120, 121, 125
Gimbels, 137
Glenmore Distilleries, 211
Gold Mines, 189
Goodyear Tire, 186
Gore, W. L., Association, 149
Great Dane Trailers, 208
Greyhound, 244
Grove Manufacturing, 162
Grumman, 133

GTE, 120, 125
Gulf Stream, 208

Halliday, 127
Hallmark, 224
Hanover Foods, 162
Harbert International, 195
Harley-Davidson, 180
Hartford, 112
Hazeltines, 133
Hercules, 149
Hershey Foods, 158
Hewlett-Packard (Ca.), 255; (Col.), 220; (Del.), 149; (Ga.), 205; (Mass), 123; (Pa.), 159
Honeywell (Fla.), 200; (Mass.), 125
Hooker, 140
Hospital Corp. of America, 215
Houston Port City and Oil City, 236
Howmet, 158
HRB Singer, 161
Hughes Aircraft, 246, 249, 250
Hunt Foods, 246
Huntington-Melville Industrial Park, 133
Hunt-Wesson, 249
Hy-Line International, 183

IBM (Ariz.), 243; (Ca.), 252; (Col.), 219-221; (Conn.), 112; (Ga.), 205; (Mass.), 120, 121; (Mich.), 174; (N.C.), 154; (N.Y.), 131, 141; (Tex.), 236, 239
ICI, 149
Intalco Aluminum, 190
Intel, 188
Interco, 232
Interface, 126
International Circuit Technology, 167
International Paper (Ala.), 196; (Miss.), 213
Itek, 120

Jacobs Engineering, 245
James River Corp. of Virginia, 169
Jantzen, 188
Jet Propulsion Lab, 245
Jim Walters, 200
John Deere, 183
John Hancock, 121, 125
Johns-Manville, 213

Kaibab Industries, 244
Kelloggs, 158
Kimberly-Clark, 249
Knoll International, 156
Knouse, 162
Kodak, *see* Eastman Kodak
Koss, 180
Kraft, 173

Lahey Clinic, 126
Lancaster Colony, 178
Landis-Teledyne Machine, 162
Landis Tool, 162
Langley Air Force Base, 170
Leterkenny Army Depot, 162
Lever Brothers (Ohio), 178
Lever House (N.Y.), 137
Levi Strauss (Ca.), 254; (Ga.), 207
Liebert, 178
Lincoln Electric, 176
Lindsay Manufacturing, 186
Lockheed, 212, 239
Lynchburg Foundry, 167

McDonnell Douglas (Ca.), 250; (Mo.), 231, 232
Mack Truck, 156, 162
Macy's, 137
Martin Marietta (Col.), 221; (Fla.), 203; (Md.), 152; (Pa.), 161
Masonite, 212
Massachusetts Eye and Ear Hospital, 118
Massachusetts General Hospital, 118, 126

Masterlock, 180
Maytag, 183
Meredith/Burda, 167
Meredith Publishing, 183
Micro Electronic Research, 239
Miller Brewery, 180
Millstone Nuclear Plant base, 111
Mobil Oil Refinery, 190
Monsanto (Mass.), 120; (Mo.), 231,232
Morrison, 196
Motorola (Ariz.), 243; (Col.), 221; (Ill.), 173; (Tex.), 239
Musselman Foods, 162

NASA, 170
Natchez Port, 213
National Center for Atmospheric Research, 219
National Institute of Health, 151
National Services Industries, 205
Naval Air Station (Tex.), 235
Naval Training Center at Orlando, 203
Naval Underwater Systems Center, 145
Naval Weapons Station, 170
NBI, 219
NCR, 157
Neodata, 219
Nestlés, 131
Newsday Publishers, 141
Nissan, 215
NLT, 215
NORAD, 220
Northern Telecom, 215
Northrop, 249
Northwest Mutual, 180
NPPD Power, 186

Oasis, 178
Ocean Spray, 127
Omark Industries, 188
Optical Coating, 255
Oregon Steel Mills, 188
Oster, 180
Owens-Corning, 212

Pabst Brewery, 180
Pacific Telephone, 245
Palmer Johnson, 179
Paradyne, 200
Parsons, 245
Peat, Marwick, Mitchell (Va.), 169
Pella Windows, 183
Pendleton Woolen Mills, 188
Pepsico, 131
Perdue, 152
Peterson Builders, 179
Pet Foods, 162
Pfizer (Conn.), 111
Philadelphia Navy Yard, 149
Philco, 249
Philip Morris, 169
Pilgrim Nuclear Plant, 127
Pillsbury, 156
Pioneer Hibred International, 183
Plough, 214
Polaroid, 120, 121, 123, 125
Port of Anchorage, 263
Prime Computer, 118, 121
Proctor & Gamble, 178
Prudential, 157

Quaker Oats, 183
Quality Micro Systems, 196

Ralston, 231
Ramada Inns, 244
RAX, 178
Raytheon (Mass.), 117, 118, 121; (R.I.), 145
RCA, 121
Regency Printers, 162
Rexnord, 180
Reynolds Aluminum (Ore.), 188; (Tex.), 235
Reynolds Metals, 169
Robins, A. H., 169
Rockwell, (Ca.), 246, 249; (Col.), 219; (Iowa), 183; (Ohio), 178; (Pa.), 156

Rohm & Haas, 160
Rotary International, 173
Rouse & Company, 152
Rust Engineering, 195

Sacramento Tomato Co., 252
St. Mary's Hospital, 175
St. Regis Paper, 115
Sauer, C. T., 169
Savannah Foods, 208
Schlitz Brewery, 214
Scientific Atlanta, 205
Scott Paper, 196
Searle, G. D., 173
Sears (Ill.), 173; (Canada), 273
Service Merchandise, 215
Sharp Electronics, 214
Silicon Valley, 248, 254
Smith Kline, 160
Snyder Industry, 186
Sohio, 176
Solar, 253
Space Command, 220
Sperry (Ariz.), 243; (Neb.), 186
Sperry Flight Systems, 244
Sperry-Rand (Fla.), 200
Sperry Univac, 160
State Farm Insurance, 255
Stauffers (Ala.), 196; (N.Y.), 131
Stone & Webster, 120
Storage Tech, 219
Sunnyland Meat Packing, 210
Sun Recording Studio, 214
Sylvania (Mass.), 125; (N.Y.), 135

Tab Books, 162
Tennessee Chemical, 207
Teradyne, 120
Texaco (N.Y.), 131; (Tex.), 235
Texas Instruments, 234, 236, 239
3M (Canada), 276; (Tex.), 239

Toledo Scale, 178
Transcom, 145
Travelers, 112
TRW (Ga.), 210; (Ohio), 176, 178

Underwater Sound Lab, 111
Union Camp, 208, 209
Union Carbide (Ala.), 196; (N.Y.), 140
Union-Pacific Railroad, 186
U.S. Fidelity & Guaranty, 152
U.S. Government agencies, 151
U.S. Homes, 200
U.S. Naval Academy, 151
Universal Leaf Tobacco, 169
University Hospital (Canada), 274
University Hospitals of Cleveland, 176
Upstate Medical Center, 143
Usingers, 180

Valley Lab, 219
Vermeer, 183
Vernon, 183
Virginia Electric and Power, 169
Vulcan Materials, 195

Wachenhut, 199
Wang (Conn.), 117; (Mass.), 121, 126
Wendy's, 178
Western Electric (Pa.), 156; (Va.), 169
Westinghouse, 204
Westinghouse Oceanic, 151
Westminster-Canterbury, 167
Weyerhauser, 212
White Stag, 188
Winnebago, 183
Woods, T. B., 162
World Airways, 152
Worthington Industries, 178

Xerox (Col.), 221; (N.Y.), 134, 135; (Ohio), 178

312 • INDEX

ATTRACTIONS

Acadia National Park, 115
Acadian country, 227
Adirondack Museum, 136
Adirondack State Park, 136
Air Force Academy, 221
Alamo, The, 238
Alaskaland, 265
Alaska Oil Pipeline, 263
Alaska Railroad, 263
Alaska Salmon Bake, 265
Allenberry Playhouse, 162
"Alt Friedrichsburg," 237, 239
Amagansett Marine Museum, 132
Amana Colonies, 183
American Royal, 224
American Tennis Classic, 223
Americas Cup Races, 144
Amish Country, 157, 160
Amish Homestead, 158
Angeles National Forest, 245
Annapolis Naval Station, 152
Antique Automobile Club of America, 158
Antique Car Museum, 156
Appalachian Trail, 114, 162, 166, 207
Appomattox National Park, 167
April Historic Garden Week, 166
April Rose Festival, 210
Aransas Wildlife Refuge, 235
Arch (St. Louis), 232
Arlington Cemetery, 151
Armstrong State Park, 255
Asheville/Biltmore Home, 154
Ash Lawn (James Madison's home), 166
Asia Pacific Museum, 245
Astrodome, 234
Audubon Center, 180
Audubon Highland Sanctuary, 117, 128
Audubon Park and Zoo, 225, 226
Austin State Capitol, 239

Avon Valley Hiking Trail, 281
Azalea Trails, 236

Bahai Temple, 173
Bahia Honda State Park, 198
Baltimore Inner Harbor, 152
Bar Harbor, 115
Baseball Hall of Fame, 131
Beacon Hill, 118, 120
Beacon Hill Park, 272
Beale Street, 214
Belgian Orchestral Organ, 162
Belle Carol Riverboat, 215
Belle Mead mansion, 215
Belleville Amish Market, 161
Bellevue House National Historic Site, 275
Bellingrath Gardens, 196
Bell Museum, 273
Bertrand Steamboat, 186
Bethlehem (Pa.), 156
Bethpage Recreation Village, 142
Betsy Ross House, 160
"Bird City," 279
Black Hills, 189
Blandwood Estate, 155
Blue Knob Ski Resort, 161
Blue Ridge Mountains, 161
Blue Ridge Parkway, 166, 167
Boalsburg (Pa.), 161
Bob Marshall Wilderness Area, 185
Bodego Bay, 255
Bonneville Dam Fish Hatchery, 188
Boscobel Mansion, 131
Boston attractions, 117-121, 124-126
Boston Ballet, 120
Boston Pops, 120, 125
Boston Symphony, 120, 125
Botanical Gardens (Canada), 283
Botanical Gardens (Ga.), 204
Botanical Gardens (Wis.), 180
Boys Town, 186

INDEX • 313

Brandywine Battlefield, 159
Brandywine River Museum, 149, 157, 159
Bras D'Or lakes, 274
Breckenridge Park, 238
British Art Museum, 113, 146
Broadmoor Zoo, 221
Broadway theaters, 137-139
Bruce Trail, 278
Bryant, William Cullen, Homestead, 129
Bryce National Park, 260
Buchanan, James, birthplace, 162
Bureau of Printing and Engraving, 151
Burt Reynolds Dinner Theater, 198, 199
Busch Gardens (Fla.), 200, 201
Busch Gardens (Va.), 169, 170
Busch Stadium, 232
Butchart Gardens, 191, 272

Cabot Trail, 274
Cajun bayou tours, 227
Caledonia State Park, 161
Calgary Exhibition, 271
Calgary Stampede, 271
Calgary Zoo, 271
Calistoga hot springs, 256, 259
Camp Topridge, 136
Canada's Wonderland, 282
Canadian National Exhibition, 282
Canal Museum, 156
Cape Cod, 122, 124, 126, 128
Cape Kennedy, 203
Cape Playhouse, 128
Capitol Building, 150, 151
Caramoor Music Festival, 131
Car Collectors' Hall of Fame, 215
Carpenter's Hall, 160
Carthage Home, 236
Central City Opera House, 221
Central Park, 137, 138
Charleston attractions, 163-164
Charlie Russell Museum, 185
Chateau Frontenac, 284

Chattahoochie National Forest, 207
Cheekwood Botanical Gardens & Fine Arts Center, 215
Chesapeake Bay, 152, 168
Chesterfield Gorge, 129
Chevalier House, 284
Children's Museum, 151
Chinatown (Boston), 120
Chinatown (San Francisco), 254
Chocolate World, 158
Christian Science Church, 120
Chrysler Museum, 168
Cincinnati Opera, 178
Cincinnati Zoo, 178
Circus World, 200
Citadel and Governor's Promenade, 284
Civil War monuments, 205
Clemens Amphitheater, 231
Cleveland Museum of Art, 176
Cleveland Natural History Museum, 176
Cleveland Zoo, 176
Cliff Walk, 145
CN Tower, 282
Cockaigne, 135
Coconut Grove Village, 199
Cohutta Wilderness, 207
Cold Spring antiquing, 131
Columbus Pilgrimage, 212
Commonwealth Winery, 127
Concord, 118, 123, 126
Cooper-Hewitt Mansion, 137
Coors International Bicycle Race, 219
Coral Castle, 197
Corning Glass, 131, 135
Corpus Christi Art Museum, 235
Country Music Hall of Fame and Museum, 215
Cowan's Gap State Park, 162
Craigdarroch Castle, 272
Cranberry World, 127
Cranbrook Art Museum, 174
Crawford Auto Museum, 176
Crocker Art Museum, 252
Croton Clearwater Revival, 131

Crown Center, 224
Cumberland National Seashore, 208
Cyclorama, 204, 205
Cypress Gardens, 200

Dali Museum, 201
Dania Jai-Alai, 199
Danish Museum, 183
DAR State Park, 129
Dauphin Islands, 196
Davenport House, 208
"Days of '47" Rodeo, 260
Deerfield (Mass.), 129
Delaware Natural History Museum, 159
Del Coronado Hotel, 253
Del Mar Racetrack, 251
Denver Art Museum, 221
Denver Zoo, 221
De Sota Bend Wildlife Refuge, 186
Detroit Zoo, 174
Devonian Gardens, 271
Dillard Mill, 231
Discovery Place, 154
Disneyland, 248-251, 253, 258
Disney World, 200, 201, 203
Dodger Stadium, 245, 258
Dorney Park Velodrome and Art Museum, 156
Dufferin Terrace, 284
Durango Silverton Narrow-Gauge Railroad, 222
Dutch Wonderland, 158

Eastman House of Photography, 134
Eaton Centre, 282
Edaville Railroad, 127
Edgar Allan Poe Museum, 169
Edmonton Art Gallery, 271
Edmonton Wildlife Park, 271
Eisenhower, Mamie, birthplace, 183
Emerson Ralph Waldo, home, 123
Empress Hotel, 191
Enchanted Rock National Pack, 237
Epcot, 200

Everglades National Park, 199
Everson Museum, 143

Fairhope Village, 196
Fairmount Park, 160
Falcon-Braves Stadium, 204
Fall foliage, 116, 124
Falmouth Playhouse, 128
Faneuil Hall Marketplace, 118, 120
Farmers' Market, 195, 258
Fatima Shrine, 140
Faulkner, William, home, 212
Fenway Park, 119
Fine Arts Museum, 125
Finger Lakes, 135, 143
Fire Island, 142
Fishermen's Wharf, 254
Fisher Theater, 174
Flagler Museum, 199
Flipper's Sea School, 198
Florida White House, 198
Foliage tours, 116, 124
Forest Park Zoo, 232
Fort Atkinson Museum, 186
Fort Conde, 196
Fort Museum Artillery Park, 284
Fort Niagara, 140
Fortress Louisborg, 274
Fort Ross Russian settlement, 255
Fort Vancouver, 187
Fox Theater, 232
Franklin Institute, 157
Franklin Museum, 160
Fredericksburg, 239
Freedom Trail, 118, 120, 126
French Creek State Park, 156
French Quarter, 214, 225-227
Friedericksburg, 237, 239

Galena, 173
Galveston Bay, 236
Gamble House, 245
Game Farm and Zoo, 142
Garden of the Gods, 221
Gardner Museum, 119, 120

INDEX • 315

Genessee Country Museum, 134
Gerald R. Ford Museum, 175
German Village, 177
Gettysburg, 161
Glacier National Park, 185
Glencoe Botanic Garden, 173
Glencove Historic Hotel, 191
Governor Curtin Mansion Village, 161
Graceland, 214
Grady, Taylor, home, 204
Grand Avenue Mall, 180
Grand Canyon, 243, 244
Grand Prix racing, 174
Grand Theater, 276
Great River Road attractions, 231
Greek Theater, 258
Greenfield Village, 174
Green Hill Center for North Carolina Art, 155
Green Lake State Park, 143
Greensboro Historical Museum, 155
Greenwich Village, 137
Grey, Zane, home, 243
Griffith Park Observatory, 258
Guild Hall Art Exhibits, 141
Guild Hall Summer Theater, 132
Gulf Coast, 196, 200, 202, 227
Gulf of Mexico, 230, 236
Guthrie Theater, 184

Habitat, 117
Hagley Museum, 149, 157
Halsey Homestead, 141
Harbor Whaling Museum, 142
Hargreaves Vineyards, 142
Harness classic 178
Hawthorne's home, 123
Hearst Castle, 247
Heavy Water Plant, 272
Hemingway, Ernest, home, 197-199
Henry, Patrick home, 167
Henry Doorly Zoo, 186
Henry Ford Museum, 174
Heritage Hill District, 175
Heritage Plantation, 128

Herman Park, 234
Hermitage and Tulip Grove, 215
Hershey Chocolate Factory, 156
Hershey Museum of American Life, 158
Hershey Park, 158
Hershey Rose Gardens, 158
Hialeah Race Track, 199
High Museum, 206
Hilton Head, 209
Holland Tulip Festival, 175
Holly Springs Pilgrimage, 212
Hollywood, 250, 258
Hollywood Bowl, 258
Hollywood Park race track, 258
Home Sweet Home Museum, 141
Hoover, Herbert, birthplace, 183
Hopewell Village, 156
Hopi village, 244
Hot Sulphur Springs, 221
House of Cash, 215
Howe Caverns, 131, 135
Huntington Library & Gardens, 245
Hutterite Colony, 189
Hyde Park mansion, 131

Ice caves, 131
Ile D'Orleans, 284
Independence Hall, 157, 160
Indian Caverns, 161
Indian Market, 233
Indian Monuments, 243
Indian reservations and ancient ruins, 260
Iowa Great Lakes, 183
Iowa State Fair, 183
Irish Hills, 174
Irvine Meadows, 249

Jack London House and Museum, 255
Jackson Laboratory, 115
Jackson Square Artists, 226
Jackson State Capitol, 212
Jacob's Pillow Dance Festival, 114, 129
Jai Alai, 197

James River Plantations, 169
Jamestown, 170
Japanese Art Museum, 235
Japanese Botanical Gardens, 236
Jekyll Island, 208, 209
Jimmy Rodgers Festival, 212
John Drew Theater, 141
John F. Kennedy Center for the Performing Arts, 151
John F. Kennedy Library, 120
John Pennekamp State Park, 198, 199
Jones Beach, 142
Jones Memorial Library, 167
Junior Miss Pageant, 196

Kansas City Zoo, 224, 229
Kenai Penn, 264
Kennedy Center for the Performing Arts, 151
Kennedy Library, 120
Key West, 198
Kingdom of Dancing Stallions, 249
King Ranch, 235
Kings Dominion, 169
Kings Island, 178
Kingston Harbor sailing events, 275
Kissing Bridge, 135
Kitt Observatory, 244
Kleinhans Music Hall (Buffalo), 140
Klondike Jet Boats, 271
Knott's Berry Farm, 249, 250, 258
Kutztown Folk Festival, 156

Laclede's Landing, 232
Laguna Beach Arts Festival, 51
Lake Blue Ridge, 207
Lake Burton, 204
Lake Geneva, 173
Lake Havasu, 243
Lake Huron beaches, 281
Lake Michigan, 173, 175, 180
Lake Ontario, 134
Lake Powell, 243
Lake Sunapee, 130
Lake Winnipesaukee, 130

Laura Ingalls Wilder Pageant, 189
Lemon Dam, 222
Letchworth State Park, 134, 143
Lewiston Art Park, 140
Lexington, 118, 123, 126
Lexington Bluegrass, 211
Liberty Bell, 160
Libertyland, 214
Library of Congress, 150
Lime Rock car racing, 114
Lincoln Center, 137
Lion Country Safari, 248, 250
Little Brown Jug, 178
Living History Farms, 183
Lobster festivals, 116
Long Key State Park, 198
Longvue Gardens, 227
Long Wharf Theater, 113
Longwood Gardens, 149, 157, 159
Los Angeles Art Museum, 258
Los Angeles County Arboretum, 245
Los Angeles Zoo, 245
Lowell Observatory, 243, 244
Lyndhurst Castle, 131
Lyndon B. Johnson State and National Historic Park, 237, 239

McArthur Memorial, 168
Macaulay House, 279
McCormick Place, 173
MacLachlan Woodworking Museum, 275
Madison, James, home, 166
Magazine Street antique shops, 227
Mammoth Cave, 211
Mardi Gras, 196
Marietta River Festival, 178
Marineland, 250
Marine Museum, 275
Mark Twain National Forest, 231
Marshall, John, house, 169
Marshall Homes Tour, 174
Martha's Vineyard cruise, 128
Martin Luther King Memorial Site, 206
Mayflower Site, 127, 146

Mayo Clinic, 184
Meadow Brook Hall, 174
Melody Tent, 128
Mennonite country, 157
Merrimack Valley, 130
Mesa Verde National Park, 221, 222
Mesquakie Indian area, 183
Metro Toronto Zoo, 280
Metro Zoo, 197
Mexico missions, 250
Miami Seaquarium, 197
Michigan Space Center, 174
Military Shrine & Museum (28th Division), 161
Miller Outdoor Theater, 234
Milwaukee Zoo, 180
Miner's Museum, 274
Mining Valley at Alaskaland, 265
Minneapolis Art Institute, 184
Mint Museum, 154
Minuteman National Historic Park, 146
Missions of California, 248
Mission Trail, 238
Mississippi Gulf Coast, 212
Mississippi River, 226
Missouri River fishing, 189
Misty Fjords National Monument, 267
Mobile Bay, 196
Mobile Greyhound Park, 196
Molly Brown House, 221
Monkey Jungle, 197, 199
Montauk Hither Hills State Park, 141
Montauk Lighthouse, 132, 142
Monticello, 166
Montmorency Falls, 284
Monument Valley, 244
Mormon Temple Square, 260
Moscone Convention Center, 254
Mound Builders' Sites, 178
Mountain Music Shows, 228
Mt. Bachelor skiing, 188
Mt. Baker Ski Resort, 190
Mt. Hood National Forest, 188
Mt. McKinley, 264
Mt. Rainier National Park, 191

Mt. Royal Park, 283
Mt. Rushmore, 189
Mt. St. Helens, 187, 191
Mt. Vernon, 151, 165
Movieland Wax Museum, 249
Mud Island, 214
Muirfield Golf Course, 178
Muny Outdoor Opera Theater, 232
Murcoot Park, 131
Murney Tower, 275
Museum of Fine Arts, 119, 120, 283
Museum of Science, 125
Museum of the Confederacy, 169
Museum Row, 137
Mystic Seaport and Aquarium, 111-113, 124, 146

Nantucket, 124, 128
NASA Space Center, 234
Natchez Bluffs, 213
Natchez State Park, 213
Natchez Under the Hill, 213
National Archives, 151
National buildings, 150-151
National Bison Range, 185
National Civil War Park, 212
National Historic Preservation, 211
National parks, *see* specific park
National Zoo, 151
Nature Museum, 154
Naval War College, 144
Navajo village, 244
NBC Studios, 245, 258
N.E. Aquarium, 120
Nelson Art Gallery, 224
Nemours, 149
Newfoundland Ferry, 274
New Haven Coliseum, 113
New Jersey attractions, 153
New Orleans Museum of Art, 226
Newport mansions, 124, 145, 146
New York Academy of Sciences, 137
New York city, 137-139
Niagara Falls, 135, 140
Norfolk Naval Base, 168

North Carolina Zoological Park, 155
North Cascades National Park, 190
Northern States Nuclear Power Plant, 184
North Pole, The (Santa's home), 136
Norton Simon Museum, 245
Nova Scotia cruise, 116

Oakleigh, 196
Ocean Beach Amusement Park, 111
Ocoee River Rafting, 207
Ohio Historical Center, 178
Okefenokee Swamp, 208
Old Fort Henry, 275
Old Kentucky Home, 211
Old Louisville, 211
Old Montreal, 283
Old New Castle, 149
Old Sturbridge Village, 125
Oldtown, 252
Olivera Street, 258
Olympic sites, 283
   summer (1984), 253, 247
   winter (1980), 136
Onondaga Cave, 231
Ontario Science Center, 282
Opryland, 215
Owen-Thomas House, 208

Pacific Ocean, 253
Padre Island, 235
Pageant of the Masters, 249
Parliament Buildings of Canada, 277
Parrish Museum, 141
Parrot Jungle, 197, 199
Peabody Museum, 113, 146
Pebble Hill Plantation Museum, 210
Penn Dutch country, 159
Pennekamp Coral Reef, 198, 199
Penns Cave, 161
Pennsylvania Farm Museum, 158
Petrified Forest, 244
Philadelphia Art Museum, 157, 160
Philadelphia Zoo, 160
Phillips Mushroom Museum, 159

Phoenix Zoo, 243
Pike's Peak 221
Pint Mt. Observatory, 188
Pioneer Town, 239
Pittock Mansion, 188
Place d'Armes, 284
Place des Arts, 281
Plains of Abraham, the, 284
Planet Ocean, 197, 199
Plimouth Plantation, 118, 127
Plymouth, 124, 127, 146
Plymouth Rock, 127, 146
Plymouth Wax Museum, 127
Poe, Edgar Allan, Museum, 169
Portland Zoo, 188
Ports O'Call, 250
Powder Ridge Ski area, 113
Provincial Museum, 191, 272
Puget Sound, 190
Pump House Museum, 275
Purgatory Ski Area, 222

Queen Elizabeth Planetarium, 271
Queen Mary, 250
Quincy Market, 120, 125

Railroad Museum, 252
Ravinia Festival, 173
Red Mountain Museum, 195
Red Rocks, 221
Redwood Forest, 255
Rideau Canal, 277
Rockport Art Colony, 235
Rocky Mountain National Park, 219, 221
Rodin Museum, 157, 160
Roger Williams Park and Zoo, 146
Rose Bowl, 245
Rose Garden, 188
Rothman's Art Gallery, 280
Royal Ontario Museum, 282
Russian River Resorts, 255, 256
Rye Playland, 131

INDEX • 319

SAC Air Base, 186
Sagamore Hill, 142
Sag Harbor Customs House, 141
Sag Harbor Museum and Custom House, 142
Sag Harbor Whaling Museum, 132
St. Charles Ave., 226
Ste. Anne de Beaupre, 284
St. George Island, 202
St. George Resort Area, 260
St. John's Church, 169
St. Joseph Oratory, 283
St. Louis Art Museum, 231
St. Louis Repertory Theater, 231
St. Louis Zoo, 231
St. Mark's Wildlife Preserve, 202
St. Simon's Island, 208, 209
Salmon Locks, 191
San Antonio River, 238
San Antonio Zoo, 238
San Diego Sea World and Zoo, 251
San Diego Zoo, 248, 253
San Francisco cable cars, 254
San Jacinto Monument, 234
Santa Ana race track, 258
Santa Anita Race Track, 245
Santa Barbara Missions, 247
Sandwich, 122
Sandwich Glass Museum, 128
Saratoga, 131, 135
Saratoga Raceway and Center for Performing Arts, 135
Savoy Theater, 274
Science Museum of Virginia, 169
Scripps Aquarium, 253
Scripps Institute of Oceanography, 253
Sea Island, 209
Seal Island Bridge, 274
Seaquarium, 197, 199
Seattle Center (World Fair '61), 191
Sea World (Fla.), 200, 201, 203
Sea World (Ca.), 250, 253
Sequoia National Park, 248
Serpentarium, 197, 199
Seven Mile Bridge, 198

Severance Hall, 176
Shaker Museum, 135
Shakespeare Festival, 219
Shark Valley, 197
Sharon Playhouse, 114
Sheldon Art Gallery, 186
Shenandoah National Park, 166
Shinnecock Indian Reservation, 141
Shubert Theater, 113
Silver Dollar City, 228
Silver Springs, 200
Simpsonville, 211
Ski Liberty, 161
Skippack Village, 157
Skyline Drive, 166
Sleeping Bear Dunes National Park, 174
Sleepy Hollow Restorations, 131
Sloss Furnace Restoration, 195
Smithsonian, 150, 151
SOHO, 137
Song Mountain Ski and Alpine Slide, 135
Sonnenberg Gardens, 134
Sonoma Old Spanish Mission, 255
South Ferry, 137
South Street Seaport, 137
Spanish Governor's Palace, 238
Stanley Park, 191
State Archives, (Va.), 169
Statue of Liberty, 136
Stephens, Alexander H., home, 204
Sterling Clark Museum, 129
Sternwheeler "Columbia Gorge," 188
Stone Mountain Park, 204-206
Stony Brook Museum Complex, 142
Strasburg Railroad, 158
Stratford Shakespeare Theater, 280, 281
Stratford Summer Music, 281
Strong Toy Museum, 134
Sturbridge Village, 112, 124
Sunken Gardens, 201
Sunken Gardens Mexican Market, 238
Sunken Meadow State Park, 142
Sunrise Theater, 197

Superdome, 226
Sutter's Fort, 252
Syracuse Dome, 135

Table Rock lakes fishing, 228
Taliesin West, 244
Tall Timbers Research Station, 202
Tampa Bay Football Stadium, 200
Taneycomo fishing, 228
Tanglewood Music Festival, 114, 129
Telfair Academy, 208
Tennessee State Museum, 215
Texas Medical Center, 234
Texas Safari Wild Game Park, 236
Texas Stadium, 236
Theater of the sea, 198
Thoreau Lyceum, 123
Thousand Islands, 135, 143, 275
Tijuana, Mexico, 250, 253
Toccoa River, 207
Topiary Gardens, 144
Torrey Pines Golf Course, 253
Totem Pole Playhouse, 162
Tournament of Roses Mansion, 245
Touro Synagogue, 145
Truman, Harry S., home, 229
Truman Library, 224
Tucson Zoo, 243
TVA, 207
Twain, Mark, home, 231
28th Division Military Shrine & Museum, 161
Twitty City, 215

United Nations, 137
U.S. Mint, 221
U.S. Government Buildings, 150-151
Universal City and Studios, 245, 250 258
Ursuline Convent and Museum, 284
USS Alabama, 196
USS Drum, 196
Utah Shakespeare Festival, 260

Vail skiing and winter events, 223
Valleoto Lake, 222
Valley Forge, 157, 159
Valley Junction Antiques, 183
Vancouver (B.C.)-1986 World's Fair, 190, 191
Vandalia Trap Shoot, 178
Vanderbilt Mansion, 131
Vanderbilt Planetarium, 142
Vicksburg historic homes, 212
Virginia Beach, 168
Virginia Historical Society, 169
Virginia House & Garden Tour, 167
Virginia Museum, 169
Virginia Ten Miler Road Race, 167
Virginia Theater for the Performing Arts, 169
Vizcaya, 197, 199

Walden Pond, 123
Walker Art Center, 184
Wall Street, 137
Washington, D.C. attractions, 165
Watermill Museum, 132
Watermill Old Mill Museum & Windmill, 141
Waterside Festival Marketplace, 168
Wayne, John, birthplace, 183
Westbury Music Fair, 142
Western Bluffs, 183
Whale watching, 122, 127, 188
Whaling Museum, 141
White Chapel Meeting House, 279
Whiteface Highway, 136
Whitefish Big Mountain Ski Area, 185
White House, 150
White Mountains, 124, 130
White Water Fun Park, 228
Wild Animal Park, 248, 250
Wildwood Conservation park, 281
William Penn Museum, 158
Williams, Tennessee, home, 197, 199
Williamsburg, 169

Williamstown Theater, 114, 129
Winter Carnival, 284
Winter Park Arts Festival, 203
Winterthur Museum and Gardens, 149, 157, 159
Woodland Zoo, 191
Woodruff Art Center, 205
Woodward Cave, 161
World Affairs Conference, 219
World Congress Center, 205
World's Fair sites
    New Orleans (1984), 225-227
    Seattle (1961), 191
    Tennessee (1983), 214
    Vancouver (1986), 190, 191
Worlds of Fun, 224
World Trade Center, 137

York Fairgrounds, 162
Yorktown, 170
Yosemite National Park, 248

Zion National Park, 260

NOW, SAVE MONEY ON ALL YOUR TRAVELS!
Join Arthur Frommer's $25-A-Day Travel Club

Saving money while traveling is never a simple matter, which is why, over 23 years ago, the **$25-A-Day Travel Club** was formed. Actually, the idea came from readers of the Arthur Frommer Publications who felt that such an organization could bring financial benefits, continuing travel information, and a sense of community to economy-minded travelers all over the world.

In keeping with the money-saving concept, the annual membership fee is low—$18 (U.S. residents) or $20 (Canadian, Mexican, and foreign residents)—and is immediately exceeded by the value of your benefits which include:

(1) The latest edition of any TWO of the books listed on the following page.

(2) An annual subscription to an 8-page quarterly newspaper *The Wonderful World of Budget Travel* which keeps you up-to-date on fastbreaking developments in low-cost travel in all parts of the world—bringing you the kind of information you'd have to pay over $25 a year to obtain elsewhere. This consumer-conscious publication also includes the following columns:

Hospitality Exchange—members all over the world who are willing to provide hospitality to other members as they pass through their home cities.

Share-a-Trip—requests from members for travel companions who can share costs and help avoid the burdensome single supplement.

Readers Ask ... Readers Reply—travel questions from members to which other members reply with authentic firsthand information.

(3) A copy of *Arthur Frommer's Guide to New York*.

(4) Your personal membership card which entitles you to purchase through the Club all Arthur Frommer Publications for a third to a half off their regular retail prices during the term of your membership.

So why not join this hardy band of international budgeteers NOW and participate in its exchange of information and hospitality? Simply send $18 (U.S. residents) or $20 U.S. (Canadian, Mexican, and other foreign residents) along with your name and address to: $25-A-Day Travel Club, Inc., 1230 Avenue of the Americas, New York, NY 10020. Remember to specify which *two* of the books in section (1) above you wish to receive in your initial package of members' benefits. Or tear out this page, check off any two books on the opposite side and send it to us with your membership fee.

FROMMER/PASMANTIER PUBLISHERS Date_____
1230 AVE. OF THE AMERICAS, NEW YORK, NY 10020

Friends, please send me the books checked below:

$-A-DAY GUIDES
(In-depth guides to low-cost tourist accommodations and facilities.)

☐ Europe on $25 a Day $11.95	☐ New Zealand on $20 & $25 a Day $10.95
☐ Australia on $25 a Day $10.95	☐ New York on $35 a Day............. $9.95
☐ England on $35 a Day $10.95	☐ Scandinavia on $35 a Day........... $9.95
☐ Greece on $25 a Day $10.95	☐ Scotland and Wales on $35 a Day..... $10.95
☐ Hawaii on $35 a Day................ $10.95	☐ South America on $25 a Day $9.95
☐ India on $15 & $25 a Day........... $9.95	☐ Spain and Morocco (plus the Canary
☐ Ireland on $25 a Day................ $9.95	Is.) on $35 a Day $9.95
☐ Israel on $30 & $35 a Day $10.95	☐ Washington, D.C. on $40 a Day...... $10.95
☐ Mexico on $20 a Day $9.95	

DOLLARWISE GUIDES
(Guides to accommodations and facilities from budget to deluxe, with emphasis on the medium-priced.)

☐ Austria & Hungary $10.95	☐ Caribbean $12.95
☐ Egypt............................. $11.95	☐ Cruises (incl. Alaska, Carib, Mex,
☐ England & Scotland $10.95	Hawaii, Panama, Canada, & US) $10.95
☐ France............................ $10.95	☐ California & Las Vegas $9.95
☐ Germany.......................... $11.95	☐ Florida $10.95
☐ Italy.............................. $10.95	☐ New England $11.95
☐ Japan & Hong Kong (avail. Apr. '86) .. $11.95	☐ Northwest......................... $10.95
☐ Portugal (incl. Madeira & the Azores) . $11.95	☐ Skiing USA—East $10.95
☐ Switzerland & Liechtenstein $11.95	☐ Skiing USA—West $10.95
☐ Bermuda & The Bahamas............ $10.95	☐ Southeast & New Orleans........... $11.95
☐ Canada $12.95	☐ Southwest $10.95

THE ARTHUR FROMMER GUIDES
(Pocket-size guides to tourist accommodations and facilities in all price ranges.)

☐ Amsterdam/Holland $4.95	☐ Mexico City/Acapulco $4.95
☐ Athens............................ $4.95	☐ Montreal/Quebec City $4.95
☐ Atlantic City/Cape May $4.95	☐ New Orleans $4.95
☐ Boston............................ $4.95	☐ New York......................... $4.95
☐ Dublin/Ireland $4.95	☐ Orlando/Disney World/EPCOT....... $4.95
☐ Hawaii $4.95	☐ Paris $4.95
☐ Las Vegas $4.95	☐ Philadelphia....................... $4.95
☐ Lisbon/Madrid/Costa del Sol........ $4.95	☐ Rome $4.95
☐ London $4.95	☐ San Francisco $4.95
☐ Los Angeles $4.95	☐ Washington, D.C. $4.95

SPECIAL EDITIONS

☐ Bed & Breakfast—N. America $7.95	☐ Museums in New York $8.95
☐ Fast 'n' Easy Phrase Book	☐ Shopper's Guide to England, Scotland
(Fr/Ger/Ital/Sp in *one* vol.) $6.95	& Wales $10.95
☐ Guide for the Disabled Traveler....... $10.95	☐ Swap and Go (Home Exchanging) $10.95
☐ How to Beat the High Cost of Travel... $4.95	☐ Travel Diary and Record Book........ $5.95
☐ Marilyn Wood's Wonderful Weekends	☐ Urban Athlete (NYC sports guide) $9.95
(NY, Conn, Mass, RI, Vt, NJ, Pa) $9.95	☐ Where to Stay USA (Lodging from $3
	to $25 a night) $9.95

In U.S. include $1 post. & hdlg. for 1st book; 25¢ ea. add'l. book. Outside U.S. $2 and 50¢ respectively.

Enclosed is my check or money order for $_____

NAME_____

ADDRESS_____

CITY_____ STATE_____ ZIP_____